RESPECTING STATE COURTS

Recent Titles in
Contributions in Legal Studies

Constitutional Politics in the States: Contemporary Controversies and Historical Patterns
G. Alan Tarr, editor

Law and the Great Plains: Essays on the Legal History of the Heartland
John R. Wunder, editor

Judicial Entrepreneurship: The Role of the Judge in the Marketplace of Ideas
Wayne V. McIntosh and Cynthia L. Cates

Solving the Puzzle of Interest Group Litigation
Andrew Jay Koshner

Presidential Defiance of "Unconstitutional" Laws: Reviving the Royal Prerogative
Christopher N. May

Promises on Prior Obligations at Common Law
Kevin M. Teeven

Litigating Federalism: The States Before the U.S. Supreme Court
Eric N. Waltenburg and Bill Swinford

Law and the Arts
Susan Tiefenbrun, editor

Contract Law and Morality
Henry Mather

The Appearance of Equality: Racial Gerrymandering, Redistricting, and the Supreme Court
Christopher M. Burke

Religion, Law, and the Land
Brian Edward Brown

The Supreme Court's Retreat from Reconstruction: A Distortion of Constitutional Jurisprudence
Frank J. Scaturro

RESPECTING STATE COURTS

The Inevitability of Judicial Federalism

Michael E. Solimine
and James L. Walker

Contributions in Legal Studies, Number 92

GREENWOOD PRESS
Westport, Connecticut • London

Library of Congress Cataloging-in-Publication Data

Solimine, Michael E., 1956–
Respecting state courts : the inevitability of judicial federalism / Michael E. Solimine and James L. Walker.
p. cm.—(Contributions in legal studies, ISSN 0147–1074 ; no. 92)
Includes bibliographical references and index.
ISBN 0–313–30634–6 (alk. paper)
1. Courts—United States—States. 2. Judicial power—United States—States. 3. Federalism—United States. 4. Judicial power—United States. I. Walker, James L., 1942– . II. Title. III. Series.
KF5130.S66 1999
347.73′3—dc21 99–22141

British Library Cataloguing in Publication Data is available.

Library of Congress Catalog Card Number: 92–22141
ISBN: 0–313–30634–6
ISSN: 0147–1074

First published in 1999

Greenwood Press, 88 Post Road West, Westport, CT 06881
An imprint of Greenwood Publishing Group, Inc.
www.greenwood.com

Printed in the United States of America

The paper used in this book complies with the Permanent Paper Standard issued by the National Information Standards Organization (Z39.48–1984).

10 9 8 7 6 5 4 3 2

Copyright Acknowledgment

The author and publisher gratefully acknowledge permission to quote from the following:

Solimine, Michael E., & James L. Walker. *Constitutional Litigation in Federal and State Courts: An Empirical Analysis of Judicial Parity*, 10 Hastings Constitutional Law Quarterly 213 (1983). © 1983 by University of California, Hastings College of Law. Reprinted from *Hastings Constitutional Law Quarterly*, Vol. 10, No. 2, pp. 213–253, by permission.

To our mentors:

United States District Judge Walter H. Rice
—M.E.S.

Professor William S. "Sandy" Muir, Jr.
—J.L.W.

Too little consequence has been attached to the fact that the courts of the States are under an obligation equally strong with that resting upon the courts of the Union to respect and enforce the provisions of the Federal Constitution as the Supreme Law of the Land, and to guard rights secured or guaranteed by that instrument. We must assume—a decent respect for the States requires us to assume—that the state courts will enforce every right secured by the Constitution.

U.S. Supreme Court Justice John Marshall Harlan,
dissenting in Ex Parte Young, 209 U.S. 123, 176 (1908).

Most essentially, federal and state courts are complementary systems for administering justice in our Nation. Cooperation and comity, not competition and conflict, are essential to the federal design. A State's dignitary interest bears consideration when a district court exercises discretion in a case of this order.

U.S. Supreme Court Justice Ruth Bader Ginsburg,
writing for the Court in Ruhrgas AG v. Marathon Oil Co.,
119 S.Ct. 1563, 1571 (1999).

Contents

Tables ix

Preface xi

Chapter 1: The Once-and-Future Federalism 1

Chapter 2: Rights and Judicial Federalism 13

Chapter 3: Beyond Paradigms: State Court Adjudication of Federal Rights 29

Chapter 4: Judicial Federalism, Civil Law, and the New Forum Shopping 63

Chapter 5: Federalism, Liberty, and State Constitutional Law 87

Chapter 6: Special Problems for Judicial Federalism: Race, the Death Penalty, and Habeas Corpus 105

Chapter 7: Judicial Federalism: Power, Ideology, and Community 129

Bibliography 143

Table of Cases 161

Index 167

Tables

3.1	Results of All Cases	47
3.2	Results by Court System	47
3.3	Outcome Versus Forum by Case Type	49
3.4	Outcome by Forum for Five Subsamples	61
4.1	Published State Courts Section 1983 Cases	76
4.2	Results of Sample of Published Federal Appellate Court Section 1983 Cases in 1987	78

Preface

This is a book about the relationship between America's court system and the structure of federalism. For a long time now, the nagging fear of anyone daring to write about federalism is that, in Plutarch's words, we are "misusing that love of inquiry and observation which nature has implanted in us on objects unworthy of the attention." The subject has been marginalized by some of the best minds of the last two generations. It has been vilified and associated with most of the evils of modernity. We hope only that our willingness to rush in where angels fear to tread is a sign not of foolishness but of a desire to take the road less traveled.

Like most books, this one developed over several years. First as student and teacher, the two authors have long discussed the relative merits of the state and federal courts and judges. The older and more leftist of the two had written a doctoral dissertation on state trial courts. The younger, and more centrist of the two, had clerked for a federal judge. They were surprised, therefore, that despite their ideological predispositions and experiences, they agreed that there was not as much difference between the two systems as the conventional wisdom of the time assumed. Over the next several years, they would write, separately and together, on various aspects of this point of view.

This volume is an attempt to summarize many of these arguments and to give a more mature voice to the ideas first expressed over two decades ago. We hope that anyone interested in law and courts, whether they be of the academic, political, or citizen, will find something of interest in these pages. But most importantly, we hope that it will provoke further debate and discussion on what we consider to be a vital national topic, the best road to just, self-government.

In the chapters that follow, the dear reader will find little stridency, much conviction, but little passion. We hope to gently persuade not that our Constitution is the "greatest document ever struck off in the history of man," or even that it is the greatest thing since sliced bread. We simply desire, in a quiet and, we hope, intellectually honest way, to write an appreciation of the unique qualities of the American federal system of law and courts.

As mentioned, we have already written on this topic. In particular, three of our chapters are based on heavily edited, updated, and rewritten law review articles: Solimine & Walker, *Constitutional Litigation in Federal and State Courts: An Empirical Analysis of Judicial Parity*, 10 Hastings Constitutional Law Quarterly 213 (1983) (chapter 3); Solimine, *Rethinking Exclusive Federal Jurisdiction*, 52 University of Pittsburgh Law Review 383 (1991) (chapter 4); and Solimine & Walker, *Federalism, Liberty and State Constitutional Law*, 23 Ohio Northern University Law Review 1457 (1997) (chapter 5). We are grateful for and acknowledge the permission of the copyright owners of these articles, who are, respectively: the University of California, Hastings College of Law; Michael E. Solimine; and the Ohio Northern University Law Review.

We are grateful to the many individuals without whom this book would not have been possible. A necessarily incomplete list starts with the colleagues, students, and staff at our respective institutions who aided us in the three articles mentioned above. For more recent assistance, we are indebted to students Maria Bevington, Ann Koize, Andrew White (all of the University of Cincinnati College of Law), Jan Konya (Wright State University), and for their indispensable word processing and clerical assistance, Connie Miller (UC) and Pat Browder (WSU). We also acknowledge the financial assistance of the UC College of Law summer research grants, and of the faculty development fund of WSU, The production of this book was greatly facilitated by Dr. James Sabin and his colleagues at the Greenwood Publishing Company. Finally, we, as always are grateful for the patience and support of our wives and children.

1

The Once-and-Future Federalism

A continuous thread runs through the history of our nation's politics. That thread is federalism: the doctrine and practice of sharing power between two sorts of government, acting on behalf of, and regulating, the same people. We use the term "sorts of government" rather than the more common "levels of government." This is because a key premise of this book is that Washington, D.C. on the one hand, and all of the state capitals on the other, are home to governments that are very different in concept, scope of authority, and, sometimes, political culture.[1] And, we

1. The questions of size seems obvious enough. There are few if any states, or even regions of the country, that compare with the federal government in terms of size; most, in fact, are positively tiny by comparison. For a discussion of the impact of size on political participation and the formation of civic virtue see Michael J. Sandel, Democracy's Discontent 347 (1996). See also David L. Shapiro, Federalism: A Dialogue 93–94 (1995).

As for scope, although it is true that over the last sixty years a severe complacency has set in about the existence of a "federal police power" that virtually eliminates the distinction between state and federal government, that position has never been truly adopted in constitutional law. In fact, in the 1990s, the Supreme Court has held to the contrary, e.g., United States v. Lopez, 514 U.S. 549 (1995) (holding part of Gun Free School Zones Act of 1990 beyond Congress' Commerce power); Printz v. United States, 521 U.S. 898 (1997) (invalidating provisions of Brady Handgun Violence Prevention Act of 1993, which imposed background check duties on state officials), and may be willing to make even more reaffirmations about the distinction between delegated and reserved powers. See Ann Althouse, *Theoretical and Constitutional Issues: Enforcing Federalism After United States v. Lopez*, 38 Ariz. L. Rev. 793 (1996); Vicki C. Jackson, *Federalism and the Uses and Limits of Law: Printz and Principle?*, 111 Harv. L. Rev. 2180 (1998); Evan H. Caminker, *Printz, State Sovereignty, and the Limits of Formalism*, 1997 Sup. Ct. Rev. 199; Matthew D. Adler & Seth F. Kreimer, *The New Etiquette of Federalism: New York, Printz, and Yeskey*, 1998 Sup. Ct. Rev. 71.

Political culture, on the other hand, is more contentious. For a classic statement of the phenomena see Daniel Elazar, American Federalism: A View From the States (3d ed. 1984) or the work of V.O. Key, Jr., especially Southern Politics in State and Nation (1949). More

believe, this is more significant than the rather obvious fact that when there is a conflict between the state and the federal government, the Constitution requires that it be settled in favor of the federal government, thus leading to the simplistic use of the term "levels," indicating higher and lower positions.[2]

Five easy pieces of evidence for the claim of a thread unbroken are quickly related. The ratification of the Constitution itself by the states was, in great part, a result of the successful marketing of federalism. The Civil War fought eighty years later was essentially over slavery but had at least as much to do with the nature of the federal union. In the early part of the twentieth century, the Great Depression challenged the ability of the federal government to respond to national problems because of perceived limitations the federal system had placed on it. In the 1960s, it took an enterprising and creative use of the federal commerce power to overcome state resistance to civil rights. Finally, more recently, the continuing national debate over the right of a woman to secure an abortion can be reduced to an argument over the reach of state power in the face of a judicially discovered (or created) federal right.

From this thumbnail sketch one gathers that interest in federalism becomes more intense from time to time. The last decade or so has provided us with an illustration of this phenomenon because the evidence abounds that the topic engages our attention as much, or more, than ever. There are many high-profile study groups, associations, Supreme Court decisions, articles in law reviews, the popular press, books, and even television shows that argue the merits or flaws of the federal system.[3]

---

recently some authors have questioned the existence of a separate state political cultures. E.g., G. Alan Tarr, *State Constitutional Politics: An Historical Perspective* in Constitutional Politics in the States: Contemporary Controversies and Historical Patterns 5 (G. Alan Tarr ed., 1996). We will have more to say about state political cultures in chapter 5, and in our conclusions.

2. Article V, § 2 of the U.S. Constitution states that "the Constitution, and the laws of the United States which shall be made *in pursuance thereof*, . . . shall be the Supreme Law of the Land, . . . the laws of any state to the contrary notwithstanding." (Emphasis added.)

3. During the course of the following chapters we will of course be discussing many of the decisions and published works referred to. A few examples of the other categories are Alan Brinkley, Nelson W. Polsby & Kathleen M. Sullivan, New Federalist Papers: Essays in Defense of the Constitution (1997); a television series that deals directly with the topic, Fred W. Friendly's *Whose Law Whose Order,* which is based on an article written by Joan Greco, *Forgotten Federalism*; and the earlier program produced by Friendly, *The Constitution, That Delicate Balance*, which included *Federalism: The National Government Versus the States*, December 11, 1984; The Reagan administration, which commissioned a study, The Status of Federalism in America, authored by an interagency working group on Federalism of the Domestic Policy Council in November 1986. And finally there is the Federalist Society and its publications an forums, all of which should more properly be labeled "anti-federalist" for their concentration on restoring state power, if not sovereignty.

FEDERALISM AND IDEOLOGY

The current heightened interest in federalism is not just a function of a particular issue, such as the aforementioned abortion controversy, it is also ideological. A keen appreciation of the potential of federalism was the opening wedge in what has become the transformation—perhaps renaissance is a better word—of the conservative movement in the United States (as well as the transformation of the Democratic party, at least at the presidential level).

For those who witnessed it, the marginal candidacy of the late Barry Goldwater seems now almost surreal. The country was New Deal, Keynesian, and was about to agree that poverty could be eliminated through governmental action. Aggressive federal protection of civil rights was a consensus, bipartisan position. The price of things like airline tickets and moving services were fixed by the federal government, and the ideas that Social Security might be "privatized," or that the monopoly of the postal service might be eased were considered to be beyond the fringe.[4] But the capture of the Republican party by the Western establishment and the newly Republican South,[5] was a warning shot across the bow of the ship of state by those who questioned this orthodoxy. Although thoroughly trounced in the balloting, Goldwater's efforts foreshadowed the election of one of the most unlikely presidents in history, Ronald Reagan, who made two of his major priorities the reduction of federal power and the return of sovereignty to the states.[6]

But even before Reagan's election, the conservative transformation in the judiciary had been set in motion by Richard Nixon's appointments to the U.S. Supreme Court—appointments that eventually would contribute to placing federalism on the national political agenda with a vengeance, and would eventually lead to a continuing judicial dialogue on the nature of the "states qua states," transforming the Tenth Amendment to the Constitution from a truism to a legitimate topic of discussion.[7]

---

4. Soon after his death, the story of his candidacy was remembered positively in Lee Edwards, *In Our Hearts We Know Goldwater Was Right,* Kansas City Star, June 4, 1998, p. C7. A negative retelling can be found in Theo Lippman, Jr., *"Mr. Conservative" Was a Loser of World-Class Proportions*, The Baltimore Sun, June 2, 1998, p. 9A. Whether one accepts the former or the latter, it is clear that he was the first politician of national stature since the New Deal to successfully make federalism a political issue.

5. For a good statistical summary of the real impact of the effect of the 1964 election on the Roosevelt consensus, see Michael Barone, Our Country: The Shaping of America From Roosevelt to Reagan 378–380 (1990).

6. Very early in his presidency, Reagan spoke about "restoring the constitutional symmetry between the central government and the states and reestablishing the freedom and variety of federalism" in this same speech he spoke about "initiat(ing) a debate on the fact that over the past 40 years federalism . . . has nearly disappeared as a guiding force in American politics and government," President Ronald Reagan, Address to the National Conference of State Legislatures, (17 Weekly Comp. Pres. Doc. 836, July 30, 1981).

7. New York v. United States, 505 U.S. 144, 157 (1992) ("[T]he Tenth Amendment confirms that the power of the Federal Government is subject to limits that may, in a given instance, reserve power to the States. The Tenth Amendment thus directs us to determine,

Of course the trend toward reducing the power of the federal government and the devolution to the states is not an exclusively Republican phenomenon. The new Democrats led by Al Gore and Bill Clinton were reinventing government, and the size of the federal government workforce actually shrank much more under the Clinton administration than it ever did under Ronald Reagan.[8] The final ignominy for the vestigial New Dealers in the electorate was the signing in 1996 of the welfare reform bill by President Clinton, thus repealing an entitlement to federal benefits that had lasted for sixty years.

JUDICIAL FEDERALISM: THE TERM

The meaning of the term judicial federalism itself has not yet jelled.[9] It continues to appear in a variety of different contexts with meanings that are not always the same, or even consistent with one another. One of the goals of this book, if not to resolve these inconsistencies, is at least to set us on the path of doing so.

There are three general ways in which the term is used. The first is the descriptive or structural context where the relationship between the courts created in the federal Constitution and those created in the constitutions of the states are compared. In this, the broadest of meanings, judicial federalism is merely the parceling out of law work between each set of courts. In this context, the most important topics discussed are such things as federal jurisdiction. Under what circumstances are issues to be resolved by the federal courts rather than the state courts? Should cases where the parties are citizens of different states, for example, still be heard in federal courts even though the reasons for allowing this have long since (for the most part) evaporated?[10]

A second and more nuanced meaning of the term is the devolution of more responsibility to the state courts and away from the federal courts. This use of the term is best illustrated by the 1995 report on the future of the federal courts.[11] As one commentator put it, one purpose of the report would be to "curb federal usurpation of state court prerogatives and to handle the remaining federal business more efficiently." Among the many topics that tend to generate the most heat in

---

as in this case, whether an incident of state sovereignty is protected by a limitation on an Article I power.") (O'Connor, J.).

8. At the beginning of the Clinton administration, the total federal civilian workforce stood at 3,456,873. By 1997, it had shrunk to 2,807,077, for a drop of 17.7 percent. The number of federal workers went up by close to 200,000—nearly 8 percent—during the eight Reagan years. Of course, this number is only one indication of total federal activity. For a libertarian view of total federal impact in the two administrations see Richard B. McKenzie, *Clinton Confidential: The Best-Kept Secret of the Clinton Years Is Economic*, Reason, November 1996, p. 40.

9. Indeed, the term itself has apparently only come into use since the 1970s. See Louise Weinberg, *The New Judicial Federalism*, 29 Stan. L. Rev. 1191 (1977).

10. See discussion in chapters 3 and 4.

11. Judicial Conference of the United States, Committee on Long Range Planning, Long Range Plan for the Federal Courts (1995) (hereinafter Long Range Report).

this second meaning of the term are claims within the states for vindication of federally guaranteed rights. As the report suggests, these cases should be heard in the federal courts only when there is a clear need for national uniformity on an issue that cannot be dealt with at the state level.[12]

A third and most specialized use of the term is the increased use of state courts to protect individual rights based on the state constitutions. This is often referred to as the "new judicial federalism," and the parentage of this usage is often attributed to the late Justice William Brennan.[13] In this sense of the word, the major arguments are over the extent that state courts should be more active in seeking to enhance the rights of their citizens, even, or especially, in the face of the perceived reluctance of federal courts to do so. Among the most popular topics of discussion related to this meaning of the term are enhanced protections of privacy, rights of criminal defendants, and freedom of speech.

JUDICIAL FEDERALISM IN CONTEXT

When federal and state power are debated, whether at the bar or in the bar, usually *legislative* and *executive* powers are at issue. The power of the judiciary is at most an afterthought. This is to be expected given the perceived immediacy of law-making and law-executing versus the esoteric machinery of justice. In addition the arcane nature of topics such as federal jurisdiction, removal, habeas corpus, and diversity jurisdiction do not as readily admit of free-wheeling discussion and sound bites as abortion, pollution, gun control, and drinking ages—especially *in* the bar.

Therefore, this book is not in the mainstream of federalism literature, most of which concentrates on law-making and the bureaucracy. Indeed, there has recently been renewed attention to federalism themes in the academic community, revisiting the putative virtues of a federal system of government: states are closer to and more responsive to the wishes of people, can check the aggrandizement of authority by the federal government, can more efficiently deliver at least some public goods, and can experiment with policies in ways the national government cannot.[14] Our book, in contrast, is about *judicial* federalism, the sharing of the judicial power by two *court systems* over the same land and people. While judicial federalism has been frequently explored in the legal literature, as the succeeding chapters will indicate, it has suffered from a relative lack of attention by political scientists and

12. Harlon L. Dalton, *Judicial Federalism and Individual Rights*, 31 Trial 56 (Oct. 1995); Long Range Report, *supra* note 11, at 21–30 (chapter labeled "Judicial Federalism").

13. William J. Brennan, Jr., *State Constitutions and the Protection of Individual Rights*, 90 Harv. L. Rev. 489, 503 (1977).

14. Our quick summary, of course, cannot do full justice to the large literature on federalism. For good recent summaries of, and contributions to, that literature, see Jackson, *supra* note 1; Larry Kramer, *Understanding Federalism*, 47 Vand. L. Rev. 1485 (1994); Michael W. McConnell, *Federalism: Understanding the Founders' Design*, 54 U. Chi. L. Rev. 1484 (1987); Shapiro, *supra* note 1.

other non-legal academics.[15] Moreover, our view of judicial Federalism is itself somewhat out of the mainstream, as we hope to make apparent in the chapters that follow.

Actually, it is often difficult to say where the mainstream of judicial federalism is. Opinions on the topic vary widely. Terms such as "our federalism," "dual federalism," "normative federalism," and "tamed federalism," and even "fear of federalism" are some of the descriptors used.[16] A few commentators view judicial federalism as more of a nuisance or accident of history rather than a positive benefit, going so far as to call federalism itself a "national neurosis."[17] Judicial federalism is seen by some as a path to injustice and a denial of human rights. Hypothetically, some seem to long for a unitary government.

We cannot hope to counter an argument based solely on a hypothetical, i.e., what if the original structure of "Middle North America"[18] were unitary? We can't engage those who wonder if we would be better off without federalism any more than we can imagine what the world would be like if Hitler had been assassinated in 1940 or if Mozart had lived to a ripe old age. Instead we will concentrate on what is.

We are a nation of states; judicial federalism is inevitable. And, this much we believe: our country would either not exist in its current shape (literally) or would be a much less pleasant and prosperous place to live, if it had a unitary government, based in Washington, D.C. So our thesis, briefly, is that judicial federalism is essential to the health, and even to the existence, of a successful system of power sharing, and it has been consistently undervalued in that role.

Although more constrained by federal power than at any time in our history, states continue to maintain a broad field of independent action and innovation. Rather than be fated to proceed in lock step with the federal courts, the state courts present a unique opportunity and a unique challenge. It is true, it cannot be denied, that the state courts are also much more influenced by the federal judiciary than ever before in our history. The federalization of many areas of the substantive criminal law, the national application of rules of criminal procedure, the national-

---

15. There are, of course, exceptions, such as the work of G. Alan Tarr, who we cite in note 1 in this chapter, and elsewhere in the book. For another recent exception, see Donald J. Farole, Jr., Interest Groups and Judicial Federalism: Organizational Litigation in State Judiciaries (1998).

16. See Louise Weinberg, *Fear and Federalism*, 23 Ohio N. U. L. Rev. 1295 (1997).

17. Edward L. Rubin & Malcolm Feeley, *Federalism: Some Notes on a National Neurosis*, 41 UCLA L. Rev. 903 (1994).

18. Obviously, this hypothetical country couldn't be called "The *United States.*"

ization of libel law standards, have all had a dramatic impact on the way state courts do business.[19] But it is the other side of the coin, the way courts in the states remain, fundamentally *state* institutions, that concerns us.

APPROACHES TO JUDICIAL FEDERALISM

As with all renderings of complex structures, the picture one paints will depend on the perspective one takes. For the sake of discussion, let us posit five different perspectives on the relationship between the state and federal judicial systems. Naturally each of these perspectives is a composite of many different authors and scholars, and does not pretend to be a "model" or "theory" of judicial federalism, merely a heuristic device that we will refer to from time to time throughout the book. We are confident that the reader will be able to advance yet other perspectives that we do not here consider.

The Structural Approach

From this perspective, the bulk of American law is made by the states and enforced by the states. One would expect this body of law to differ from state to state and from time to time. However, there will be some attempts to standardize the law, both through the adoptions of codes such as those promulgated by the private American Law Institute,[20] driven mostly by commercial interests and those seeking economic efficiency in a national, and now-global market. Federal attempts at standardization have mainly served federal interests and are generally limited in scope. Federal law itself is usually very specialized and will only attempt to "fill

19. Two examples of the former are the large areas of preemption of narcotics laws by the federal government leaving the states with limited discretion in this area. In chapters 2 and 7 we will discuss situations where innovative state policies have been stymied by federal action. There is also a large area of federal intrusion into traditional state criminal law enforcement involved in RICO statutes and other measures based on the commerce power (U.S. Const. Art. 1, § 8), though recent cases have circumscribed this intrusion, see note 1. The rules of state criminal procedure have been revolutionized by federal court decisions, most notably by the imposition of the exclusionary rule on the states, Mapp v. Ohio, 367 U.S. 643 (1961) The law of libel was altered to some degree in almost every state by Gertz v. Robert Welch, Inc., 418 U.S. 323 (1974).

20. For a broad-ranging discussion of the pros and cons of such endeavors, see Alex Elson, *The Case for an In-Depth Study of the American Law Institute*, 23 Law & Soc. Inquiry 625 (1998). The ALI promotes standardization by its promulgation of "restatements" of various areas of laws, which can be voluntarily adopted by state supreme courts. Standardization can also occur through the adoption of uniform acts by state legislatures, the Uniform Commercial Code being the most prominent example. See Larry E. Ribstein & Bruce H. Kobayashi, *An Economic Analysis of Uniform State Laws*, 25 J. Legal Stud. 131 (1996).

in the gaps."[21] Of all of the perspectives on the relationship between the state courts this one is arguably the most "value free" perspective because it seems to flow naturally and logically from the constitutional structure of delegated and reserved powers.

The Functional Approach

According to this perspective, the dynamism of American law has been primarily due to the existence of the states and their legal systems. Innovations in the states diffuse through the national system and are sometimes adopted by the federal government.[22] Some who share this perspective actually see the states as virtually indispensable to federal action or adoption of legal innovation. Of course much of the legal innovation in the states is the result of legislative rather than judicial action. But that does not preclude significant contributions by state courts and judges, especially appellate judges.[23] Obviously, those who share this perspective will see judicial federalism as a bounteous source of progress, and a positive feature of American government.

The Qualitative Approach

Best known from the arguments over the "parity" of state and federal courts (a topic we consider in chapter 3), the qualitative approach starts from a very simple premise and reasons to a rather disturbing conclusion. The simple premise is that the state courts are inferior to federal courts. Because of a disparity in resources training and attitude, state judges cannot, and sometimes will not, fairly and fully protect the Federal Constitutional rights of the litigants who appear before them.[24] Although the arguments against parity are of greater moment in those cases where a potential loss of liberty is involved, there is little distinction made, in the qualitative perspective, between criminal and civil litigation. The rather disturbing conclusion reached from this premise is that litigants should always prefer a federal to a state forum and that federal courts should never shrink from policies that result

21. "Federal law is interstitial in nature. It rarely occupies a legal field completely. It builds upon legal relationships established by the states, altering or supplanting them only so far as necessary for the special purpose." Henry M. Hart, Jr. & Herbert Wechsler, The Federal Courts and the Federal System 435 (1953). While over forty years old, we think the statement remains largely true today. See, e.g., Atherton v. FDIC, 519 U.S. 213, 218 (1997) (quoting Hart & Wechsler).

22. The classic statement is that of Justice Brandeis dissenting in New State Ice Co. v. Liebman, 285 U.S. 262, 311 (1932), the source of the "laboratories of experimentation" metaphor. The diffusion of state innovations through the nation has been the subject of much literature, including Jack L. Walker, *The Diffusion of Innovations Among the American States*, 63 Am. Pol. Sci. Rev. 880 (1969).

23. Kermit Hall, The Magic Mirror: Law in American History 104–105 (1989); Kermit L. Hall, William M. Wiecek, & Paul Finkleman, American Legal History ch. 10 (2d ed. 1996).

24. Burt Neuborne, *The Myth of Parity*, 90 Harv. L. Rev. 1105 (1977).

in maximum review of state action through appeal, habeas corpus, diversity jurisdiction, etc.

The Economic Approach

In the economic approach the concentration is on winners and losers. State and local governments are often looked upon as the bastions of protection for entrenched economic interests and the state courts as their handmaidens.[25] As the classic theory goes, it is easier for industrial and commercial interests to "capture" policy-making at the state level than it is at the federal level, where a variety of regional interests must compete with each other for attention, thus diffusing the power of any one interest. It is logical, it is argued, for those who favor the status quo, the current winners, to favor more decision-making at the state level. Those on the side of the losers, those disadvantaged by the economic status quo, should correlatively favor increased decision-making at the federal level. There are of course examples on both sides of this issue to support the competing claims.[26]

The Philosophical Approach

Finally, there are several commentators who view judicial federalism through the prism of political philosophy or theory. In their view we must be conversant with the "ism" in federalism, or understand the "norms" that are both expressed and implied by the structure of a dual court system. We are generally sympathetic with the fact that one is unable to appreciate the foundations of judicial federalism without understanding the myths and principles that underpin it. And, we will have much more to say about this approach in our concluding chapter. For the next few chapters, however, the actual results of judicial federalism will capture more of our attention.

THE PLAN OF THE BOOK

In this volume we will discuss judicial federalism in all of its manifestations. But our focus is on evaluating judicial federalism as it actually operates. We believe that there should be more empirical work on the operation of judicial federalism and less angst over whether those of us who like the idea are neurotics. Barry Friedman and Larry Kramer have persuasively argued that, with few exceptions, the contemporary debate over federalism has been conducted at a highly abstract level. With, again, some exceptions, much of the legal discourse on the topic has done little to empirically study the values, the pros and cons, of

---

25. Kenneth M. Dolbeare, Trial Courts in Urban Politics (1967).

26. For examples of the economic literature on federalism, see Richard A. Posner, Economic Analysis of Law 695–714 (5th ed. 1998); Robert P. Inman & Daniel L. Rubinfeld, *Rethinking Federalism*, 11 J. Econ. Perspectives 43 (1997); Thomas S. Ulen, *Economic and Public-Choice Forces in Federalism*, 6 Geo. Mason L. Rev. 921 (1998).

federalism.[27] While neither Friedman nor Kramer specifically mentions judicial federalism, we think their critique applies to the literature on that topic as well.

Indeed, their critique is symptomatic of a larger problem of a relative lack of dialogue between legal and social science scholars on topics of mutual interest. At least until quite recently, many political scientists and other social scientists rarely relied on law review articles, or took seriously on their own terms the technical guideposts provided by procedural and substantive law, which lawyers and judges purport to follow. Likewise, most legal scholars rarely if ever engage in any minimal empirical research, or make much effort to utilize the social science research of others.[28] Our goal in this book is to speak to both audiences: to measure the values of judicial federalism, and to inform our measurement by social science research.

In chapter 2 we will discuss the effect of our bifurcated judicial system on rights. Opinion is widely divergent on this issue. There are those who claim that judicial federalism is a roadblock to the protection of rights while other see it as a work of genius in securing and even enhancing rights enforcement. We will attempt to take a balanced view of the evidence, and to show that how one thinks about the nature of rights has a direct bearing on an evaluation of judicial federalism.

Chapter 3 will concentrate on the role of state courts in adjudicating federally protected rights. Once again, this has been a contentious issue over the last twenty years or so. In shorthand it has come to be know as the "parity" debate. Many see the state courts as intellectual and political backwaters, unable to litigate fairly and boldly when federally protected rights are concerned. Others see no discernible difference in the way rights are litigated in federal and state courts, and even see some distinct advantages in encouraging state court litigation of federally protected rights.

Chapter 4 will discuss the choice of courts that confronts many litigants, and will discuss the strategy in trying to select the place for deciding issues. It will be

27. Barry Friedman, *Valuing Federalism*, 82 Minn. L. Rev. 317, 317–319 (1997); Kramer, *supra* note 14, at 1490. Other writers have also recently called for more functional analysis of legal issues raised by federalism. E.g., Lynn A. Baker, *The Revival of States' Rights: A Progress Report and a Proposal*, 22 Harv. J. L. & Pub. Pol'y 95 (1998); Erwin Chemerinsky, *Formalism and Functionalism in Federalism Analysis*, 13 Ga. St. U. L. Rev. 959 (1997); Michael C. Dorf, *Instrumental and Non-Instrumental Federalism*, 28 Rutgers L. J. 825 (1998).

28. Frank B. Cross, *Political Science and the New Legal Realism: A Case of Unfortunate Interdisciplinary Ignorance*, 92 Nw. U. L. Rev. 251 (1997). There are, of course, many exceptions on both sides. Probably legal scholars have overall done a better job of incorporating social science research in their work, rather than the reverse. Edward L. Rubin, *The New Legal Process, the Synthesis of Discourse, and the Microanalysis of Institutions*, 109 Harv. L. Rev. 1393 (1996). On the other hand, perhaps political scientists are now paying more attention to law review literature, as evidenced by, e.g., the presentations by law professors at the annual meetings of the American Political Science Association and the Law and Society Association, and the cross-disciplinary dialogue found in the Law and Courts Section of the APSA and its e-mail discussion list.

shown that some issues formerly decided only in the federal courts are now showing up on state court dockets, thus reversing the forum shopping patterns that many civil libertarians recommend.

Chapter 5 will discuss the ability of state courts to protect liberty by using the state constitutions to provide additional liberties, not provided by the federal courts in interpreting the U.S. Constitution. In some ways this is the mirror image of the parity argument because it assumes that the federal government is retreating or even abandoning the protection of some rights, especially in the criminal justice and privacy areas. We will discuss the problem of balancing the need for national uniformity of rules with the desire for innovation and cultural diversity in the states.

Chapter 6 is entitled "Special Problems for Judicial Federalism: Race, the Death Penalty, and Habeas Corpus." In this chapter we address the legitimate criticism that has been leveled at the performance of the structure of judicial federalism. Of obvious concern is the penchant for racism and parochialism that is often latent, and sometimes disturbingly manifest in courts. But we point out that these problems are neither peculiar to the state courts nor are they bereft of solutions, many of which have been attempted and successful.

In our concluding chapter, we summarize our argument, and relate it to questions of community power and ideology. We end the volume by suggesting future directions for judicial federalism, and for policy initiatives that might be undertaken to facilitate and improve it.

2

Rights and Judicial Federalism

Whether one is looking at judicial federalism as the apportionment of the nation's law work, as the initiatives of state courts, or even as the devolution of responsibility from federal to state courts, the question of rights intrudes. Most often the question is posed thusly: Does judicial federalism serve to expand or contract rights? A straightforward question? Perhaps. A simple one? Certainly not.

MEASURING RIGHTS

To ask the question is to speak of rights as if they were commodities, like corn or electricity. It is not at all clear that rights may be so quantified as to allow measurement of their expansion or contraction. When one speaks of a commodity, it is intuitively clear what it more or less means. If we sought to know whether a certain method of farming, or a certain fertilizer would lead to more or less corn, or perhaps would have no effect on the yield, a simple experiment, ending in a commonly accepted measurement, would demonstrate to all, with perfect clarity, the truth of the matter. No such experiment exists for rights.

But quantifying is only the beginning of any inquiry, not the end. For we would want to know the costs associated with different methods or fertilizers, and whether there was environmental damage associated with either. Is the fertilizer dangerous to produce? Perhaps most importantly, do we need to produce more corn? Is there a glut or a shortage in the market? Thus, does having more corn make us better off or worse off? To ask the question is to illustrate the problem.

Some rights advocates seem to have no such worries. To them you can never be too thin, or too rich, or have too many rights to paraphrase a common 1980s fallacy. Were we to engage in *reductio ad absurdum* we could finally ask what a person would be to whom every possible right had been given? Well, the words king or queen come to mind.

Corn and rights are not fungible because rights are reciprocal. They impose obligations on others. They have costs associated with them. They are personal. They only make sense in the context of a society.[1] Although it has become commonplace to speak of rights adhering to states, to other creatures, and to groups, we realize that the unit of analysis is the person, a human being. In this sense, all rights are ultimately human rights. When one attempts to make the claim that there are more rights or less rights under some system or another she encounters an extremely difficult logical problem as well, which can be best illustrated in the area of criminal procedure.

Many who are skeptics of judicial federalism say that the criminal defendant has fewer rights in state courts than in federal courts, or is protected less ardently in state courts. How does one attempt to measure such a thing? What is the empirical referent for right? Certain things can be quantified. For example, we can enumerate a specific right, say the right to be free from unreasonable searches and seizures, and then design a study that could calculate the instances where that right was denied, using as a benchmark the motion for suppression of evidence by a court.[2] The more suppressions the more evidence of denials of rights. But perhaps the greater rate of suppression signaled a greater solicitude for rights, thus indicating the presence of more rights. In other words do we count a court's correcting the police as the existence of more or fewer rights? The default position seems to be the success of a rights claim. That is, the more successful rights claimants are, the more rights there are. Put another way, the easier it is to convict someone the fewer rights they have had enforced. Therefore we are constrained to say that the more unsuccessful prosecutions of accused criminals there are, the more rights are present. Of course, just the opposite could be true.[3] Consider the following example.

Let us say that there were a jurisdiction where the police, prosecutors, trial courts, prisons, and so forth, never make mistakes, nor do they ever intentionally violate the constitutional rules that previous courts have discovered or invented. In this wonderful place, we hypothesize, any claims of rights would be denied as unsupportable. The criminal won't go free because the constable has not blundered. Whereas in an adjoining jurisdiction where all of these agencies make a lot of mistakes, or intentionally fail to follow procedures, many more rights claims would be upheld. In which place are there more rights? In which place would it be preferable to live?

1. Richard H. Fallon, Jr., *Individual Rights and the Powers of Government*, 27 Ga. L. Rev. 343 (1993); Barry Friedman, *Trumping Rights*, 27 Ga. L. Rev. 435 (1993).

2. Some examples of studies in this area are Jerome H. Skolnick, Justice Without Trial (1964); Jonathan Simon & Jerome H. Skolnick, *Federalism: The Exclusionary Rule and the Police* in Power Divided: Essays on the Theory and Practice of Federalism 75 (Harry N. Scheiber & Malcolm M. Feeley eds., 1989); James J. Fyfe, *Enforcement Workshop*, 19 Crim. Law Bulletin 253 (1983).

3. It must be pointed out, as respectfully as possible, that one's attitude on this issue could be related to one's occupation. A criminal defense attorney or American Civil Liberties Union board member may have a different view of this than a prosecuting attorney.

As we explain in chapter 3, if one could actually see how the same case would be handled in two different places, then it would be possible to say where a person had more rights. On the other hand, if one is considering rights in a purely ontological sense, it would not even make sense to talk about more or less rights since everyone has exactly the same basket of rights, to the same degree, just for being human. It is only in their accidental characteristics that persons differ.[4] Thus it would be only in their realization or perfection, based on these accidental characteristics, that rights would likewise differ.

Let us take another example from the criminal justice system, that of the trial of a person accused of rape. In many jurisdictions defendants were, and are, allowed to present evidence relating to past sexual conduct of the alleged victim. Judges routinely gave strong instructions to the jury allowing them to consider such evidence. As more was discovered about the crime of rape, the reluctance of rape victims to come forward, and the effect of such evidence on juries and witnesses, many of these same jurisdictions, for sound public policy reasons, eliminated this evidence as irrelevant and prejudicial. (This was done, by the way, on a state-by-state basis, and not mandated by the federal courts.)[5]

The right to confront the witnesses against oneself is fundamental to the justice system.[6] Since the court allowed such inquiry by the defense, it could be said that the defendant had a right to confront the complainant in this manner. Now the obvious question is this: what would happen to the right of a hypothetical, perhaps innocent, criminal defendant to defend himself by attacking the credibility of the accuser in a given jurisdiction (that is a jurisdiction that has eliminated the defense)? It is gone, of course (as well it should be). Where did it go? Did it vanish? Or perhaps, ontologically, it never was a right to begin with. We were just "mistaken."

None of this is meant to discourage the discussion of rights in the context of federalism. It is simply to warn against a simplistic treatment of the topic. Of course structure has an impact on outcomes, including rights. There are features of judicial federalism that have positive impacts on people's rights, and lives, and there are features that have negative impacts as well. The secret, as in most things in life, is to have a balanced view and to treat the subject fairly. This, in any case, is what we will attempt.

The country has been for some time awash in "rights talk," a phrase made famous in a 1991 volume by law professor Mary Ann Glendon. In that oft-cited work she outlines her position that political discourse has been impoverished by the resort to rights claims rather than by an appeal to public policy preferences. In

4. By accidental characteristics we refer to those things that are not essential to every human being, assuming one accepts the concept of "essence" in the first place. Examples might be having been arrested, or being handicapped, or being in a protected class.

5. About half of the states in the 1980s restricted the admissibility of sex history and reputation. See John Kaplan, Jerome H. Skolnick & Malcolm Feeley, Criminal Justice 398 (5th ed. 1991).

6. U.S. Const., Amend. VI.

Glendon's view, this has had extremely bad consequences for society because it tends to freeze opposing public policy positions into absolutes and disfavors talk of compromise. It also tends to consider individuals outside of their social context. This leads, in turn, to a neglect of the concept of duties, which can be considered the reciprocal of rights.[7]

FEDERALISM AND RIGHTS

Glendon's approach is both moderate in tone and balanced in terms of policy positions. In general we find her arguments persuasive and helpful.[8] And we find them particularly apposite to a discussion of judicial federalism. This is because the type of political dialogue that Glendon favors is more likely to take place at the local level, not in a national forum. And we believe that courts and judges, at the local level, are crucial elements in this political dialogue.

Until recently, the thought was often expressed that such a dialogue would not be useful.[9] The putative advantages of federalism—sensitivity to local interests, increased citizen involvement in public affairs, and policy experimentation—can be clearly seen as *potentially* leading to an increase in personal freedom. However, when commentators look at federalism in practice, most are skeptical, even contemptuous, of federalism's potential to contribute to liberty.[10] The argument runs that it is local power that most often oppresses the citizen, and that the federal government is the only center of power able, and willing, to counteract this oppression. The archetypical case in point, according to these commentators, is the enslavement of African-Americans and the century-long struggle by the freed slaves to achieve equal rights through federal action in the face of state intransigence.[11]

---

7. Mary Ann Glendon, Rights Talk: The Impoverishment of Political Discourse (1991).

8. Glendon has been criticized strongly by at least one noted commentator for failing to give rights enough credit for actually enhancing the values of community and interaction that she favors. See Cass Sunstein, Book Review, New Republic 33 (September 2, 1991). Among the rights cited by Professor Sunstein is freedom of speech, which encourages opening channels of communication and acts to facilitate the social interaction that Glendon calls for. He also questions her blaming "rights talk" for diminishing feelings of social responsibility when, according to him, "the opposite is more nearly true." The problem with Professor Sunstein's criticism is that it treats rights at a very high level of generality while Professor Glendon is dealing with rights as actuated in the political system.

9. See, e.g., Richard Briffault, *"What About the 'Ism'?": Normative and Formal Concerns in Contemporary Federalism*, 47 Vand. L. Rev. 1303, 1312–1317 (1994); Erwin Chemerinsky, *The Values of Federalism*, 47 Fla. L. Rev. 499, 525–527 (1995); Michael W. McConnell, *Federalism: Evaluating the Founders' Design*, 54 U. Chi. L. Rev. 1484, 1491–1511 (1987).

10. Harry N. Scheiber, *Federalism and the Legal Process: Historical and Contemporary Analysis of the American System*, 14 L. & Soc'y Rev. 663, 706–707 (1980).

11. Pace Jefferson McConkie, *Civil Rights and Federalism Fights: Is There a "More Perfect Union" for the Heirs to the Promise of Brown?*, 1996 B.Y.U. L. Rev. 389; Scheiber, *supra* note 10, at 706–707; David L. Shapiro, Federalism: A Dialogue 52–56 (1995).

Nonetheless, the federal government has engaged in some world-class rights trampling of its own. The Japanese internment during World War II, the "Red Scare" and McCarthyism were almost entirely federal responsibilities.[12] More recently the federal government's response to drug abuse and domestic terrorism has raised a collective eyebrow.[13] Despite these significant lapses, the federal government, mainly through the courts but also through the legislature, is still arguably the primary guarantor of personal rights for Americans in the twentieth century. Even so, the possibility that state governments, and to some extent state courts, can have a significant role in the protection of individual liberties cannot be denied.[14]

It is a fact that certain decisions of the federal courts have led to the protection of important rights, rights that a majority, or significant minority, of states did not protect. Many of these rights now seem so intrinsic to our political culture that it hardly seems possible that we once lived in a regime without them. But when rights are established or discovered in federal courts or in Congress, dialogue and political development across the entire nation is foreclosed and largely ended. State courts are less free to implement rights in ways that may be unique or experimental, or in ways that respect the wishes of political majorities in their jurisdictions.

Some critics of judicial federalism would say that this experimentation and political dialogue comes only at the expense of, and to the detriment of, individuals in the states, either because of the "tyranny of the majority,"[15] or because of the

---

12. E.g., James L. Gibson, *Pluralism, Federalism and the Protection of Civil Liberties*, 43 W. Pol. Q. 511 (1991); Scheiber, *supra* note 10, at 707 n.25.

13. See Note, *Blown Away? The Bill of Rights After Oklahoma City*, 109 Harv. L. Rev. 2074 (1996) (discussing Congressional legislation passed in 1996); Greg Hollon, Note, *After the Federalization Binge: A Civil Liberties Hangover*, 31 Harv. C.R.-C.L. L. Rev. 499 (1996) (discussing extensive expansion of federal criminal jurisdiction over drug and gun offenses in recent Congresses).

14. See, e.g., Federalism and Rights (Ellis Katz & G. Alan Tarr eds., 1996) (essays from various authors discussing how federalism can promote liberty under certain circumstances); Akhil Reed Amar, *Five Views of Federalism: "Converse-1983" in Context*, 47 Vand. L. Rev. 1229 (1994) (suggesting that in some situations state court actions premised on state law can provide remedies when federal officials violate federal constitutional rights); Gibson, *supra* note 12 (empirical study of state governmental repression of communists during McCarthy era, showing that some states acted less repressively than the federal government); Shapiro, *supra* note 11, at 97–103 (general discussion); Tom Stacy, *Does Federalism Promote Liberty?*, 5 Kan. J. of L. & Pub. Pol'y 15 (1996) (general discussion); Richard B. Stewart, *Federalism and Rights*, 19 Ga. L. Rev. 917 (1985).

15. The concept is often associated with Alexis De Tocqueville, Democracy in America 9 (Richard D. Heffner ed., New American Library 1956) (1835). Today it is problematical, in that the nature of decision-making does not favor numerical majorities as much as it favors those who, for one reason or another, have better access to decision-makers. For an individualist perspective on this issue see Clint Bolick, Grassroots Tyranny (1993). For a modern recasting of the problem coupled with some novel political solutions, see Lani Guinier, The Tyranny of the Majority: Fundamental Fairness in Representative Democracy (1994).

inferiority of state and local structures. But to the claim that judicial federalism is a structural barrier to full enjoyment of individual rights either because of the attitudes of the majority or because of the inferiority of state courts, we respectfully demur. The remaining chapters will address this. But as a precursor to that discussion, we first look at the topic rights generally in the context of courts and federalism.

RIGHTS, RECONSIDERED

The term itself has come under intense scrutiny over the last several years. As Austin Sarat and Thomas Kearns have pointed out, every discussion of law in American society today seems to eventually turn to the subject of rights.[16] This question has occupied some of the best minds of this and previous generations, but there is no consensus position on what a right is or, for that matter, what the Constitution says, or was intended to say, about the nature of rights.

Even the briefest recounting of various positions on rights demonstrates a wide spectrum of approaches that have been taken to explaining their nature.[17] On one end of the spectrum are those who approach rights in a way that emphasizes the individual and equal justice. Among the leading exponents of this view are John Rawls, who argues that "citizens of a just society ought to have the same basic rights" (basing this conclusion on the classic premise of an equal value for each citizen), and Ronald Dworkin, who views rights as barriers to collective action:

> Individual rights are political trumps held by individuals. Individuals have rights when, for some reason, a collective goal is not a sufficient justification for denying them what they wish, as individuals, to have or to do, or not a sufficient justification for imposing some loss or injury upon them.[18]

Many of the modern conceptions depend on similar views of rights as based on traditional "higher law" foundations. It is claimed that without such basis there is no principled way for judges and courts to vindicate unenumerated rights, those

---

Tocqueville spent considerable time in his work discussing American federalism. For modern discussions of his views, see Barbara Allen, *Alexis de Tocqueville on the Covenantal Tradition of American Federal Democracy*, 28 Publius: The Journal of Federalism 1 (Spring 1998); John Kincaid, *Federal Democracy and Liberty*, 32 PS: Political Science & Politics 211 (1999); G. Alan Tarr, Understanding State Constitutions 118 & n.108 (1998). Amazingly, he even spoke to judicial federalism, as recounted in Lawrence Lessig, *Translating Federalism: United States v. Lopez*, 1995 Sup. Ct. Rev. 125. In *Democarcy in America*, Tocqueville at one point argues that "the common people in America [could] easily perceive . . . the point where the competence of federal courts commences and that of the state courts ends." *Id.* at 125 (quoting *Democracy in America*, p. 165).

16. Legal Rights: Historical and Philosophical Perspectives (Austin Sarat & Thomas R. Kearns eds., 1996) (hereinafter Legal Rights).

17. For a compressed and engrossing litany of rights see Peter Schlag, *Rights in the Post-Modern Condition* in Legal Rights, *supra* note 16, at 263–264.

18. Ronald Dworkin, Taking Rights Seriously xi (1977).

without a clear reference in the constitution. Michael Perry goes so far as to argue that only a religious foundation will ultimately support the claim that universal rights exist. His claim is that any idea of human rights must be "ineliminably" religious, a view shared by many other legal philosophers.[19]

Still there are those others who as legal positivists who tend to defer to the will of the majority and would give much less trumping power to the individual, especially absent a clear textual basis for such power. Among these are John Hart Ely, who views the role of courts as increasing the representative character of the political system. Farther across the majoritarian part of the spectrum are James Buchanan and Robert Bork, who would arguably would give almost all power to local majorities, as long as the right to move freely about the country was preserved.[20]

Some, writing in the post-modernist vein, deny either that there is any ontological meaning for "right," or claim that our current search for such meaning has failed:

> The aesthetics that shape the legal conceptualization of "law" and rights are increasingly turning out to be intellectually incredible. Not to be credited. Not warranting faith.[21]

Whatever grounding rights may still find, their *expression* remains in the laws and in the decisions of courts about those laws. Even the most ardent of individualists must look askance at self help. The routinization of conflict concerning rights is maintained. Anyone seeking the vindication or elimination of a right, ultimately still depends on the decision of a court making or interpreting a law. In simpler days Oliver Wendell Holmes, Jr. could say, apparently without irony or cynicism, that the law was simply a prophesy of what the courts will do in a given case, and therefore the protection of rights depended on the actions of courts or of persons anticipating the actions of courts.

Rights are still court-centered. Old maxims hold that there is no right without a remedy and the role of a common law court is to either fashion or adjust remedies. Often, the main reason for enumerating a given right is to give guidance to a court.[22] Although courts are by no means the only guarantor of rights, it is hard to imagine any regime of rights succeeding without the existence of an independent judiciary. As one commentator has eloquently stated the case:

---

19. See Michael J. Perry, *Is the Idea of Human Rights Ineliminably Religious?* in Legal Rights, *supra* note 16, at 205.

20. Robert H. Bork, The Tempting of America: The Political Seduction of the Law 52–53 (1990); James M. Buchanan, *Federalism and Individual Sovereignty*, 15 Cato J. 259 (1995); John Hart Ely, Democracy and Distrust: A Theory of Judicial Review (1980).

21. Schlag, *supra* note 17 at 303.

22. It cannot be denied that the responsibility for protecting rights rests on more than the shoulders of judges. An individual must seek to preserve his or her own rights. Other agencies of government, from the legislature to the street-level bureaucrats, such as police officers and driver's license examiners, can be both guardians and, unfortunately, abusers of rights.

> [T]he courts are integral to democracy. They are not to be sure the only instruments of justice, perhaps not the most significant in the day to day life of the individual. But at certain crucial moments when his life, his liberty or his property are in jeopardy, the judiciary is the most immediately available resource.[23]

Both the breezy realism of a young Judge Holmes and the optimism of Professor Jaffe may both be thin gruel to some nowadays. Such talk leaves them with a feeling of emptiness, perhaps disillusionment. We may certainly long for a much more complex, and some would say better anchored, body of thought about the nature of rights. In other words, many find the naked positivism of Holmes's statement to be philosophically unsatisfying, or even morally bankrupt. But what is desired, ultimately, is a persuasive vocabulary of rights, one that will achieve a just society.[24]

So if one's major concern is the rationalization of judicial federalism, how should we view rights? One cannot argue simultaneously for the law as a "brooding omnipresence in the sky" and celebrate the virtues of diversity. It is clear that those who speak in praise of judicial federalism are intellectually closer to those who believe that rights talk is rather more divisive than unifying, has supplied the union more callus than sinew. There is also little doubt that judicial federalism creates a situation where the success of a rights claim is at least partially dependent on jurisdiction. The more important question, we think, is whether that fact is helpful or hurtful to American democracy.

The first imperative for a judicial federalist is to view rights broadly, that is to say to realize that rights encompass much more than the limitation of government in a very narrow area such as criminal procedure. Most laws in some way create rights, and it is perfectly natural to speak as if they do. For example, the Americans with Disabilities Act (ADA) both sprang from "rights talk" and created rights through legislation.[25] Some rights are revocable, like the right to deduct the cost of mortgage interest from your tax returns. Others are more difficult to revoke, like the right not to be taxed on your income at all unless apportioned by state. That right took a constitutional amendment to take away. It would not take a constitutional amendment to take away the rights of the disabled, but it would probably be harder than taking away the mortgage interest deduction.

The language of rights also contributes to the problem because politicians discovered, fairly early on, that the word "right" resonates. However, in campaigning on rights not much intellectual heavy-lifting is apparent. The right-to-work laws never guaranteed a single job to an individual (although they may have created an economic environment where businesses were free to create more jobs at lower salaries). The Right to Life Society does not campaign against capital

---

23. Louis Jaffe, English and American Judges as Lawmakers 33 (1969) (as edited).

24. Consider, for example, the criticism of rights vocabulary. Mark Tushnet, *An Essay on Rights*, 62 Texas L. Rev. 1394 (1984). See also the discussion in Jeremy Waldron, *Rights and Needs: The Myth of Disjunction* in Legal Rights, *supra* note 16, at 87.

25. Stephen L. Percy, *ADA, Disability Rights, and Evolving Regulatory Federalism*, 23 Publius: The Journal of Federalism 87 (Fall 1993).

punishment (although the Catholic Bishops, maintaining their pre-modern consistency, do). Right to die really means right to die somewhat earlier, and animal rights, well, what can I say? (Trees apparently don't have rights, but they might have standing.)[26]

Some folks hate talking about rights like this; they want the term reserved for things no government can ever take away. They may even be offended. To them we apologize and hope they will keep reading. But if one is wedded to the notion that rights are of one, and only one, type, that they are universal and flow from a higher law or religion, or reflect some quality that inheres in all human beings, then judicial federalism is nigh impossible to defend. For if judicial federalism has any meaning (independent of mere decentralized administration of universal law), then it must countenance some diversity of both rights and outcomes of "rights claims."

If, on the other hand, rights are seen as mainly the product of political dialogue, not its antecedent, a case can be made for the salubrious effects of diversity and therefore of judicial federalism. We believe that there is no contradiction in not denying the metaphysical basis of some rights and yet favoring the existence of judicial federalism, in other words of positing a hierarchy of rights claims.

Lest this appear to be watering down the basis of rights, consider the fact that regardless of the lofty rhetoric about rights, the ultimate normative goal is to have rights succeed at something, not be neatly justifiable. Some rights claims appear, at first blush, to be so obviously universal that they must be uniformly enforced everywhere, at all times. Take, for example, the right to live. What could be more straightforward? Human beings, having some intrinsic special value, must not be killed except in the most extreme and rare of circumstances, narrowly constrained by the rule of law. As Jeremy Waldron points out though, even this is a tough sell:

> Those who found themselves falling back upon the elemental claim that simply because one is human, one deserves to live, have had to discover that this is sometimes the weakest, not the strongest claim that people can make to one another.[27]

Not to belabor the point, rights are only as good as their persuasive power, either to raise up a majority or bring down a tyrant. To say that certain rights simply cannot be denied, anytime anywhere, is to ignore the fact that rights are denied everyday, everywhere, with impunity. It may make one feel good to talk about the right to life of those in Bosnia, Rwanda, Kosovo, or Chechnia, but if nothing is done to keep them alive, including deciding, through *political* action to use force against their killers, then the cry of universal rights become nothing more

---

26. See Christopher Stone, *Should Trees Have Standing? Toward Legal Rights for Natural Objects*, 45 S. Cal. L. Rev. 450 (1972).

27. Waldron, *supra* note 24, at 94. He was in part paraphrasing Michael Ignatieff, The Needs of Strangers (1984). He also quotes Hanna Arendt, The Origins of Totalitarianism 299 (2d ed. 1958) ("The world found nothing sacred in the abstract nakedness of being human.").

than "sounding brass and tinkling cymbal."[28] The value of rights lies not in universality but in potency.

The argument for a diversity of rights ultimately depends, therefore, not on defeating a universalistic conception of rights, but rather on championing an alert, talented, and independent, state judiciary working alongside of a federal judiciary, to guarantee the maintenance of a republic. Both state and federal courts have this maintaining function. There is *essentially* no difference between a state and a federal court. Both fashion or adjust remedies, and both are designed, in pursuance of a "republican form of government,"[29] to be independent of the political branches of government. It is not a difference in fundamental attitudes toward rights that creates the conditions for judicial federalism. It is simply the relationship between the two courts that does so.

JUDICIAL FEDERALISM AND RIGHTS

It is important to distinguish the relation of rights to federalism itself[30] from their relationship to judicial federalism. Much has been written on the topic of federalism and some of this writing does discuss its impact on rights, since rights are often created by legislatures and implemented by agents of the executive branch. In fact, society could not function if every right depended solely on the courts. But it is clear that, under federalism, the citizens of the different states have different rights that are discovered and enforced by their own political systems, irrespective of the actions of the federal courts or the federal legislature. For many this is problematic.

In general, progressives have been suspicious of federalism. They believe either that it promotes a natural conservatism at best, or that it is the reification of hypocrisy, at worst. It is seen both as a way of guaranteeing the victory of the

28. I Corinthians 13:1

29. Although never definitely tested, the U.S. Constitution does, of course, call for such a government in each state (Art. IV, § 4.). See Vicki C. Jackson, *Printz and Testa: The Infrastructure of Federal Supremacy*, 32 Ind. L. Rev. 111, 119–122 (1998) (discussing whether general constitutional plan requires states to create courts to, *inter alia*, enforce federal law); Michael E. Solimine, *Constitutional Restrictions on the Partisan Appointment of Federal and State Judges*, 61 U. Cin. L. Rev. 955, 962 n. 39 (1993) (discussing whether Guarantee or Due Process clauses require each state to maintain an independent judiciary). Every state has an independent judiciary in that it can't be directly overruled or controlled by the other branches. But since rights are most often cast in the role of restraint on governmental action, courts must also be relatively independent of the pressures that are normal and welcome in the other branches of government. See Steven P. Croley, *The Majoritarian Difficulty: Elective Judiciaries and the Rule of Law*, 62 U. Chi. L. Rev. 689 (1995).

30. On the question of whether there is such a thing as "federalism itself," see Harold M. Hyman, *Federalism: Legal Fiction and Historical Artifact?*, 1987 B.Y.U. L. Rev. 905; Briffault, *supra* note 9.

haves over the have-nots, and posing severe dangers to certain minorities.[31] Some criticize federalism on the ground that the states are irrelevant, that there is but one national political culture and therefore that there should be one set of American rights.[32] Some say that federalism is merely fear or neurosis, a longing for a simpler mode of yesteryear that is as comfortable as it is fictitious.[33] We will have more to say about all of these perspectives, especially about the progressive critique, in chapter 7. For now, we will restrict our comments strictly to the relationship of state and federal rights as interpreted by the courts.

The framers of the constitution, each representing his own state,[34] were obviously concerned about rights. The promise of a Bill of Rights was seen, by most, as a *sine qua non* for the ratification of the Constitution, and thus for the union. What they feared most, and therefore wanted protection from, was the Congress. It is not trivial that the bill begins with the expression "*Congress* shall make no law." Nor is it trivial that John Marshall and the court thought that the word "Congress" meant exactly that in the case of *Barron v. Baltimore*,[35] which held that the Bill of Rights does not serve as a limitation of state power.[36] Then, the state constitutions were seen as the primary repository of citizens' rights against the states. Each state had its own constitution and most had a bill of rights. Early on, the range of rights protected was wide and the enforcement of these rights robust.[37]

---

31. One of the most elegantly argued statements is that of Grant McConnell, Private Power and American Democracy 178 (1966). Consider also, for example, the following: "The general effect of federalism in a developed economy, then, is to make it difficult for local majorities to adopt substantial social welfare programs." Mark Tushnet, *The Politics of Constitutional Law* in The Politics of Law 223 (David Kairys ed., rev. ed. 1990); see also James F. Blumstein, *Federalism and Civil Rights*, 47 Vand. L. Rev. 1251 (1994).

32. Mark Tushnet, *What Then Is the American?*, 38 Ariz. L. Rev. 873 (1996).

33. Edward L. Rubin & Malcolm Feeley, *Federalism: Some Notes on a National Neurosis*, 41 UCLA L. Rev. 903 (1994). For careful and sharp criticism of the neurosis argument, on the grounds that (like many *defenses* of federalism) it is premised on many abstract and untested assumptions, *see* Barry Friedman, *Valuing Federalism*, 82 Minn. L. Rev. 317 (1997).

34. This is merely stating a fact. It is not intended to imply a particular theory of the constitution or of federalism. However, there is an extended colloquy on the structure of the original federal government in the case of U.S. Term Limits Inc. v. Thornton, 514 U.S. 779 (1995) that has caused extensive academic comment. See for example Robert F. Nagel, *The Term Limits Dissent: What Nerve*, 38 Ariz. L. Rev. 843 (1996).

35. 32 U.S. 243 (1833).

36. This is not meant to celebrate the result of the case. Perhaps Barron deserved the $4,500 that the state court awarded him but that the state appellate court took away. John Marshall certainly thought there was a taking involved, even though there was no actual possession of his property (and even though the subject of when a taking occurs is still a hotly contested issue). See Richard Epstein, Private Property and the Power of Eminent Domain (1985). See also J.M. Balkin, *Learning Nothing and Forgetting Nothing: Richard Epstein and the Takings Clause*, 18 Urban Lawyer 707 (1986).

37. Ellen A. Peters, *Capacity and Respect: A Perspective on the Historic Role of the State Courts in the Federal System*, 73 N.Y.U. L. Rev. 1065 (1998).

The passage of the Fourteenth Amendment eviscerates much of the decision in *Barron*, but it doesn't overturn it, the late great Justice Black not withstanding.[38] But no unbiased reading of the history of the Fourteenth Amendment can lead to the conclusion that the Congress sought to create one, national culture of rights. The evidence is overwhelming that the intention was to destroy the capacity of the states to reimpose involuntary servitude and to insure the complete citizenship of the freed slaves.[39]

As the U.S. Supreme Court has been called upon over the years to invalidate state laws or practices on the basis of the due process clause of the Fourteenth Amendment, we have come to refer to the "selective incorporation" of the Bill of Rights. This has occurred, for the most part, not because the provision guaranteeing the right did not exist in the relevant state constitutions, but almost always because the federal court did not believe that the way a particular state court was interpreting its own laws and constitution, particularly in the area of criminal procedure, comported with the minimum rights guaranteed under the federal due process standards. The problem is that the Supreme Court cannot pick and choose among the states. For example. It cannot say, "Mississippi, why can't you behave like Massachusetts in your handling of tainted evidence?" Or, "Florida, go check with Oregon on giving people adequate representation at trial." It must, instead, proclaim a national right and then require all the states to observe it.

States are thus marginalized: That is, they must tinker with policies, if they wish to, at the margins. The poster child for this process is the development of trial by jury. The constitution says a jury trial is a right in both criminal and civil cases. In federal court in criminal cases the size must be twelve and the verdict unanimous. States may have fewer members on a jury and, up to a point, may allow nonunanimous verdicts.[40] But this is the exception rather than the rule. Usually the result is that state procedures become lockstep with the federal procedures.[41] With the end of experimentation comes the end of creativity and responsibility. Some federal rules have had beneficial effects on state procedures. Certainly one would

38. Justice Black believed that the Fourteenth Amendment Due Process Clause incorporated the totality of the Bill of Rights as a limitation against the states. His view never commanded a majority on the Court. Adamson v. California, 332 U.S. 46 (1947) (Black J., dissenting).

39. Jacobus ten Broek, Equal Justice Under Law (1965); Akhil Reed Amar, *The Bill of Rights as a Constitution*, 100 Yale L.J. 1131, 1201–1202 (1991); Akhil Reed Amar, *The Bill of Rights and the Fourteenth Amendment*, 101 Yale L.J. 1193 (1992).

40. The constitutional provisions are found in the Sixth and Seventh amendments to the U.S. Constitution. Fed. R. Crim. P. 23 and 31 requires a twelve-person jury that renders a unanimous verdict. How much states can depart from this model is addressed in Ballew v. Georgia, 435 U.S. 223 (1978).

41. Jerold Israel, *Federal Criminal Procedure as a Model for the States*, 543 Annals Am. Acad. Pol. & Soc. Sci. 130 (Jan. 1996). However, state constitutions can serve as an independent basis for developing criminal procedure. See in general chapter 5, and in particular Nina Morrison, Note, *Curing "Constitutional Amnesia": Criminal Procedure Under State Constitutions*, 73 N.Y.U. L. Rev. 880 (1998); Special Project, *The Continuing Evolution of Criminal Constitutional Law in State Courts*, 47 Vand. L. Rev. 795 (1994).

have to include the exclusionary rule in this category. The prophylactic and didactic dimensions of excluding ill-gotten evidence are now commonly accepted.[42]

Some other experimentation by the states has occurred. But then the problem is that the fruit of the experiment is subsequently imposed on all other states rather than allowed to stand and be observed. A typical example is the good faith exception to a defective warrant.[43] What would be wrong with saying that a police officer may plead the good faith exception in Florida, but not in Vermont? Another example of experimentation stifled is in the area of campaign finance reform. The city of Cincinnati, Ohio attempted to strictly limit the amount of money spent on local political campaigns. A federal district judge, believing that the issue was disposed of by the U.S. Supreme Court case of *Buckley v. Valeo*[44] struck down the law as unconstitutional. Now *Buckley* is a very complex case with many parts to it, but none of the case has anything to do with local political campaigns. The problem is that at the highest level of generality, *Buckley* stands for the idea that spending money in state and national campaigns is functionally the equivalent of speech, and thus cannot be restrained. If the Cincinnati case had been reviewed by the Supreme Court, it may have been able to carve out some areas for exception, for example political campaigns where face-to-face communication is not only possible but preferred. In other words, the restriction on spending money might actually encourage speech, rather than discourage it. Yet, given the few cases that the Supreme Court chooses to review each year, it is unlikely that it would get to this. It didn't,[45] and thus the experiment in Cincinnati died aborning.

The burden of supporting a defense of judicial federalism is, we admit, made heavier by the realization that rights will be different in different states. It is almost instinctive to the human being to be suspicious of differential treatment. Obviously all citizens are guaranteed equal protection of the law. But that phrase is no more self-defining than "freedom of speech," "cruel and unusual punishment," or "excessive bail." Each requires a context, a set of facts, and a court to have an impact. Economic theory suggests that even putatively national rights can be subject to somewhat different interpretations and application within each state, without harming the federal system as a whole. The exercise, or curtailment, of many rights are not apt to have much interstate spillover effects. The benefits or detriments of policies with respect to many rights will in many cases be largely felt within the state involved. Moreover, many if not most people enjoy some degree of interstate mobility, so they can flee (exit) states with restrictive rights regimes,

42. Simon & Skolnick, *supra* note 2.

43. Developed in United States v. Leon, 468 U.S. 897 (1984) and other cases.

44. 424 U.S. 1 (1976) (per curiam).

45. Kruse v. City of Cincinnati, 142 F.3d 907 (6th Cir. 1998), *cert. denied*, 119 S.Ct. 511 (1998).

and enter states with (in their view) more favorable rights climates. Thus, to some degree, states can compete to provide more favorable rights.[46]

We believe there are some simple truths that should allay fears that judicial federalism will lead, inexorably, to unfair treatment. Plain error on the part of the states in interpreting settled national law, reflecting national consensus on certain rights of American residents and citizens, is not allowed to exist under judicial federalism. The supremacy clause makes clear that the Constitution, treaties, and laws of the United States are the supreme law of the land. The right to appeal the decision of a state court that contradicts any of these is not eliminated by judicial federalism. Furthermore, there is no logical requirement that judicial federalism leads to limiting access to federal courts.

By the same token, nothing in the concept or operation of judicial federalism has made it impossible, or even difficult, for the federal government, or the federal courts from implementing any policy development through a national consensus.[47] A problem does sometimes develop when a state achieves consensus on a matter before the nation does and there is a question of whether the federal government preempts the field. In the 1990s, for example, several state and local jurisdictions have adopted softer approaches to drugs such as marijuana, but the national government is still firmly wedded to a zero-tolerance policy. Some states have adopted a right-to-die policy and one was threatened by a federal official with prosecution of doctors for using federally controlled substances.[48] The Geogia Supreme Court legitimated consensual sodomy even though the U.S. Supreme Court (in a case from Georgia!) had refused to do so.[49]

Sometimes the federal courts mistake the existence on a national consensus on rights and sometimes they are successful in helping to create one.[50] Although the

---

46. This point is developed in Richard A. Posner, The Federal Courts: Challenge and Reform 280–302 (1996); Shapiro, *supra* note 11, at 94–96, and Nelson Lund, *Federalism and Civil Liberties*, 45 Kan. L. Rev. 1045 (1997), and in chapter 4. Perhaps the best, and in our view largely successful, example of this theory is the Supreme Court's delegation in Miller v. California, 413 U.S. 15 (1973) to local communities to determine what works are obscene and thus beyond First Amendment protection. Cf. Donald J. Farole, Jr., Interest Groups and Judicial Federalism: Organizational Litigation in State Judiciaries 159 (1998) (pointing out that obscenity decisions in courts of one state don't directly affect other states). See generally Mark Rosen, *Our Nonuniform Constitution: Geographical Variations of Constitutional Requirements in the Aid of Community*, 77 Texas L. Rev. 1129 (1999).

47. See Louise Weinberg, *Fear and Federalism*, 23 Ohio N.U. L. Rev. 1295 (1997) for a discussion of recent revivals of limitations, or at least discussions of limitations, of federal power. Her general conclusions is that supporters of federalism ultimately fear "the consolidation catastrophe," the subsuming of all power by the national government, an event she views as extremely unlikely.

48. The Justice Department eventually rescinded its threat. See Thomas Maier, *Suicide Law: Year 1 / Few in Oregon Have Asked for Help in Dying*, Newsday, Nov. 3, 1998, p. C3.

49. The Supreme Court case is Bowers v. Hardwick, 478 U.S. 186 (1986). The Georgia case is Powell v. State, 510 S.E.2d 18 (Ga. 1998).

50. See Michael E. Solimine & James L. Walker, *The Supreme Court, Judicial Review, and the Public: Leadership Versus Dialogue*, 11 Const. Comm. 1 (1994).

Supreme Court has declared that securing an abortion is some kind of right, it is in state courts that the outlines of the right are being drawn, not in the federal courts.[51] One can hardly fault the states for attempting, in their smaller universes, to solve a problem that the nation as a whole has not been able to solve.

MAJORITIES AND RIGHTS

The last aspect of judicial federalism that we would like to address is what might be referred to as the problem of majorities. In a sense, judicial federalism forces us to address several difficult questions about the operation of government. Such as the amount of required insulation of the judiciary from the will of the majority, the best means to protect minorities, and the existence, or nonexistence, of dual majorities (state and federal).

Many critics of federalism seem to deny the possibility of dual majorities. As William H. Riker has written,

> To one who believes in the majoritarian notion of freedom, it is impossible to interpret federalism as other than a device for minority tyranny. To those who wish to enforce it, the plea for maintaining the guarantees of federalism is simply a hypocritical plea for the special privilege to disregard the national majority.[52]

To these commentators, majorities in the states become minorities in the nation in order, perhaps, to abuse minorities in the states. The state court system, because of its lack of isolation from the electorate, becomes, in this scenario, the tool of national minorities (state majorities) in denying rights. But we believe that the worry about (state) majoritarian pressures on the courts is overdrawn. The major reason we believe so is that ultimately, all rights are majoritarian. When a *continuing* majority disfavors a right it must eventually disappear. Unless a minority, or discrete, and possibly insular, majority, such as women, are able to persuade the rest of society to restrain itself from taking advantage, they may very well do so.

The political minority cannot prevail in the long run; they can only hope to educate the majority. Judges and courts are educators. Rights are teaching tools. We offer the proposition that it may be better to have fifty sets of teachers than only one. Thus to speak disparagingly of majorities is ultimately counterproductive. This is the real lesson of judicial federalism and rights. Preservation of

---

51. Steven A. Holmes, *Right to Abortion Quietly Advances in State Courts*, N.Y. Times, Dec. 6, 1998, § 1, p.1. Indeed, a woman's right to seek an abortion illustrates our point. It can be argued that the Supreme Court decision in Roe v. Wade, 410 U.S. 713 (1973) had the (perhaps unintended) effect of polarizing views on the issue, and prevented states from evolving different approaches to that contentious issue. See Ruth Bader Ginsburg, *Speaking in a Judicial Voice*, 67 N.Y.U. L. Rev. 1185, 1199–1209 (1992); Solimine & Walker, *supra* note 50, at 4–5.

52. William H. Riker, Federalism: Origin, Operation, Significance 142 (1964) (as edited).

dialogue is a necessary but not sufficient condition of the maintenance of rights. It is our contention that this dialogue is enhanced by judicial federalism, not hindered by it.

We believe that the most important function of rights is the protection of free government and the promotion of civil society, not the facilitation of radical individualism. As one commentator has put it, "The central virtue of federalism is not heterogeneity but self government."[53] We further believe that an important part of this protection and promotion flows from what we refer to as the didactic function of courts.

There are, and there have always been, major shortcomings in the U.S. rights regimen. There is no doubt that some of this is attributable to judicial federalism. This is a truism, since structures have consequences. But the converse is not true. There is no evidence that without judicial federalism many of the same, or even worse, insults to rights would not have taken place. Throughout most of our history, the federal courts have often come up very short when it comes to protecting the basic rights of Americans.[54] We often forget what an aberration the Warren Court was in our federal judicial history. Fifty-eight years of "separate but equal" and the endorsement of McCarthyism and the obscenity of Japanese exclusion were not attributable to judicial federalism.[55]

We believe that there is no conclusive evidence, taking into consideration any definition of right, that judicial federalism should be restrained, much less done away with. Although it is sometimes tempting and important to concentrate on the lonely innocent man, caught up in the wheels of state justice, abused by the system, it is difficult to imagine that grinding would be less painful in a unitary system, comprising a quarter of a billion people, operated from a central location hundreds, or even thousands, of miles away.

---

53. The quote is in Gary Jeffrey Jacobsohn, *Contemporary Constitutional Theory, Federalism, and the Protection of Rights*, in Federalism and Rights, *supra* note 14, at 48.

54. See Henry Steele Commager, *Judicial Review and Democracy*, 19 Va. Q. Rev. 417 (1943).

55. Plessy v. Ferguson, 163 U.S. 537 (1896); Dennis v. United States, 341 U.S. 494 (1951); Korematsu v. United States, 323 U.S. 214 (1944).

3

Beyond Paradigms: State Court Adjudication of Federal Rights

The federal structure of the United States was, in part, intended to insure individual liberty. It must by now be obvious that we think it has, in part, succeeded. In this chapter, we focus on one way that these individual rights are tested, that is by litigation in state courts. We are interested particularly in those rights derived from federal law (i.e., the U.S. Constitution and federal statutes). The litigation of federally guaranteed rights in state courts has been common from the birth of the republic to the present day. But it remains, to some, deeply problematic. In short, many criticize the state courts as not being up to the task of "rights protection." We hope to demonstrate in this chapter that the criticisms of state courts and judges in the protection of individual liberties are greatly overstated.

From their inception, federal court doctrine assumed that state courts are ready and able to fully and fairly adjudicate federal rights. There is, however, a line of cases, and some scholarly authority, that continues to question that assumption. In this chapter we summarize and critique the empirical evidence that has been brought to bear on this difference of opinion. In shorthand, this is the debate over the "parity," between state and federal courts, i.e., the availability and qualitative receptivity of state courts to adjudicate and, where appropriate, uphold federal rights. Although difficult to measure and evaluate, we conclude that relative parity exists between state and federal courts to do just that.

THE MADISONIAN COMPROMISE AND BEYOND

The debate over the existence of parity springs from the initial establishment of the lower federal courts by the Constitution. Article III of the Constitution provides that there "shall" be one Supreme Court, but the Congress "may" establish lower federal courts.[1] Providing Congress with the discretion to create the latter courts was the culmination of a debate at the Constitutional Convention. Some of the framers argued for the mandatory creation of federal tribunals inferior to the U.S. Supreme Court, to properly manage large caseloads and to serve as an enforcement arm for the president and the Congress. The opponents contended that such courts would be unnecessary and duplicative, since *state* courts were available to adjudicate federal cases. James Madison and James Wilson ultimately offered a plan to resolve the conflict, which has taken the name of the first of its authors. The Madisonian compromise gave Congress the option to create or not to create lower federal courts; this compromise was adopted at the convention as a part of Article III.[2]

The significance of the compromise has not so much in the discretion to create (since inferior federal courts were, in fact, established by the First Judiciary Act of 1789), as in the contemplation that federal cases would be litigated in state courts. Indeed, not until 1875 did Congress expand the jurisdiction of the federal district courts to include cases involving general federal questions.[3] Congress unquestionably has the power to *exclude* the state courts from adjudicating federal cases, though as described in the next chapter in practice such exclusion has been the exception, not the rule. In adjudicating these cases, state courts are bound by the Supremacy Clause to apply relevant federal law, and thus are endowed with the same power and responsibility to enforce federal constitutional principles as are their federal counterparts.

Bound by federal law and under the review of state appellate courts and, ultimately, the U.S. Supreme Court, state courts seem to be, in the abstract, appropriate forums for the adjudication of federal rights. These assumptions undergird other important aspects of federal court doctrine.[4] Consider first what are

---

1. U.S. Const. art. III, § 1, provides in part that "[t]he judicial Power of the United States, shall be vested in one supreme Court, and in such inferior Courts as the Congress may from time to time ordain and establish."

2. See Richard H. Fallon, Daniel J. Meltzer & David L. Shapiro, Hart & Wechsler's The Federal Courts and the Federal System 7–9 (4th ed. 1996) (hereinafter Hart & Wechsler). There remains, however, a considerable scholarly debate on what limits, if any, there are on Congressional power to restrict the jurisdiction of the lower federal courts it does create. *Id.* at 348–387. That debate implicates the parity issue, since the effect of a reduction might force a case raising federal issues to be litigated in a state court. *Id.* at 351–354.

3. See Judiciary Act of Mar. 3, 1875, ch. 137, 18 Stat. 470 (codified at 28 U.S.C. § 1331).

4. Other federal court doctrines are premised to varying degrees on some assumption of parity. For example, the Eleventh Amendment has been interpreted to prohibit many actions for damages in federal court by private litigants asserting that a state has violated their federal rights. In such cases, the Supreme Court often observes that a state court is presumably open to hear the claim. E.g., Seminole Tribe of Florida v. Florida, 517 U.S. 44, 71 n.14 (1996); Atascadero State Hosp. v. Scanlon, 473 U.S. 234, 238 n.2 (1985). Cf. Idaho v. Coeur d'Alene Tribe of Idaho, 521 U.S. 261, 267–280 (1997) (opinion of Kennedy, J., joined by Rehnquist, C.J.) (two Justices arguing that exceptions to Eleventh Amendment

called the abstention doctrines. The prosecution of criminal actions in a state court can potentially raise a variety of federal constitutional questions, such as the suppression of evidence under the Fourth Amendment or the constitutionality of the state statute under which the prosecution is brought. Traditionally, a defendant in such an action must raise these issues in the state court system. However, a state court defendant can also seek an equitable remedy in federal court, such as enjoining the state proceeding if he can show irreparable harm as a result of the prosecution. Federal courts were long reluctant to flesh out this narrow federal remedy, but the doctrine seemingly flourished with the Warren Court decision in *Dombrowski v. Pfister.*[5] The plaintiffs in *Dombrowski* sought to enjoin the enforcement of state laws alleged restrictive of their First Amendment rights. After restating the traditional reluctance of federal courts to exercise their equitable powers against state courts, the majority nevertheless held that an injunction must issue since protracted litigation in state court would have a chilling effect on the exercise of First Amendment rights. Justice Harlan in dissent argued that the majority's approach was premised on the notion that state courts will not vindicate constitutional rights as effectively as federal courts—or, in other words, that parity was being ignored.

Harlan's dissent in *Dombrowski* effectively became the majority position six years later in the celebrated Burger Court decision of *Younger v. Harris.*[6] *Younger* held that, in the absence of extraordinary circumstances, a federal court could not enjoin a state criminal proceeding. The majority opinion by Justice Hugo Black relied on traditional principles of equity doctrine, the notion of comity between federal and state courts, and the values underpinning what he called "Our Federalism." *Younger's* progeny have come to rely explicitly on the values of parity,[7] and have expanded *Younger* to preclude the use of injunctive or declaratory

---

jurisprudence should be limited to situations where no state forum is open to the litigant). (One of those exceptions is derived from Ex Parte Young, 209 U.S. 123 (1908), referenced in the opening pages of this book, which permits litigants under certain circumstances to sue state officials for injunctive relief in federal court.) See generally Vicki C. Jackson, *Coeur D'Alene, Federal Courts and the Supremacy of Federal Law: The Competing Paradigms of Chief Justices Marshall and Rehnquist*, 15 Const. Comm. 301, 321–322 & n.100 (1998) (observing that parity debate informs Eleventh Amendment jurisprudence). For more discussion of the Eleventh Amendment, see the end of this chapter.

In the balance of this chapter, and elsewhere in the book (e.g., chapters 4 and 6), we address other examples of federal courts doctrine that are shaped by the parity debate, such as abstention, habeas corpus, and exclusive federal jurisdiction. This list is not exhaustive. For a useful overview of a broad range of statutes and court decisions that impact the allocation of cases between and among federal and state courts, see Thomas E. Baker, *A Catalogue of Judicial Federalism in the United States*, 46 S.C. L. Rev. 835 (1995).

5. 380 U.S. 479 (1965).

6. 401 U.S. 37 (1971).

7. In *Younger,* Justice Black described "comity" as the "proper respect for state functions." 401 U.S. at 44. This preference for comity can be construed as shading into the concept of parity—that is, avoiding "affront" to state courts by suggesting that they cannot

relief by federal courts to interfere with "quasi-criminal" state court proceedings, civil contempt proceedings, or civil litigation involving "important state interests."[8]

For another example, consider the use of the writ of habeas corpus. Although federal courts had possessed the power to issue writs of habeas corpus on petitions by state prisoners since 1867, that power usually was limited to considering only the validity of the jurisdiction of a sentencing court. The scope of the writ was expanded in 1953 by the landmark decision of *Brown v. Allen,*[9] where the Court held that a federal court could review the validity of a state court conviction when it rested on a determination of a federal constitutional claim. The writ was further expanded in such cases as *Fay v. Noia,*[10] where habeas corpus relief was permitted despite the state prisoner's failure to properly appeal his conviction in the state court system.

Some commentators, such as Justice Lewis Powell, expressed disquietude over this expansion of relitigation of federal claims already addressed in state courts. Their concern was based particularly on the fact that the decisions of an entire state court hierarchy would thus be subordinated to the opinion of a single federal district judge.[11] These reservations were adopted by the Court in the years since as a rationale for curtailing the expansion of the writ in the review of state court convictions. The most significant expression of this trend came in *Stone v. Powell,*[12] where the Court held that Fourth Amendment claims could be relitigated on habeas corpus only upon a showing that the petitioner did not have a full and fair opportunity to have that claim considered in the state court system. In the course of the opinion, the Court expressly reiterated the concept of parity as providing the basis for deference to state court decision-making.[13]

Cases like *Younger* and *Stone* are examples of what Richard Fallon calls the

---

properly adjudicate federal rights. Nevertheless, only *Younger's* progeny were to explicate the concept of parity. See, e.g., Moore v. Sims, 442 U.S. 415, 429–430 (1979); Huffman v. Pursue, Ltd., 420 U.S. 592, 610–611 (1975); Deakins v. Monaghan, 484 U.S. 193, 203 (1988).

While derided by some commentators, the "Our Federalism" mantra of Justice Black in *Younger* continues to resonate in Supreme Court opinions, even by liberal justices. E.g., Ruhrgas AG v. Marathon Oil Co., 119 S.Ct. 1563, 1571 (1999) (Ginsburg, J., writing for a unanimous Court, quoting "Our Federalism" passage from *Younger*).

8. See Hoffman v. Pursue, Ltd., 420 U.S. 592 (1975); Juidice v. Vail, 430 U.S. 327 (1977); Pennzoil v. Texaco, 481 U.S. 1 (1987).

9. 344 U.S. 443 (1953).

10. 372 U.S. 391 (1963). *Fay* was severely undercut by the "cause" and "prejudice" rule developed in Engle v. Isaac, 456 U.S. 107 (1982), and Wainright v. Sykes, 433 U.S. 72 (1977) (requiring the habeas applicant to show good cause for the failure to follow state procedure, and prejudice to him if the procedures had to be followed), and was formally overruled in Coleman v. Thompson, 501 U.S. 722 (1991).

11. See, e.g., Schneckloth v. Bustamonte, 412 U.S. 218, 259–261 (1973) (Powell, J., concurring).

12. 428 U.S. 465 (1976).

13. *Id.* at 493 n.35. We further consider habeas corpus in chapter 6.

federalist model.[14] But there is another theme in the cases, which Fallon terms the nationalist model, premised on seemingly different assumptions about parity. For example, in *Mitchum v. Foster*,[15] decided only a year after *Younger*, the Court unanimously held that the cause of action utilized most by private parties to vindicate federal rights, 42 U.S.C. § 1983, was an exception to the strictures of the federal Anti-Injunction Act. The Court reached this conclusion in part on its review of the legislative history of section 1983, which reveals that the Reconstruction Congress was motivated in large part by the gross failures of state courts, particularly in the South, the enforce federal rights, especially those of the newly freed slaves. Similarly, in *Patsy v. Florida Board of Regents*,[16] the court held that plaintiffs suing under section 1983 were not required to exhaust any remedies they might have under state law. The Court relied in large part, as it did in *Mitchum*, on the legislative history of section 1983, and concluded that Congress intended that federal courts had the "paramount role in protecting constitutional rights." Of course, the cases in the nationalist and federalist models do not necessarily contradict each other, and can be reconciled depending on the particular statute and precedent at issue, and the procedural postures of the case. But their differing visions of the breadth of the role state courts ought to play in protecting federal rights is in tension.

COMPETING PARADIGMS

Even sharper tensions are clearly evident in the academic commentary on federal court doctrine. The legal process paradigm is akin to the federalist doctrinal model, and is most often associated with Henry Hart and Herbert Wechsler and their influential federal courts casebook. Hart and Wechsler and their disciples attempt to resolve the jurisdictional tensions inherent in a dual court system by emphasizing the need for finality, minimizing friction between federal and state courts, and assigning cases on the basis of institutional competence. The Hart and Wechsler paradigm largely assumes that both federal and state courts share the responsibility to define and enforce federal rights, and that state courts, on the whole, are capable of respecting federal rights. Thus, entry into federal court should be limited, or rejected entirely, if litigants had full and fair opportunities to adjudicate their federal rights in state tribunals.[17]

---

14. Richard H. Fallon, Jr., *The Ideologies of Federal Courts Law*, 74 Va. L. Rev. 1141 (1988).

15. 407 U.S. 225 (1972). The Court held that the Anti-Injunction Act, 28 U.S.C. § 2283, did not prohibit a federal court from ordering equitable relief under 42 U.S.C. § 1983, as § 1983 was encompassed by the "expressly authorized" exception found in the act itself.

16. 457 U.S. 496 (1982).

17. See Richard H. Fallon, Jr., *Reflections on the Hart and Wechsler Paradigm*, 47 Vand. L. Rev. 953 (1994); Michael E. Solimine, *Against Judicial Devolution*, 78 Judicature 313 (1995) (review of Larry W. Yackle, Reclaiming the Federal Courts (1994)); Michael

There is a long line of commentators who sympathize with the nationalist line of cases, and thus reject some or all of the assumptions of the legal process model. Perhaps the most prominent recent proponent of the alternative model is Larry W. Yackle.[18] The academy has not settled upon a name for the alternative model, but we think the new legal realism would be a fitting one.[19] Yackle and other advocates of this model are highly critical of any notion of parity, and would make it far easier for litigants to bring suit and obtain remedies in federal court. Thus, they would overrule or limit virtually all of the cases found in the federalist model.

There's no denying that the legal process model, at least as originally articulated, had demonstrable shortcomings. Critics have observed that the Hart and Wechsler casebook had remarkably little to say about concurrent developments in substantive civil rights and constitutional law, which would presumably impact (and be impacted by) the allocation of litigation between federal and state courts.[20] And despite its implicit assumptions about parity, the casebook only its fourth edition in 1996 began to address the issue from an empirical perspective.[21] The new legal realism has its own shortcomings. Yackle's work, for example, has been taken to task for its static vision of the quality of state courts, and its often dismissive attitude toward the virtues of a judicial federal structure.[22]

THE MYTHS AND REALITIES OF PARITY

From our perspective, perhaps the most serious weakness of the new legal realism model is its refusal to take a serious look at how state courts are actually litigating federal rights. The best support for this conclusion is demonstrated by a

---

Wells, *Who's Afraid of Henry Hart?*, 14 Const. Comm. 175 (1997) (review of Hart & Wechsler, *supra* note 2).

18. Larry W. Yackle, Reclaiming the Federal Courts (1994) (hereinafter Yackle, Reclaiming). Other scholars, like Yackle, have also to varying degrees criticized broad swaths of present federal court doctrine and advocated alternative models. See, e.g., Daan Braveman, Protecting Constitutional Freedoms: A Role for Federal Courts (1989); Martin H. Redish, Federal Jurisdiction: Tensions in the Allocation of Judicial Power (2d ed. 1990); Judith Resnik, *Rereading "The Federal Courts": Revising the Domain of Federal Courts Jurisprudence at the End of the Twentieth Century*, 47 Vand. L. Rev. 1021 (1994). A helpful summary of the various models is found in Larry W. Yackle, Federal Courts 13–26 (1999).

19. Ann Althouse, *Federal Jurisdiction and the Enforcement of Federal Rights: Can Congress Bring Back the Warren Era?*, 20 Law & Soc. Inquiry 1067, 1082–1083 (1995) (review of Yackle, Reclaiming, *supra* note 18) (arguing that Yackle's model is similar to the Legal Realism movement of the early twentieth century).

20. A point developed in Wells, *supra* note 17; Michael Wells, *Naked Politics, Federal Courts Law, and the Canon of Acceptable Arguments*, 47 Emory L. J. 89 (1998).

21. See Hart & Wechsler, *supra* note 2, at 351–354. However, only lately have other federal courts casebooks also begun to refer to and evaluate the empirical literature on point. Wells, *supra* note 17, at 192–193.

22. E.g., Althouse, *supra* note 19, at 1070–1074; Barry Friedman, Book Review, 12 Const. Comm. 441 (1995) (review of Yackle, Reclaiming, *supra* note 18).

law review article by Professor Burt Neuborne, *The Myth of Parity*,[23] being the "favorite citation" of the new legal realists, a reference that has now achieved a "mythic status of its own."[24] Neuborne's article neatly encapsulates some empirical arguments *against* trusting state courts with the adjudication and possible vindication of federal rights, and for that reason deserves an extended look on our part.

Neuborne and other skeptics of parity typically settle on two rationales to suggest a litigant's preference for a federal forum. First, they argue that historical considerations—notably, the outcome of the Civil War and the passage of the constitutional amendments during the Reconstruction era—have elevated the federal government in general, and federal courts in particular, to a place of prominence over their state counterparts. In addition, they assert that contemporary institutional differences between federal and state courts justify preference for the former over the latter.

The first rationale provides a starting point for those who question the existence of parity. The debate over parity, as they see it, was largely settled with the defeat of the secessionist states in the Civil War.[25] Centralized government and the federal judicial power were enhanced by the passage of the Reconstruction constitutional amendments, by the broadening of the federal question jurisdiction of the federal courts in 1875, and by the passage of section 1983 to enforce civil rights. These developments were hastened, to a large extent, by the perceived hostility of state courts to the enforcement of federal rights created by the amendments. Moreover, it is often said, the asserted dismal performance of state courts (particularly in the South) in the modern civil rights era lends modern validity to this historical construct.[26]

---

23. Burt Neuborne, *The Myth of Parity*, 90 Harv. L. Rev. 1105 (1977).

24. Althouse, *supra* note 19, at 1069, 1071. A computer search in the LEXIS law review database conducted in June of 1999 revealed that the article had been cited in at least 264 law review articles. This number would place it in or near the top 100 most-cited law review articles of all time. See Fred R. Shapiro, *The Most-Cited Law Review Articles Revisited*, 71 Chi.-Kent L. Rev. 751 (1996). (Interestingly, a parallel search indicated that the article had been cited only six times by federal courts.)

25. See, e.g., Redish *supra* note 18, at 2; Neuborne, *supra* note 23, at 1114–1115. We also note that the justices of the Supreme Court who have criticized parity have also relied mainly on historical considerations, and have eschewed any reference to empirical data discussed later in this chapter. See, e.g., Fair Assessment in Real Estate Ass'n v. McNary, 454 U.S. 100, 124 n.11 (1981) (Brennan, J., concurring); Stone v. Powell, 428 U.S. 465, 526 (1976) (Brennan, J., joined by Marshall, J., dissenting); Steffel v. Thompson, 415 U.S. 452, 463–464 (1974) (Brennan, J.).

26. Southern state courts in that period were perceived as being generally hostile to civil rights. See Michael Meltsner, *Southern Appellate Courts: A Dead End,* in Southern Justice 136 (Lawrence Friedman ed., 1965); Michal R. Belknap, Federal Law and Southern Order: Racial Violence and Constitutional Conflict in the Post-Brown South 120–121 (1987); David L. Shapiro, Federalism: A Dialogue 54 (1995). While the hostility of many state government officials in the South toward civil rights in that period hardly requires

We do not quarrel, of course, with the supremacy of the national government, nor with the evidence of hostility of some courts to the enforcement of federal rights, after the Civil War. Doubters of parity, however, can marshall little evidence to suggest that state courts continued to be *systematically* hostile to federal rights after Reconstruction. To the extent that the hostility was revived in some state courts during the 1950s and 1960s, it was an unfortunate aberration not reflected on a nationwide basis today.[27] Whatever the historical scorecard of state courts in enforcing federal rights, such a record has only a tangential relevance to the *modern* debate over parity.

The second rationale—alleged institutional incompetence—ultimately is also lacking in significant force. Although most critics of parity have been content to rely on rather abstract, conclusory assertions as to historical changes in federalism, others have also asserted empirical evidence concerning the comparative expertise of federal and state courts. The primary source of this evidence has been the much-

---

documentation, the hostility of state courts is more problematic. Indeed, one study of all race relation cases in Southern state supreme courts between 1954 and 1963 indicated that 33 % of dispositions were favorable to the black parties. See Kenneth Vines, *Southern State Supreme Courts and Race Relations,* 18 W. Pol. Q. 5 (1965). The Vines study concluded that the record of Southern judges "is more favorable to Negro claimants than in any other part of the state political system." *Id.* at 18.

27. See Neuborne, *supra* note 23, at 1119. To his credit, Professor Neuborne (writing over 20 years ago) points out that the "widespread breakdown of Southern justice which motivated enactment of the Civil Rights Act of 1871, and similar breakdowns during the height of the civil rights movement which provoked calls for significant expansions of federal jurisdiction, do not exist today." *Id.* at 1119 n.55 (citations omitted). He reiterates the point in Burt Neuborne, *Parity Revisited: The Uses of a Judicial Forum of Excellence*, 44 DePaul L. Rev. 797, 798–799 (1995). While doubts as to fairness of Southern justice (and, presumably Southern judging) persist even thirty years after the civil rights era, e.g., Stephen B. Bright, *Can Judicial Independence Be Attained in the South? Overcoming History, Elections, and Misperceptions About the Role of the Judiciary*, 14 Ga. St. U. L. Rev. 817 (1998); Alabama v. Engler, 85 F.3d 1205, 1210 (6th Cir. 1995) (Jones, J., concurring) (wondering whether African-Americans being extradited from Michigan to Alabama, will receive justice given that state's treatment of, *inter alia*, the Scottsboro Boys), modern assessments of the judicial branch in the Deep South are much more favorable. See G. Alan Tarr & Mary Cornelia Aldis Porter, State Supreme Courts in State and Nation 69–123 (1988) (case study of Alabama Supreme Court); Mark Curriden, *The Changing Faces of Southern Courts*, 79 ABA Journal 68 (June 1993) (focusing on state supreme courts). For a critical view of the argument that the South in general and Southern legal institutions have been somehow distinctive from the rest of the nation, see James A. Gardner, *Southern Character, Confederate Nationalism, and the Interpretation of State Constitutions: A Case Study in Constitutional Argument*, 76 Tex. L. Rev. 1219 (1998). See also Robert J. Glennon, *The Jurisdictional Legacy of the Civil Rights Movement*, 61 Tenn. L. Rev. 869 (1994) (arguing that Supreme Court in 1950s and 1960s modified some federal court doctrines that would otherwise have presented jurisdictional obstacles to its support for the civil rights movement, but that subsequent changes in the South's legal and political systems have diminished the need for expansive federal jurisdiction).

cited article by Neuborne, which, after an extensive review of social science data, concludes that federal courts are institutionally more competent than state courts to enforce federal rights. Neuborne deserves much credit, we think, in grounding his criticism of parity in evidence derived from the social sciences. After reviewing his arguments, however, we suggest that they are ultimately inconclusive and do not provide a compelling basis to discard parity.

In his article, Neuborne advanced three reasons supporting a preference for federal courts over state courts. First, federal courts will have a higher level of technical competence in dealing with complex legal issues. Second, the "psychological set" of federal judges insures their greater receptivity to enforcing the interpretations of federal rights outlined by the Supreme Court and other federal courts. Finally, the federal judiciary's insulation from majoritarian pressures suggests that federal judges will be more likely to reach decisions that *may* require challenging the power of local interest groups. These three factors, Neuborne concludes, make the notion of parity, at least on a nationwide basis, a dangerous "myth."

In arguing the existence of "technical competence" of federal—as opposed to state—judges, Neuborne focuses on the individual members of the bench. He argues that a higher level of quality will be reflected in the federal judiciary, since the requirement of Senate approval of federal judicial appointments establishes a floor of competence higher than that in the states. In addition, the prospect of high compensation leads a greater number of qualified individuals to seek federal, rather than state, judicial positions. In contrast, the selection processes for state judges are based either on political patronage systems or on elections. The disparity is exacerbated, Neuborne contends, by the necessity of comparing federal district judges with state *trial* judges, rather than with those on state appellate courts.[28] Finally, the assistants to a federal judge, particularly the law clerks, may tend to outstrip their state counterparts in ability and dedication.

These arguments, we think, are not compelling. At the outset, we think, the proper comparison is between federal judges and the *entire* state court system, including appellate courts. As discussed below, such a comparison considerably ameliorates the asserted failings of state courts. In any event, modern state trial judges and courts are not functioning at the antediluvian level suggested by Neuborne. Surveys of current state trial judges, for example, indicate that increasingly they are paid more and are organized on a more professional basis.[29]

---

28. Neuborne, *supra* note 23, at 1116 n.45, 1118–1119. Neuborne argues that three factors require the comparison between federal district courts and state *trial* courts. First, delay in reaching decisions at the trial and appellate levels may deter individuals from litigating the denial of their constitutional rights. Second, appellate court ability to review the findings of fact by lower courts is limited. Third, appellate court judges may be subject to the same majoritarian pressures as are their state counterparts.

29. The salaries of state judges are annually reviewed in the State Court Journal. On the improving caliber of state trial courts, see John Paul Ryan, Alan Ashman, Bruce D. Sales & Sandra Shane-DuBow, American Trial Judges: Their Work Styles and Performance

An earlier study by Kenneth Dolbeare characterized state trial judges as largely uncreative defenders of the status quo.[30] More recent scholarship depicts a quite different image, suggesting that the qualities of state judges will vary from state to state and city to city, depending on their organizational environment, their ties to the local political system, and the judicial role in which they see themselves.[31] Moreover, the staff support for state trial judges has been increasing so that many judges now have or share law clerks, as do their federal colleagues.[32] Finally, the alleged disparity in selection procedures is somewhat overdrawn. On the one hand, the selection process for *federal* judges has always been, and continues to be,

---

(1980) (hereinafter cited as American Trial Judges); Robert J. Sheran & Barbara Isaacman, *State Cases Belong in State Courts,* 12 Creighton L. Rev. 1, 47–50, 60–61 (1978). While systematically collected, much of this evidence, we admit, impacts only indirectly on the competence of state judges to adjudicate federal rights. The same can be said, however, of virtually all of the evidence, much of it impressionistic, marshalled by Neuborne.

The increasing professionalism of state courts is indicated by the many state judicial systems that have adopted, in whole or in part, the Federal Rules of Evidence and the Federal Rules of Civil Procedure. See 1 Gregory P. Joseph & Stephen A. Saltzburg, Evidence in America: The Federal Rules in the States xxv (Supp. 1992) (thirty-five states have adopted various forms of the Federal Rules of Evidence); John B. Oakley & Arthur F. Coon, *The Federal Rules in State Courts: A Survey of State Court Systems of Civil Procedure*, 61 Wash. L. Rev. 1367 (1986) (thirty-five states, by court rule or statute, substantially replicate the provisions of the Federal Rules of Civil Procedure). See also Helen Hershkoff, *Positive Rights and State Constitutions: The Limits of Federal Rationality Review*, 112 Harv. L. Rev. 1131, 1175–1179 (1999) (arguing that many state courts have and can be efficient gatherers of facts in cases, and noting that amicus briefs, special masters and expert testimony, among other things can be used by state judges in this regard as needed); Daniel J. Meltzer, *State Court Forfeitures of Federal Rights*, 99 Harv. L. Rev. 1128, 1155 (1986) ("[I]n many areas state and federal rules are sufficiently similar that the application of federal rather than state standards would make little difference.").

30. See Kenneth M. Dolbeare, Trial Courts in Urban Politics: State Court Policy Impact and Functions in a Local Political System (1967). Neuborne cited Dolbeare's highly caustic appraisal as "[t]he only serious study" of state trial benches. See Neuborne, *supra* note 23, at 1116–1117 n.46.

31. Neuborne was correct in pointing out that as of 1977 relatively little work had been done on the performance of state trial judges, particularly on the civil side. More recent work, however, qualifies or contradicts many of Dolbeare's broad conclusions. Lynn Mather, *Policy Making in State Trial Courts* in The American Courts: A Critical Assessment 119–157 (John B. Gates & Charles A. Johnson eds., 1991) (hereinafter Critical Assessment).

32. See American Trial Judges, *supra* note 29, at 227–243. Law clerks for federal judges are typically recent graduates of law school, serving for one- or two-year terms, while those for state judges are sometimes "career" clerks and serve for considerably longer periods. See, e.g., John B. Oakley & Robert Thompson, *Law Clerks in Judges' Eyes: Tradition and Innovation in the Use of Legal Staff by American Judges,* 67 Calif. L. Rev. 1286 (1979) (study of California judges). The former, some contend, will be more attuned to recent developments in federal law than the latter, and will, in turn, serve as more valuable sources of information for judges. *Id.* at 1287–1289.

"political" in nature.[33] On the other hand, many states now *appoint,* rather than elect, judges, suggesting that selection based on patronage by local machine politics is, at least, ameliorated to some extent by the use of an ostensible merit selection.[34] The proper perspective, we acknowledge, is a comparative one: even if state trial judges have fewer shortcomings than asserted by the critics of parity, the quality of federal judges (however measured) is clearly higher. However, the evidence indicates that the disparity is *not* so great as to be able to discard parity out of hand.

In contrast to the technical competence argument, the "psychological set" thesis focuses on the receptivity of state judges to the directives of the Supreme Court. Neuborne suggests that a "series of psychological and attitudinal characteristics" make federal judges more likely to enforce federal institutional rights. The psychological characteristics, he says, draw on the elite tradition of the federal judiciary, as well as the enhanced bureaucratic receptivity of federal judges to the rulings of the Supreme Court. Similarly, the attitudinal characteristics of state judges make it more likely that they will share the socioeconomic values of the defenders of the status quo in constitutional cases, and be more likely to rule accordingly.

Again, we cannot deny the institutional élan of the federal judges or their increased familiarity with and receptivity to Supreme Court pronouncements. There is little evidence, however, that state judges have, deliberately or unknowingly, evaded the implementation of Supreme Court decisions. Indeed, the evidence indicates that state supreme courts have, for the most part, uniformly

33. With respect to the appointment of lower federal court judges, it is well-documented that presidents often defer to the wishes of one or both senators from the state in question (particularly those from his party), and that most judges share the political background of the president. Sheldon Goldman, Picking Federal Judges: Lower Court Selection from Roosevelt Through Reagan (1997). On the other hand, the apparent widespread assumption that federal judges in the lower courts invariably render decisions on some sort of party-line basis is considerably overblown, not supported by careful empirical studies, and ignores the constraining influence of precedent and facts that guide most judges in most cases. See Orley Ashenfelter, Theodore Eisenberg & Stewart J. Schwab, *Politics and the Judiciary: The Influence of Judicial Background on Case Outcomes*, 24 J. Legal Stud. 257 (1995); Gregory C. Sisk, Michael Heise, & Andrew P. Morriss, *Charting the Influences on the Judicial Mind: An Empirical Study of Judicial Reasoning,* 73 N.Y.U. L. Rev. 1377 (1998). We reach some of the same conclusions below with respect to *state* judges.

34. As of the mid-1990s, members of state supreme courts (and for most intermediate appellate courts, for those states that have them) were selected in the following ways: partisan election (9), nonpartisan election (13), merit selection, usually with retention election (20), gubernatorial appointment (5), and legislative appointment (3). The breakdown for trial courts was 11, 17, 15, 5, and 2, respectively. Robert A. Carp & Ronald Stidham, Judicial Process in America 263 (4th ed. 1998); Charles H. Sheldon & Linda J. Maule, Choosing Justice: The Recruitment of State and Federal Judges (1997).

enforced U.S. Supreme Court mandates.[35] This suggests that state judges have their own sense of the necessity to comply with Supreme Court directives. Some writers seem to assume that state judges are not psychologically ready to enforce federal rights because, for among reasons they rarely adjudicate such rights.[36] In fact, studies indicate that healthy percentages of cases on state dockets (particularly on the criminal side) involve adjudication of federal rights.[37]

---

35. Two studies of the decisions of state supreme courts, for example, have found that they have "generally enforced the requirements" of Miranda v. Arizona, 384 U.S. 436 (1966). See John Gruhl, *State Supreme Courts and the U.S. Supreme Court's Post-Miranda Rulings,* 72 J. Crim. L. & Criminology 886, 911 (1981); Neil Romans, *The Role of State Supreme Courts in Judicial Policy Making:* Escobedo, Miranda *and the Use of Judicial Impact Analysis*, 27 W. Pol. Q. 38 (1969). On the civil side, Professor Franklin, in his survey of federal and state court decisions implementing the Supreme Court's libel decisions, found that New York Times v. Sullivan, 376 U.S. 254 (1964), and its progeny were enforced to such an extent in state courts that virtually no plaintiffs recovered. See Marc Franklin, *Suing Media for Libel: A Litigation Study,* 1981 Am. B. Found. Research J. 795; Marc Franklin, *Winners and Losers and Why: A Study of Defamation Litigation,* 1980 Am. B. Found. Research J. 455.

This isn't to say that all such studies point in one direction. For example, one study found that prisoners' rights cases were handled more sympathetically in federal appeals courts than in state supreme courts. See Kenneth C. Haas, *The "New Federalism" and Prisoners' Rights: State Supreme Courts in Comparative Perspective,* 34 W. Pol. Q. 552 (1981). However, the Haas study was not as broad as others, and even he acknowledged that state courts have been as liberal as their federal counterparts on other criminal and civil rights issues. *Id.* at 569.

In arguing that "the impact of state hostility to Supreme Court mandates has been noted," Neuborne cited Jerry K. Beatty, *State Court Evasion of United States Supreme Court Mandates During the Last Decade of the Warren Court,* 6 Val. U. L. Rev. 260 (1972). The Beatty study, in fact, found that in only 27 percent of cases remanded by the U.S. Supreme Court to state courts, did the party obtaining the remand eventually lose. Beatty concluded that, "at a time when disunity, disobedience and defiance persist in many aspects of intergovernmental relations, it is refreshing to find that most state courts of last resort have an admirable record of compliance."

On the implementation of Supreme Court decisions by lower courts, see generally Carp & Stidham, *supra* note 34, at 350–357; Bradley C. Canon, *Courts and Policy: Compliance, Implementation and Innovation* in Critical Assessment 435–466, *supra* note 31.

36. E.g., Redish, *supra* note 18, at 3 ("It seems intuitively appropriate to provide *federal* courts the primary responsibility for adjudicating *federal* law, and leave as the primary function of state courts the defining and expounding of state policies and principles.") (Emphasis in original, footnote omitted.)

37. E.g., Daniel J. Meador, *Federal Law in State Supreme Courts*, 3 Const. Comm. 347 (1986) (comparison of decisions from state supreme courts in 1959, 1979, and 1983 showed that the percentage of decisions dealing with federal law rose from 14 in 1959 to 49 in 1983); Meltzer, *supra* note 29, at 1131 n.7 (by 1970, almost 50 % of criminal cases before state supreme courts presented an issue of federal constitutional law).

Meador's study covered seven states (Arizona, Colorado, Georgia, Minnesota, Mississippi, New Jersey, and Ohio). To replicate his study, we surveyed all of the published decisions on the merits from the supreme courts of those states for 1995. The data generated

The last argument Neuborne makes is that the lifetime tenure of federal judges provides a barrier against local political pressures influencing a decision. In contrast, the necessity of elections may force their state brethren to heed the wishes of the future electorate. Such majoritarian pressures can endanger the enforcement of institutional rights protecting minorities. The superiority of a lifetime appointment in countering majoritarian pressures is rightly praised. It does not follow, however, that elections of state judges, to the extent they are still held, will influence the subsequent decisions of elected judges. Almost without exception, uncontradicted evidence shows that judicial elections are plagued by very low turnout and a lack of information for voters to make a truly informed choice. Many judges are initially appointed to fill a vacancy, and whether incumbents or not, many judges run unopposed. For those few elections that are contested, the low level of information available has meant that voters use cues such as party affiliation, name recognition or incumbency to select a candidate.[38]

None of this is particularly surprising. Voters have few incentives or easy ways to investigate the decision-making or courtroom practices of individual judges. The media does a very uneven job of covering the courts, usually focusing on sensational criminal cases. (The exception of, say, the *New York Times* in our view proves the rule. Nor are we confident that new media outlets, like Court TV, have improved matters much, in part because it too seems to focus on criminal cases and caters to the nationwide audience.) And complex ethical rules place limits on what judges and judicial candidates can say during elections.[39] While perhaps not complementary of the attentiveness of state electorates, the evidence suggests that most state judges are unlikely to feel in danger of being "punished" for decisions upholding constitutional rights.

Others have taken a different view of this evidence, asserting that the high reelection of judges shows they are beholden to local elites, and that in any event judicial elections are increasingly contested and visible, often in the basis of law-

---

was remarkably similar to Meador's data from 1983. For example, our data showed that from 23 percent to 45 percent of the coded decisions from those states either decided a federal issue of law, or at least cited federal law. In most cases the decisions that directly decided a federal issue were criminal cases. A summary of this data is on file with the authors.

38. See, e.g., Paul Dubois, From Ballot to Bench: Judicial Elections and the Quest for Accountability 36–177 (1980) (study of all elections for state supreme court justices in non-Southern states between 1948 and 1974). See generally Carp & Stidham, *supra* note 34, at 264; Lawrence Baum, *Electing Judges* in Contemplating Courts 18–43 (Lee Epstein ed., 1995); Richard L. Hasen, *"High Court Wrongly Elected": A Public Choice Model of Judging and Its Implications for the Voting Rights Act*, 75 N.C. L. Rev. 1305, 1318–1319 (1997).

39. Patrick M. McFadden, Electing Justice: The Law and Ethics of Judicial Election Campaigns (1990); Kurt E. Scheuerman, Comment, *Rethinking Judicial Elections*, 72 Or. L. Rev. 459 (1993); Maura Anne Schoshinski, Comment, *Towards an Independent, Fair, and Competent Judiciary: An Argument for Improving Judicial Elections*, 7 Geo. J. Legal Ethics 839 (1994).

and-order campaigns and the like. In both ways, the argument runs, state court adjudication of federal rights (particularly of the unpopular, countermajoritarian variety) are likely to suffer.[40] These arguments are not without some force, but ultimately they cannot undermine our conclusions. The examples given are highly anecdotal and in our view do not represent a trend. Almost all judicial races operate below the radar screen, and it is difficult to believe that state judges *systemically* forfeit federal rights with an eye on an upcoming election (though perhaps some do so in particularly high-profile (e.g., death penalty) cases, or do so for other reasons).[41]

FURTHER EVIDENCE ON PARITY

In an effort to more directly examine parity, we undertook an empirical study of federal and state cases where federal constitutional issues were raised. Our goal

---

40. Steven P. Croley, *The Majoritarian Difficulty: Elective Judiciaries and the Rule of Law*, 62 U. Chi. L. Rev. 689, 726–742 (1995); Edward Hartnett, *Why Is the Supreme Court of the United States Protecting State Judges From Popular Democracy?*, 75 Tex. L. Rev. 907, 974–977 (1997); Scott D. Weiner, Note, *Popular Justice: State Judicial Elections and Procedural Due Process*, 31 Harv. Civ. Rts.-Civ. Lib. L. Rev. 187, 192–202 (1996).

There is some evidence that *some* state supreme court races are more contested and visible, and thus in theory more salient to voters. See Baum, *surpa* note 38; Paul D. Carrington, *Judicial Independence and Democratic Accountability in Highest State Courts*, 61 Law & Contemp. Prob. 79 (Summer 1998); Melinda Gann Hall, Competition in Judicial Elections, 1980–1995 (1998) (delivered at 1998 annual meeting of the American Political Science Association, Boston, Sept. 3–6, 1998); Marie Hajnacki & Lawrence Baum, *Choosing Judicial Candidates: How Voters Explain Their Decisions*, 75 Judicature 300 (1992). In response, there have been calls, among other things, to place limits in campaign contributions and expenditures in judicial races. Carrington, *supra*, at 117–118; Mark Hansen, *A Run for the Bench*, 84 ABA Journal 68 (October 1998); American Bar Association, Task Force on Lawyers' Political Contributions, Report and Recommendations Regarding Contributions to Judges and Judicial Candidates (Part Two) (July 1998). Ohio was one of the first states to promulgate such limits, as described in Nicole C. Allbritain, Comment, *One Step Closer to Merit-Based Judicial Selection: Ohio's New Limitations on Judicial Campaign Contributions and Expenditures*, 64 U. Cin. L. Rev. 1323 (1996). Some of those limits were held unconstitutional as violative of the First Amendment (and Buckley v. Valeo, 424 U.S. 1 (1976)) in Suster v. Marshall, 149 F.3d 523 (6th Cir. 1998), *cert. denied*, 119 S.Ct. 890 (1999).

41. Barry Latzer, *Toward the Decentralization of Criminal Procedure: State Constitutional Law and Selective Disincorporation*, 87 J. Crim. L. & Criminology 63, 78–82 (1996); Hasen, *supra* note 38, at 1320 n.60. Indeed, at least one study of countermajoritarian decision-making by state supreme courts (operationally defined as declaring a state statute unconstitutional) found what it labeled as the "counterintuitive result" that the most activist courts were those selected in direct elections. James P. Wenzel, Shaun Bowler, & David J. Lanoue, *Legislating From the State Bench: A Comparative Analysis of Judicial Activism*, 25 Am. Pol. Q. 363 (1997). We discuss death penalty cases and state judicial behavior in more detail in chapter 6.

was to compare the way rights-claims were handled in state court with the way they were handled in federal court. If Neuborne is right when he claims that parity is a myth, then we should expect to see fewer rights-claims upheld in the state courts.[42] Our hypothesis was that there would be no significant difference in the way such claims were treated because there was neither ignorance nor systemwide hostility to federal rights in the state courts. Thus we sought to contradict Neuborne's implied hypothesis, that is: that state courts would uphold proportionately fewer rights-claims than federal courts would.

In our research design, the dependent variable is the disposition of the rights-claim and the independent variable is the forum. Both are dichotomous variables, i.e., a rights claim is either upheld or denied and the forum is either state or federal. But it is obvious that there are literally dozens of other factors that can affect the outcome of any case. Primary among these are strength of case and talent of the advocates. In social science research, it is seldom possible to use true experimental design methods where all possible factors that might influence the result can actually be held constant. Thus, for example, we don't have the luxury of litigating exactly the same claim in state and federal court, with the same attorneys, at the same time, etc.[43]

This problem is dealt with by randomly sampling cases from both federal and state systems. By sampling a large enough number of cases, and by carefully choosing the sample, differences such as strength of claim, talent of counsel, and so forth, can be, in effect, be averaged out,[44] and the effect of the forum in which the case is heard can then be determined.

Before proceeding with a discussion of the results of the sampling of cases, several points should be raised concerning the methodology used. The use of published opinions for empirical judicial research is neither new nor unique. As with all data sources, these opinions have strengths as well as weaknesses.[45] We

42. Of course, if we simply assume that state judges are not as talented as federal judges, we might assume that they could also err by being *too solicitous* of federal rights-claims. Neuborne, however, assumes not only ignorance but also lack of enthusiasm for federal rights.

43. For a rare study that sought to control for that variable, see Sisk, Heise, & Morriss, *supra* note 33 (studying large number of federal judges' decisions on a single, narrow issue).

44. One should be careful not to take the phrase "averaged out" too literally. Perhaps a better way to put it is this: With two random samples of cases from each of the fora, it is likely that the proportion of weak claims and strong claims, good lawyers and poor lawyers, etc., in each sample will be the same as in the universes from which the samples came, thus isolating forum as the only independent variable of interest. See Herbert M. Blalock, Jr., Social Statistics (rev. 2d ed. 1979) on the effect of random sampling.

45. There is an enormous body of literature in both law and the social sciences that uses the published opinions of courts as its data base. One of the most sanguine views of the utility of opinions for such research was that of the legendary Karl Llewellyn, set forth in the Common Law Tradition: Deciding Appeals 514 (1960). For a recent caveat an the unrestrained use of case opinion data, see Peter Siegelman & John J. Donohue III, *Studying the Iceberg From Its Tip: A Comparison of Published and Unpublished Employment*

chose state appellate and supreme courts and federal district courts. A legitimate question can be raised as to whether the data are comparable.[46] There are three reasons for choosing these courts to compare. By far the most important reason has to do with the nature of parity itself. Parity refers to the ability of the state and federal court *systems* to handle federal constitutional claims. The dynamics of state court behavior, we believe, are such that important federal constitutional claims will tend to be appealed at a higher-than-average rate, whereas in the federal system federal constitutional claims are likely to be fully litigated at an earlier stage.[47]

A second reason is that a study of opinions of state trial courts is virtually impossible. Full written opinions (as opposed to short orders or entries) are a rarity, and even the full opinions are rarely reported. On the other hand, a significant portion of state appellate and supreme court and federal trial court opinions make their way into print. Finally, the use of state appellate court opinions recognizes the

---

Discrimination Cases, 24 Law & Soc'y Rev. 1133, 1133–1134 (1990).

46. Neuborne argues that the proper comparison is between trial-level courts in the two systems but his arguments are not convincing. First, he seemingly argues that delays will characterize the litigation process in state, but not federal, courts. This broad assumption is unwarranted. Until recently, there have been virtually no statistics kept on docket congestion and delay in state or federal courts. What little data has been kept at the trial court level indicates that the median interval from the filing of a complaint to disposition in civil cases, in both systems, typically averages almost two years, with delay slightly more pronounced in state courts. See Joel Grossman et al., *Measuring the Pace of Civil Litigation in Federal and State Trial Courts,* 65 Judicature 86, 102–103 (1981). See also Joseph A. Trotter, Jr. & Caroline S. Cooper, *State Trial Court Delay: Efforts at Reform,* 31 Am. U. L. Rev. 213 (1982). Dispositions are usually quicker for criminal cases, due to plea bargaining and the application of federal and state speedy trial acts. See, e.g., James A. Martin & Elizabeth A. Prescott, *The Magnitude and Sources of Delay in Ten State Appellate Courts,* 6 Just. Sys. J. 305 (1981); Peter F. Nardulli, *The Caseload Controversy and the Study of Criminal Courts,* 70 J. Crim. L. & Criminology 89 (1979). In both areas, the disparity between federal and state court delay is hardly of a quantum nature so as to call into question the validity of parity. Second, while we admit that factual records will assume importance in criminal and other cases raising constitutional questions, the increasing use by state courts of the federal rules of evidence and of civil procedure suggests that important facts will not go unreviewed by state appellate courts. Finally, it is doubtful, as Neuborne argues, that "majoritarian pressures," to the extent that they exist on a systemic basis at all, apply with equal vigor to state *appellate* judges as they apply to state trial judges. We have already indicated that many appellate judges are appointed, not elected, and that those who are elected rarely are forced to defend unpopular decisions before the electorate.

47. We acknowledge that the decision to appeal is an understudied phenomenon, and we cannot directly support our assumptions made in the text. For some suggestive studies, *see* Donald R. Songer, Charles Cameron, & Jeffrey A. Segal, *An Empirical Study of the Rational-Actor Theory of Litigation*, 57 J. Pol. 1119 (1995); Scott Barclay, *Posner's Economic Model and the Decision to Appeal*, 19 Just. Sys. J. 77 (1997); Gregory J. Rathjen, *Lawyers and the Appellate Choice: An Analysis of Factors Affecting the Decision to Appeal*, 6 Am. Pol. Q. 387 (1978).

role of these courts as the supervisors of state court systems.[48] In the area of federal constitutional rights it is the appellate courts that must be relied on to make the major interpretation of the validity of claims, especially where the litigant has no initial choice of forum.

THE SAMPLES

Federal constitutional claims can involve a host of different issues. For our samples we decided to focus on claims based on three particular constitutional areas: the First Amendment, the Fourth Amendment, and the Equal Protection Clause of the Fourteenth Amendment. First Amendment claims were chosen because they reflect concerns that are fundamental to the political system and to federalism. They encompass a wide variety of issues, both civil and criminal. They are most likely to expose hostility and parochialism on the part of one set of judges or another. Moreover, it is most appropriate to this study that these claims be included, because two key cases in the parity issue—*Dombrowski v. Pfister* and *Younger v. Harris*—both raised First Amendment claims. Fourth Amendment claims have many of the same features as First Amendment claims. They encompass a broad spectrum of issues that are salient in the public mind. They are therefore likely to be good bellwethers of possible public pressure on a judge. Furthermore, another key "parity" case—*Stone v. Powell*—raised a Fourth Amendment claim. Finally, equal protection claims strike to the heart of the parity question and indeed to the whole question of federalism. The Fourteenth Amendment was adopted for the express purpose of establishing federal supervision over state treatment of freed slaves. It reflected belief on the part of Congress that there would not be parity of treatment between state governments and the federal government. Therefore, contemporary comparative treatment of equal protection claims by state and federal courts is a particularly apt measure of parity.

---

48. Theodore Eisenberg & Stewart J. Schwab, *What Shapes Perceptions of the Federal Court System?*, 56 U. Chi. L. Rev. 501, 509 (1989); Margaret P.P. Mason, Note, *Courting Reversal: The Supervisory Role of State Supreme Courts*, 87 Yale L. J. 1191 (1978).

As of 1995, thirty-nine states had established intermediate appellate courts. Generally, the jurisdiction of these courts is mandatory (they must hear all appeals, both civil and criminal), and the supreme courts in those states have discretion to decide what appeals to hear. Carp & Stidham, *supra* note 34, at 69–72. To be sure, those supreme courts with discretionary jurisdiction will typically agree to hear less than 10 percent of criminal appeals. O'Sullivan v. Boerckel, 119 S.Ct. 1728, 1741 (1999) (Breyer, J., dissenting) (providing statistics from 1997 for supreme courts of California, Connecticut, Georgia, Illinois, Louisiana, Minnesota, North Carolina, Ohio, Texas, and Virginia). No doubt, the precentages for appeals of *civil* cases would be equally small. So just examining the decisions of those courts does not provide a complete picture. Further study of decisions of intermediate state appellate courts would be helpful. As we explain below, our study included both types of state courts.

Obviously, many important federal constitutional claims are not included. Noteworthy are the entire broad range of due process claims in both civil and criminal cases, and cases arising under the Sixth and Eighth amendments. Therefore, this study draws its conclusion only as to the three stated areas. There is, however, no apparent reason why there should be a great difference in judicial performance in the excluded areas.

A sample size of at least 1,000 total cases was originally decided upon in order to allow for the analysis of subsamples. A time frame of approximately seven years was chosen to give the study a reasonably compact temporal dimension. In order to achieve a degree of consistency in reporting, both among the several state courts and between the federal and state courts, the West Reporting System was used exclusively. Four hundred thirty-eight federal district court cases were chosen from the *Federal Supplement.* Six hundred eight were chosen from the various regional state court reporters.[49]

For federal cases, odd-numbered volumes from 393 to 511 were chosen. Within each volume an average total of twelve cases in three targeted subject areas was chosen at random and coded by the authors. If a case raised multiple federal claims, only the first claim encountered was used. Although the number of cases of each type differed from volume to volume, on the average about half of the relevant reported cases in each volume were sampled. For state cases, the method was the same, except for the fact that a lower percentage of the reported cases raised relevant federal constitutional claims. Therefore, in most instances, the sampled cases constituted almost the entire population for the sampled volumes.

For the purposes of this study, thirteen variables were coded.[50] The most important was the relevant outcome of the case, that is, whether the federal constitutional claim was upheld or denied.[51] We believe that the 1,046 cases represent a statistically valid sample of the targeted cases for the years 1974 through 1980. The first step in the analysis of the entire sample is to establish a norm, or benchmark, for success in constitutional claims. Table 3.1 shows the overall results of all cases, federal and state, which raise the aforementioned constitutional issues.

---

49. The regional reporters are: *Atlantic Second, Northeast Second, Northwestern Second, Pacific Second, Southeastern Second, Southern Second,* and *Southwestern Second.*

50. The variables coded were: (1) case name, (2) citation, (3) year decided, (4) state, (5) court level (i.e., district, appellate, supreme), (6) state law (applicability of the Fourteenth Amendment) or federal law, (7) issue (amendment involved, subject matter), (8) type (criminal or civil), (9) outcome, (10) cases cited (number, by court level), (11) length of opinion, (12) reversal or affirmance, and (13) dissents.

51. About 10 percent of the cases were double-coded. Several dozen were recorded when routine data checks pointed out inconsistencies or clerical errors.

Table 3.1
Results of All Cases

Claim Upheld	Claim Denied
36 % (N=374)	64 % (N=672)

Given the large sample size, it is very likely that the 36 percent figure for success in rights claims in all courts, state and federal is very close to the actual proportion of success. In other words, an average litigant is going to be successful in any rights claim a little over one third of the time. Table 3.2 illustrates the outcome of the litigation of all rights claims in federal and state court.

Table 3.2
Results by Court System

Forum	**Result of Rights Claim**	
	Upheld	**Denied**
Federal Court	41.7 % (n=183)	58.3 % (n=255)
State Court	31.4 % (n=191)	68.6 % (n=417)
Chi Square p=.0001	ϕ=.11	

In federal district court, about 42 percent of all claims based on the federal Constitution or laws were upheld while about 58 percent were denied. In state appellate and supreme courts, 32 percent of the same types of claims were upheld, while 68 percent of the claims were denied.

These percentages lend themselves to several common sense interpretations. For example, one could say there is a 10 percent greater chance of success in federal court over the same range of issues. Or, one could make the conjecture that if a litigant were to take the identical case to both a state and a federal court, nine times out of ten the decision would be the same. We believe that whatever common sense interpretation is chosen, there is support for the contention that there is no clear reluctance on the part of state courts to uphold a federal claim that would be upheld in federal district courts.[52]

But there are also specific statistical measures that can be used to interpret the relationship between forum and decision and that can also help in analyzing other subsamples. In any array of data such as Table 3.2, there is always the possibility that the proportion arrived at occurred simply by chance. By this we mean that if we took another sample, the results would be different. Because we make no speculation about the parameters of the larger universe of cases, and because the sample is random, we can use the measure called chi-square to estimate the likelihood that this result would not be found in all cases, that is that the difference is statistically significant. We say that the data is significant if there is less than a 5 percent probability that such an array could be the result of chance.[53] The array in Table 3.2 is very statistically significant because the probability of getting these results from a universe of cases where there was no differences in outcomes is only slightly better than 1 in 10,000.

Of course, statistical significance and strength of relationship are not the same thing. In order to make claims about the importance of the data, one needs to know the strength of the relationship between outcome and forum. An appropriate statistical measure must be chosen to determine this relationship. The measure we have chosen is *the Phi Coefficient.* In plain language, this measure answers the following question: How helpful in predicting outcomes of cases is a knowledge of forum? If we can make no better prediction about outcome by relying exclusively on a knowledge of forum, we can say there is little relevance or importance to the data. Conversely, if we could always correctly predict outcomes simply from a knowledge of forum, there would be a "perfect" relationship and obviously much relevance to the data. *Phi* ranges from zero, meaning that there is no relationship between the variables to a one, meaning a "perfect" relationship between them. Thus a score near one would mean that you could almost always predict the outcome of a case by the forum whereas a score near zero would mean that you could almost never do so. When *Phi* is computed for the data in Table 3.2, it shows a relatively weak relationship between forum and outcome of 0.11. Therefore, we believe it is correct to characterize the difference in outcomes as statistically significant (i.e., the difference in outcomes would exist if all cases were

52. One question that arises is whether, from the point of view of the plaintiff's attorney, the 10 percent difference is, by itself, enough to encourage a preference for the federal forum. We believe not. The reason for this belief is rooted in the nature of the aggregate data. An attorney with no other information, who litigates over 1,000 cases over a seven-year period might well like the 10 percent "edge" he or she seems to have in federal court. But the attorney *does* have other information about the facts of his/her cases and about his/her clients. The attorney may also know of trends of particular courts in deciding the issues that his/her clients' cases will present. It is on this information that he must litigate, not on the aggregation of information from other similar cases.

53. The 0.05 level is a customary significance level in social science research. See Blalock, *supra* note 44, at 161.

included in the analysis), but not as important for predicting outcome as the critics of parity believe.

But even though the overall percentages are therefore, somewhat supportive of parity, they by no means settle the issue. In the first place, parity does not mean exact numerical equality. Parity, as we elaborate below, best means that there is no *systematic* bias on the part of state courts to deny federal claims (such purported bias being based on environmental factors mentioned by critics of parity). In order to test for such bias, we must break down the sample of cases and look at several categories in turn.

Table 3.3 sets out the relevant results for all cases when controlled for case type. Of the total sample, about half were criminal cases and half were civil cases.

Table 3.3
Outcome Versus Forum by Case Type

	Civil Cases		**Criminal Cases**	
Federal Court	Upheld	Denied	Upheld	Denied
	44.6 % (N=144)	55.4 % (N=179)	33.9 % (N=39)	66.1 % (N=76)
State Court	33.2 % (N=67)	66.8 % (N= 135)	30.5 % (N= 124)	69.5 % (N=282)
	Chi-Square p=.009	Phi=.11	Chi-Square p=.491	Phi=.03

As Table 3.3 demonstrates, almost all of the difference between state and federal court outcomes occurs in civil cases. The relationship between outcome and in criminal cases is neither statistically significant (that is it may be zero) and it certainly is not strong if it exists at all.

This evidence is particularly useful because it goes directly to two points raised by Professor Neuborne—that is, the espoused differences in majoritarian electoral pressures on, and the psychological set of, federal vis-á-vis state judges. Certainly a judge with one eye on the public opinion polls would be well aware of the tremendous attention that issues of crime and punishment attract with the voting public. Furthermore, accused or convicted criminals are an easy target for a judge who wants to pander to imagined public anxieties about the "corrosive" effects of granting defendants their Constitutional rights. It is a great tribute to the independence of the American state judiciary that such a parity exists between them and their allegedly more isolated brethren on the federal bench.

The psychological set argument fares no better in the face of these data. Allegedly, state judges are more hardened to constitutional claims because they deal with more examples of the impact of crime and criminals, yet our data show that they do not seem to be systematically acting on their psychological feelings by refusing to recognize constitutional claims. Perhaps the notion of psychological set is overblown, or perhaps judges who are trained to be impartial are able to overcome their personal feelings more easily than others not so trained and socialized.

In order to obtain a clearer picture of the variance between federal and state cases, Table 3.4 sets out five categories of cases and the relevant results for each.

It should be apparent now that the case for systematic bias simply can't be made. We believe that these data show no clear, across-the-board hostility on the part of state courts to claims of federal constitutional rights, and that they therefore support the existence of relative parity between the state and federal systems. In two categories—equal protection civil cases and Fourth Amendment criminal cases—there are no statistically significant differences between state and federal courts. In one category—equal protection criminal cases—there is an apparent large percentage difference, but a weak relationship generally. And in the First Amendment criminal category, the state average for upholding claims is actually somewhat *higher* than that of federal courts, although the relationship is weak.

Since forum choice alone is clearly not a powerful explanation for the statistical differences evidenced here, it is incumbent upon us to speculate as to the reason for their existence. We will do this by positing an alternative model to support the existence of parity—one that is based not exclusively on environmental components of alternative forums, but rather on factors of informational flow and organizational relationship. There is no need, for the purposes of this study, to explain in detail the reasons for each of the differences. In order to add to the persuasiveness of the data, however, we will discuss each of the categories and propose some likely explanations for apparent differences between forums.

Variances among First Amendment civil cases are the most difficult to interpret. Here both federal and state courts are likely to uphold a higher percentage of claims than the overall average would indicate. But the gap between federal and state courts is increased from 10 percent to 13.5 percent. Notice, however, that there is a roughly equal proportional rise in claims upheld by both courts. This indicates that there is some "tracking" or concordance between the general treatment of First Amendment civil cases by the courts.

First Amendment criminal cases pose a much different set of questions. In these cases there is a tendency for state courts to uphold claims at a higher rate—51.2 percent versus 36.46 percent. Although obviously puzzling, and damaging to the case of those who suspect hostility on the part of state courts to federal constitutional claims, a quite plausible explanation is available. We may be witnessing an entirely separate, yet important, parity problem—the parity between state and local legislative bodies and the Congress. An overwhelming proportion of state cases involved state and local criminal laws. Federal legislative behavior—due to better staff work, the resources of the Justice Department, the centrality of Washington, D.C., and the lesser number of federal criminal laws—may indeed be more responsive to constitutional limitations, raising the possibility that states are more likely to pass laws that run afoul of the First Amendment. This possibility would lead to a higher percentage of "worthy" claims in state courts.

Although there are some interesting Fourth Amendment civil cases in the data set, the sample sizes are too small to make any reasonable assumptions. Fourth Amendment criminal cases are, we believe, not only the strongest evidence for the existence of parity, but also invite the most plausible explanation based on our preferred model of constitutional decision-making. Although these cases would seem to be the most likely to fit the pattern assumed by the skeptics of parity, in point of fact they present the closest parallel performance levels among the categories. At work in these cases is an informal flow of information between federal and state courts—mostly on the law of search and seizure, but on other issues as well—that keeps both sets of courts on very close parallel tracks. Judges, lawyers, prosecutors, and policemen are all close to the "state of the art" in this area because of the obvious and clearly defined penalties for failure to be so—that is, imposition of the exclusionary rule.

The final two categories are civil and criminal equal protection cases. In equal protection claims raised in criminal cases there is a very large difference between federal and state performance (over two-to-one "in favor" of federal courts). We believe this shows the empirical truth of an old chestnut: that the Equal Protection Clause, like patriotism, is the last refuge of scoundrels.[54] In equal protection civil claims, there is clear statistical parity between state and federal courts. A total of 32.8 percent of the claims were upheld in federal court while 28.7 percent were upheld in state court. Thus we can't reject the possibility that in all claims of this type, there is simply no difference between the treatment afforded litigants in state and federal courts. This correlation is supportive of parity because this type of case is arguably central to the entire question of federalism. One of the consistent historical arguments offered by the skeptics of parity is the alleged hostility of state courts to attempts by the federal government to enforce the civil rights of minority groups, women, and others protected from discriminatory state action by the federal Constitution. Yet in these data there is no discernible pattern of hostility, and there is close similarity of treatment.

Several criticisms have been voiced concerning our findings. First, the study compared the wrong courts (federal district courts and state appellate courts). Second, we ignored significant differences in the results of cases in state and

54. Samuel Johnson gets credit for the quote on patriotism. See J. Boswell, The Life of Samuel Johnson, L.L.D. 115 (Macmillan, 1908). Holmes applied it to equal protection in a civil case. In denying an equal protection claim based on a state's practice of sterilizing feeble-minded inmates of an asylum while not similarly treating nonconfined persons, Holmes said: "It is the usual last resort of constitutional arguments to point out shortcomings of this sort." Buck v. Bell, 274 U.S. 200, 208 (1927).

federal courts. Third, our study was limited in scope because it relied only on reported cases in a limited number of subject areas.[55]

The choice of which courts to compare is determined by the information available and the definition of parity. Ideally, one would have access to every decision of every judge deciding a federal constitutional case. All decisions are not available and one must rely on a second-best data set. Our choice of federal district and state appellate courts is a compromise. It is based on the belief that parity must be viewed as the relative ability of state and federal court systems to fully and fairly adjudicate federal claims. The adjudicative ability of a court system is not based on the behavior of any one judge or any one level of court. Critics of this methodology have failed to offer an alternative. The available data are not ideal, but that does not make them irrelevant. The random sampling of a large number of cases in each of the two jurisdictional systems represents the most reliable and possibly the only indicator of the outcomes of the claims in the two court systems.

The comparison of federal trial courts and state appellate courts is appropriate because of the following reasons: (1) we were comparing state and federal court systems; (2) few state trial court opinions are published and accessible; and (3) significant federal issues in state court are likely to be appealed and appear in published opinions. It might be argued that a sample of only published opinions by state appellate courts is not representative of the trial level. A sample drawn from numerous courts over several years will usually provide a representative picture of activity at the trial level. To the extent that the sample is somehow "unrepresentative," the data are not rendered useless. Cases fully litigated at the trial and appellate levels are on the cutting edge of the law. Routine cases are likely to be settled or plea-bargained.[56] The pioneering cases are likely to be published, and, to a skeptic of parity, they are also likely to receive less than sympathetic treatment by a state court. The alleged skewed nature of the sample may work *against* our ultimate conclusions, although the differences, if any exist, are balanced and do not distort the data or our conclusions.

---

55. E.g., Erwin Chemerinsky, *Parity Reconsidered: Defining a Role for the Federal Judiciary*, 36 U.C.L.A. L. Rev. 233, 267–268 (1988); Susan N. Herman, *Why Parity Matters*, 71 B.U. L. Rev. 651, 658–659 n.29 (1991); Thomas Marvell, *The Rationales for Federal Question Jurisdiction: An Empirical Examination of Student Rights Litigation*, 1984 Wis. L. Rev. 1315, 1338–39; Kenneth Mitchell Mash, Uniformity in the Balance: An Examination of Section 1983 and Federal Jurisdiction 144–157 (unpublished Ph.D. dissertation, Penn State Univ. 1997).

Professor Mash was very helpful in pointing out that our use of the Lambda statistic in the original article on which this analysis is based was wrong. He correctly pointed out that Lambda is often inappropriate for dichotomous variables. That is, it will always equal zero if the modal categories of the variables do not differ, as in this case. We regret the earlier error, and have corrected it by substituting the appropriate Phi Coefficient.

56. See George Priest & Benjamin Klein, *The Selection of Disputes for Litigation*, 13 J. Legal Stud. 1 (1984).

The second criticism is that important differences between the outcomes of the relevant cases in federal and state courts were ignored. The criticism is simply in error. The source of the error is probably a misinterpretation of the percentages that were originally reported. There were percentage differences between the outcome of the relevant cases in the federal and state courts. Differences were found in every category of the analysis; it would be surprising not to find some differences. A careful analysis of the statistics must go beyond statements such as the following:

> First, the 9% difference seems rather large and it is even larger in civil cases: 45% of the civil constitutional claims were upheld in federal court as opposed to only 33% in the state court. According to these statistics there is a 36% greater chance of winning a civil constitutional claim in federal court than in state court.[57]

It is misleading to transform a 12 percent difference into a 36 percent difference with such sleight of hand. Indeed, 12 is 36 percent of 33, but the 36 percent is irrelevant. The percentage differences found in our study are relevant only to the extent they can be translated into important predictive information. If a plaintiff's attorney knew that he or she were 9 percent (or 36 percent or even 1 percent) more likely to be victorious in a federal court, and the attorney had a choice of forum and all other things were equal, then the attorney would be foolish not to choose the federal forum. The raw percentage differences were not the purpose of the statistics. The following example will illustrate their purpose.

Let us say that an attorney is given 100 cases to try. The cases were chosen at random; fifty to be tried in federal court and fifty to be tried in state court. Someone tells the attorney in advance that if she takes all 100 cases she will be victorious 40 percent of the time, (she will win seventeen state cases and twenty-three federal cases). But that if she takes only the federal cases she will be victorious 46 percent of the time. It is hardly accurate to call these six additional victories a 35 percent advantage in federal court (even though six is 35 percent of the seventeen putative state court victories). Furthermore, the comparative advantages will not actually always be in favor of the federal courts. Forum choice is a much less powerful predictive variable than subject matter, as we have shown.

Professor Erwin Chemerinsky advanced another reason for the purported limitations of our data. Only coding published opinions, he says, ignores cases that are settled prior to final decision in federal and state courts. Assuming federal courts provide a more sympathetic forum for plaintiffs, he further asserts that federal court defendants and state court plaintiffs are more likely to settle. This asymmetry would not be reflected in published opinions. He says that if it is reflected at all, then it is more likely that federal courts "would be left with comparatively weaker constitutional claims and state courts with comparatively stronger ones," thus magnifying any advantage of federal courts in the data.

---

57. Marvell, *supra* note 55, at 1338.

Professor Chemerinsky's conclusions are difficult to refute in his initial assumptions are correct, but he provides no empirical basis for the behavior of potential litigants that he posits. The available date is at best ambiguous. Some studies show that a *lower* number of cases settle in federal courts than in state courts.[58] Because the diet of cases in each court system is not identical, the study cannot precisely disprove Professor Chemerinsky's hypothesis. If the study correctly establishes that fewer civil rights actions are filed in state court than in federal court, then the lower rate of settlement in federal court suggests that the purportedly hospitable forum is not a driving force of settlements. Cases settle for a vast number of reasons, and the perceived hostility or friendliness of the forum is only one of the potential reasons. Absent other data, giving the settlement factor dispositive weight in refuting our conclusions is without merit.[59]

We make no claims that our study purported to settle the parity issue. Far from it. Our data retrieval was limited and our conclusions suggestive. More work needs to be done. But our conclusions have been bolstered by several factors in the intervening years. Critics of parity have not, to our knowledge, conducted any study similar to ours which reached different results. Indeed, several studies in the interim have reached results which, in our view, are consistent with our study. For example, one study of nearly 400 appellate court cases from nine states decided between 1975 and 1986 concluded that *Stone v. Powell*'s restriction of federal habeas review of Fourth Amendment issues did not generally diminish state court enforcement of that amendment.[60] Another study compared the disposition of Fourth, Fifth, and Sixth Amendment claims by federal and state judges in New Jersey and Pennsylvania between 1981 and 1987, and found "no support" for the proposition that elected state judges will systematically underenforce federal rights.[61]

The results of all of these studies are consistent, we think, with the richer understanding of the work of state court judges reflected in recent political literature. That work suggests that simplistic notions of judicial behavior (e.g., elected state judges will be loath to enforce federal rights) are not intuitively obvious and not supported by careful statistical studies. Rather, a judge's decision-making is likely the result of an ever shifting group of factors, from the facts and precedent at play in a particular case, the personal attributes and background of the

58. See Herbert M. Kritzer, *Adjudication to Settlement: Shading in the Gray*, 70 Judicature 161 (1986); Herbert M. Kritzer et al., *Courts and Litigation Investment: Why Do Lawyers Spend More Time on Federal Cases?*, 9 Just. Sys. J. 7 (1984).

59. For the reasons stated in the text, it is simply wrong to conclude that our study has been "demolished," Yackle, *supra* note 18, at 12.

60. Craig M. Bradley, *Are State Courts Enforcing the Fourth Amendment? A Preliminary Study*, 77 Geo. L. J. 251 (1988).

61. Craig Ducat, Mikel Wyckoff, & Victor Flango, *State Judges and Federal Constitutional Rights*, 4 Res. L. & Pol'y Stud. 155, 167 (1995).

judge, and the institutional framework in which the judge works.[62] To be sure, some of these factors (such as the apparent effect of type of judicial selection) suggest that certain types of federal rights might be subject to less enforcement by elected judiciaries. But that is simply one factor, among many, that may influence a state judge's decision. We are not oblivious to the electoral and other extra-legal pressures on state judges that can undermine parity. But we think that a dispassionate review of the current evidence, taken as a whole, does not demonstrate a wholesale abandonment of federal rights by state judges.

INFORMATION FLOW AND APPELLATE REVIEW

In discussing the issue of parity, there is a tendency to concentrate on the characteristics of individual judges. Our own study uses the products of these judges—written opinions—as its major data base. But this concentration must be tempered by a recognition of the context in which judicial decisions are made. The judge is not a totally free actor, and the judicial system is not self-executing. Before a judge can make a decision, a litigant must file suit. Judges are bound by oath to follow the Constitution and by training and temperament to follow precedent. Not every case presents the same sort of problems to the court. In some cases judges are merely asked to follow clear precedents, often those created by the U.S. Supreme Court. In others they are asked to chart new ground and begin a precedent—creating process—literally to conceive of new constitutional rights. The skills of attorneys, particularly their relative abilities to deliver information, can profoundly affect the outcome of the case, no matter what the judge is being asked to do. Furthermore, our data have shown that the outcome of cases involving federal constitutional issues does not depend strictly on forum, and that the automatic preference for federal courts evoked by the critics of parity, is shortsighted at best. Therefore, it is incumbent upon us to consider other factors involved in the outcome.

62. See Paul Brace & Melinda Gann Hall, *Studying Courts Comparatively: The View From the American States*, 48 Pol. Res. Q. 5 (1995); Paul R. Brace & Melinda Gann Hall, *The Interplay of Preferences, Case Facts, Context, and Rules in the Politics of Judicial Choice*, 59 J. Pol. 1206 (1997); Gregory N. Flemming, David B. Holian, & Susan Gluck Mezey, *An Integrated Model of Privacy Decision Making in State Supreme Courts*, 26 Am. Pol. Q. 35 (1998); Wenzel, Bowler, & Lanoue, *supra* note 41. Relatedly, these and other studies cast considerable doubt on simple attitudinal explanations (e.g., that judges with Republican backgrounds vote conservative, those with Democratic affiliations, liberal) for the voting behavior of lower court judges on the federal and state benches. See Frank B. Cross, *Political Science and the New Legal Realism: A Case of Unfortunate Interdisciplinary Ignorance*, 92 Nw. U. L. Rev. 251, 279–311 (1997) (describing various factors that undermine support for the attitudinal model); Daniel R. Pinello, *Linking Party to Judicial Ideology in American Courts: A Meta-Analysis*, 20 Just. Sys. J. 219 (1999) (meta-analysis of eighty-four studies examining linkage between judges' political background and voting behavior found that only 38 % of the variance can be explained by that variable; party found to be stronger attitudinal force in federal courts than in state courts).

Arguing that other actors besides the judge affect the decision-making process in a court system, particularly at the trial level, is perhaps to state the obvious.[63] However, virtually all of the literature on parity appears to take the obvious for granted, and assumes that the validity of parity rises (or falls) on the asserted quality of the individual judge. Even conceding that the lower "quality" of state trial judges will undermine parity (a concession we are unwilling to make), litigants' attorneys can provide a court with informational resources to overcome institutional deficiencies.[64] A judge's lack of familiarity with federal law could be corrected to some extent, for example, by the briefs filed and the oral arguments delivered by attorneys. In short, the *input* of information can be influenced by the litigants, while the conversion of the data may depend almost entirely on the judge.

An adequate flow of important information is arguably helpful to any trial judge. But information flow itself may be skewed. One side may be in a better position to deliver its version of the facts and law to a judge. Frequent litigants, or "repeat players," have advantages in this regard over the infrequent litigant, or "one shotter."[65] Likewise, the organized bar, particularly in large cities, tends to be split into professional hemispheres, with some attorneys practicing largely in federal courts and others confining their work to state courts.[66] The former undoubtedly would be more familiar with federal law than the latter. What does it benefit a criminal defendant, forced to press his constitutional claim in state court, to know that parity exists, if all the information is "flowing" across the street in federal court?

But if attorneys are willing (or are forced) to pursue federal cases in state courts, the skewed system can be rectified. Cases presenting important federal issues can

---

63. On the organizational theory of courts, see Herbert Jacob, *Decision Making in Trial Courts* in Critical Assessment, *supra* note 31, at 213–233.

64. See American Trial Judges, *supra* note 29, at ch. 4.

The studies suggesting the importance of information flow to judges were developed in connection with appellate courts, but we see no reason not to apply the model to trial judges as well. See Thomas Marvell, Appellate Courts and Lawyers: Information Gathering in the Adversary System (1978); Charles Lamb, *Judicial Policy-Making and Information Flow to the Supreme Court,* 29 Vand. L. Rev. 45 (1976); Charles Thompson & John B. Oakley, *From Information to Opinion in Appellate Courts*, 1986 Ariz. St. L.J. 1.

65. The concepts are borrowed from Marc Galanter, *Why the "Haves" Come Out Ahead: Speculations on the Limits of Legal Change,* 9 Law & Soc'y Rev. 95 (1974). Galanter argues that repeat players are not only more likely to understand the "rules" of litigation, but have the resources and incentive to shape the rules in their favor, and hence are more likely to determine outcomes in cases. *Id.* at 98–103, 125. For further applications of Galanter's model to state courts, see Stanton Wheeler, Bliss Cartwright, Robert A. Kagan, & Lawrence M. Friedman, *Do the "Haves" Come Out Ahead? Winning and Losing in the State Supreme Courts, 1870–1970*, 21 Law & Soc'y Rev. 403 (1987).

66. See John P. Heinz & Edward O. Laumann, Chicago Lawyers: The Social Structure of the Bar (1982); John P. Heinz, Edward O. Laumann, Robert L. Nelson & Ethan Michelson, *The Changing Character of Lawyers' Work: Chicago in 1975 and 1995*, 32 Law & Soc'y Rev. 751 (1998).

still be litigated by those interest groups that pursue the same cases in federal court.[67] To prevent state judges from hearing federal cases due to perceived institutional differences, it has been said, creates a self-fulfilling prophecy: "[I]f state courts are widely scorned, important matters are habitually removed from their jurisdiction and incentives to exert political or social pressures to maintain or improve their quality are removed from prospective litigants."[68]

Whatever the limitations of state trial courts (which, we have attempted at great length to suggest, are not extreme), every case raising a federal issue in a trial court can be appealed to a higher court and, in theory, to the U.S. Supreme Court. Hence, parity should be examined from the perspective of comparative court systems and not simply from that of comparative trial judges. The reviewing functions of state appellate and supreme courts help to guarantee the continued validity of parity. For state trial judges, the prospect of review and the potential for reversal by the appellate court system, are presumably incentives to respect federal constitutional rights. State appellate courts themselves are subject to review by state supreme courts and by the U.S. Supreme Court. Any systemic hostility to the enforcement of federal rights is unlikely to persist under the threat of review by higher courts.[69]

Thirty-nine states now have intermediate appellate courts,[70] and, as we have already suggested, such courts are considered to have a benign effect on state appellate review in general. This leads to a lower overall caseload, with the consideration of more constitutional and "public law" cases by state supreme courts. Such structural changes are said to encourage "activism" by state supreme courts, and, we think, lead to a heightened sensitivity to federal (and state) constitutional rights.[71] Furthermore, the model of information flow outlined above has been applied to a study of decisions by state supreme courts. The studies confirm, at least in part, the validity of these assumptions, suggesting that state courts are willing to go beyond the confines of the adversary system in uncovering

67. See Donald J. Farole, Jr., Interest Groups and Judicial Federalism: Organizational Litigation in State Judiciaries (1998). See generally Lee Epstein, *Courts and Interest Groups* in Critical Assessment, *supra* note 31 at 335–371.

68. *Developments in the Law—Section 1983 and Federalism*, 90 Harv. L. Rev. 1133, 1284 (1977) (footnote omitted). For an argument expressly based on normative political philosophy, as opposed to functional considerations, that such systemic arguments do not justify sacrificing the desire of even one litigant for a federal forum, see Evan Tsen Lee, *On the Received Wisdom in Federal Court*, 147 U. Pa. L. Rev. 1111 (1999).

69. John C. Kilwein & Richard A. Brisbin, Jr., *Policy Convergence in a Federal Judicial System: The Application of Intensified Scrutiny Doctrines by State Supreme Courts*, 41 Am. J. Pol. Sci. 122 (1997) (threat of reversal plays a role in state court adherence to federal law, as well as the norms of following precedent and the clarity of Supreme Court opinions).

70. Carp & Stidham, *supra* note 34, at 69–71 (1995 data).

71. See chapter 5.

and relying upon "social and empirical information."[72] This again, supports the ability of the state supreme courts adequately to resolve complex constitutional questions.

Justice Brennan doubted that the Supreme Court had the institutional capacity to adequately review and police state court decisions on federal law.[73] Indeed, as Arthur Hellman has documented, the number of cases the Supreme Court has decided on the merits has declined from about 150 in the 1970s to barely more than half that number twenty years later.[74] That decline might seem to accentuate and support Justice Brennan's fears. Whatever the reasons for the decline, it can have multiple and perhaps unexpected effects. It means, for example, that the Court is less likely to review (and possibly overturn) a rights-expanding decision by a state court, and Hellman adds:[75]

> The only imbalance is found in state-court cases involving governmental powers. But the imbalance favors litigants asserting federal rights, not those defending state official action. In this respect, however, the Court is simply going back to its roots. From the earliest days of the nation's history, no function of the Court has ranked higher than the protection of federal rights from hostility or misunderstanding on the part of state courts. We would not expect the Court to break with that tradition, and it has not.

BEYOND PARADIGMS

Ann Althouse has remarked that Yackle and other New Legal Realists are in favor of a pristine, liberal model of federal jurisdiction; the Court itself, she suggests, has taken a "moderate" path, and she wonders what a conservative model would look like.[76] We do not advance such a conservative model here. Rather, we have attempted to demonstrate the extant social science evidence, taken as a whole, is consistent with the postulates of the moderate model. Thus, we do not contend that all state courts are fungible with all federal courts, a concept labeled by some as "strong parity." The history of federal courts doctrine and the empirical evidence reviewed in this chapter are more consistent with "weak parity," so that state courts

---

72. See Marvell, *supra* note 64 (study from 1971 to 1975 of 112 written decisions of six state supreme courts). Interestingly, Marvell concurrently studied thirty opinions from the U.S. Circuit Court of Appeals for the Sixth Circuit, and found few differences in the manner in which information was presented to federal court, or in the citation practices of federal court. *Id.* at 134–135. Marvell also found that nearly one-half of the state court decisions cited "social facts," *id.* at 153, with most of the facts supplied by the court's own search, *id.* at chs. 9–13.

73. Merrell Dow Pharmaceuticals, Inc. v. Thompson, 478 U.S. 804, 827 n.6 (1986) (Brennan, J., dissenting).

74. Arthur D. Hellman, *The Shrunken Docket of the Rehnquist Court*, 1996 Sup. Ct. Rev. 403.

75. *Id.* at 428 (footnote omitted). We further address Supreme Court review of state court decisions in chapter 5.

76. Althouse, *supra* note 19, at 1073.

are willing and capable of giving claims of federal court a fair hearing to satisfy, at least, due process.[77] Whatever adjective is used, we think parity properly understood is a viable concept capable of appropriately informing federal courts doctrine by courts and other policy-makers.

* * *

As this book went to press, the Supreme Court at the close of its 1998 Term handed down a decision, *Alden v. Maine*,[78] which implicates some of our discussion concerning judicial federalism in this chapter and elsewhere. While we doubt that the case will prove to be the paradigm-shifting case as immediately posited by the popular press,[79] we think the decision, while important, will not and should not deeply restructure the postulates of judicial federalism we have previously outlined.

Alden was decided against the backdrop of the Eleventh Amendment to the Constitution. That amendment, as interpreted by the Court over many years, prohibits states from being sued in federal court for damages for, among other things, violations of federal law. A logical and appropriate corollary of those cases, the Court had seemed to say, was that *state* courts must be open to hear such claims. As a matter of precedent and policy, we agreed with that proposition.[80] The majority in *Alden* dismissed the Court's previous discussions on point as "isolated statements" and "footnote digressions." Acknowledging that the Eleventh Amendment by its terms did not control the case, the majority nonetheless held that as a matter of history, practice, precedent, and constitutional structure, the states should hold an immunity from suit in their own courts reciprocal to that they enjoy in federal court. Were it otherwise, the majority held, the "National Government would wield greater power in the state courts than in its own judicial instrumentalities."

We find *Alden* to be problematic. It is one thing to expansively interpret the Eleventh Amendment, as the Court has done for many decades. It is another to permit a state, without sturdy warrant in the very things the majority mentioned—constitutional history, text, and policy—to prohibit citizens from suing it for violations of federal law in its own courts. It is difficult to trust state courts with understanding and enforcing federal law when a state can close that forum in the first instance. We agree with the dissent that the purported anomalous result the majority sought to avoid was a function of the expansive application of the Eleventh Amendment. The federal government does not turn state courts against

77. Wells, *supra* note 17, at 185–186.

78. 119 S.Ct. 2240 (1999).

79. See, e.g., Linda Greenhouse, *States Are Given New Legal Shield by Supreme Court*, N.Y. Times, June 24, 1999, at A1. The case was decided by the same 5–4 conservative/liberal breakdown that has characterized the Rehnquist Court's other recent federalism decisions (see footnote 1 in chapter 1), which excited discussion of the impact of any new appointments to the Court. *E.g.*, Adam Clymer, *Federalism Awaites '00*, N.Y. Times, June 25, 1999, at A20.

80. See our brief discussion of the Eleventh Amendment in footnote 4, *supra*.

its own people (the majority's characterization) by requiring state courts to hear federal claims. It is simply upholding the rule of law, much as when federal courts hear claims against other branches of the federal government.[81]

Nonetheless, we think *Alden* is unlikely to be as disruptive to judicial federalism as many might think. The majority went out of its way to observe that exceptions to the Eleventh Amendment were still in place, so states could still be sued, in actuality or effect, in federal court. Among these exceptions are suing for equitable (*e.g.*, injunctive) relief; suing individual state officers and employees for damages; and suing political subdivisions of the state. Moreover, the federal government itself can still sue the state in federal or state court to enforce federal law.[82] And as we understand the decision, *Alden* does not *require* states to adopt this new immunity in its own courts. Rather, it merely *permits* a state to refuse to hear such cases. Many states now permit suit against themselves, for violations of state or federal law, in their own courts.[83] It is not obvious to us that all of the other states will rush to embrace the option that *Alden* has presented them. Many states may continue to permit suit by private parties on federal claims in their own courts, as an example of cooperative judicial federalism.[84]

---

81. *Alden*, 119 S.Ct. at 2288–2289 & nn. 34–35 (Souter, J., dissenting).

82. *Id.* at 2266–2267. These and other exceptions to the 11th Amendment are outlined in John C. Jeffries, Jr., *In Praise of the Eleventh Amendment and Section 1983*, 84 Va. L. Rev. 47 (1998); Carlos Manuel Vazquez, *What Is Eleventh Amendment Immunity?*, 106 Yale L.J. 1683 (1997). They point out that many state officers and employees are indemnified by the state if they are sued, meaning there is often a deep pocket for plaintiffs to sue if they cannot sue a state directly.

83. This is usually done in specialized courts of claims and the like. To be sure, these courts often lack certain perceived advantages of other state or federal courts that would hear federal claims. For example, often the right to a jury trial or a full compensation in damages is limited. See Joanne C. Brant, *The Ascent of Sovereign Immunity*, 83 Iowa L. Rev. 767, 801–803 (1998).

84. The Maine Supreme Court had asserted immunity from suit by private parties in state court under the Fair Standards Labor Act, a holding affirmed by the majority in *Alden*. The majority observed that it had granted certiorari because the Supreme Court of Arkansas had ruled the opposite. The day after *Alden* was decided the Court remanded the Arkansas case and a similarly-decided case from the New Mexico courts, for reconsideration in light of *Alden*. 119 S.Ct. 2387–2388 (1999).

To be sure, the attorneys general of thirty-six states joined in an amicus curiae brief in support of Maine in the case. But that is more likely an example of one branch of a state government advancing its organizational interests in federal court. See Eric N. Waltenburg & Bill Swinford, Litigating Federalism: The States Before the U.S. Supreme Court (1999). The judges in each state, in fashioning sovereign immunity doctrines, may have a different view. Perhaps the bigger surprise is that not all of the states joined in the brief supporting Maine.

Table 3.4
Outcome by Forum for Five Subsamples

	Upheld	Denied	Totals	
A. First Amendment, Civil Cases				
Federal Court	92 53.8 %	79 46.2 %	*171*	Chi-Square Probability: 0.048
State Court	31 40.3 %	46 59.7 %	*77*	Phi Coefficient: 0.13
	123	*125*	*248*	
B. First Amendment, Criminal Cases				
Federal Court	4 36.4 %	7 63.6 %	*11*	Chi-Square Probability: 0.381
State Court	22 51.2 %	21 48.8 %	*43*	Phi Coefficient: -0.12
	26	*28*	*54*	
C. Fourth Amendment, Criminal Cases				
Federal Court	31 33.3 %	62 66.7 %	*93*	Chi-Square Probability: 0.563
State Court	92 30.2 %	213 69.8 %	*305*	Phi Coefficient: 0.03
	123	*275*	*398*	
D. Fourteenth Amendment, Civil Cases				
Federal Court	43 32.8 %	88 67.2 %	*131*	Chi-Square Probability: 0.477
State Court	35 28.7 %	87 71.3 %	*122*	Phi Coefficient: 0.04
	78	*175*	*253*	

Table 3.4 (cont'd)

E. Fourteenth Amendment, Criminal Cases

Federal Court	4 36.4 %	7 63.6 %	*11*	Chi-Square Probability: 0.148
State Court	10 17.2 %	48 82.8 %	*58*	Phi Coefficient: 0.17
	14	*55*	*69*	

4

Judicial Federalism, Civil Law, and the New Forum Shopping

The popular consciousness is overwhelmed with an image of the law in the criminal mode. Police shows on television, action movies about terrorism, courtroom novels by former lawyers, televised actual criminal trials, and day-to-day newspaper and television news shows are generally subsumed with justice as punishment or retribution.[1] In a similar manner, as described in chapter 2, the dialogue about rights in the United States is overly concentrated on the rights of the criminal defendant. This is certainly understandable as the consequences of criminal trials can range from significant loss of liberty to ritual death by execution. The stakes are usually higher and thus the dramatic potential is greater.

A more balanced view of the life of the law in the United States would be far different. Self-governance requires not only a regime of legal rules but a pervasive respect for these rules that govern social relations. Remedies for evils in a society are just as likely, and in many cases more likely, to flow from civil actions than

---

1. Legal images in popular culture (books, movies, television shows) are, and probably always have been, dominated by *criminal* trials and lawyers and judges involved in such cases. Harry P. Stumpf, American Judicial Politics 300 (2d ed. 1998); Marc Galanter, *The Faces of Mistrust: The Image of Lawyers in Public Opinion, Jokes, and Political Discourse*, 66 U. Cin. L. Rev. 805, 810–816 (1998) (observing that "the criminal justice system has been the central focus of much of the recent research on the public. [P]eople are dissatisfied with both the criminal and civil justice systems. Moreover, these two aspects of the legal system are not especially distinct in the public's eyes.") To be sure, a few high profile (and low profile, see *The People's Court* television show) civil cases dominate public discourse, e.g., the wrongful death case against O.J. Simpson, the sexual harassment suit against President Clinton. See also Jonathan Harr, A Civil Action (1995). But even in those civil cases, criminal issues are sometimes a large part of the story, e.g., Simpson's murder trial, or claims of perjury against Clinton.

from criminal law enforcement.[2] The history of a free people will always include the development of an ability to settle disputes and nurture a stable peace and confidence in authority through a rule of civil law. From tax law, what Holmes called the price of civilization, to property both real, intangible, and now intellectual, to domestic relations and torts, civil rights and commercial transactions, the life of the law has not been the suppression of crime, but the establishment of civil society.[3]

As much as we must be aware of the problems of criminal law and the rights of criminal defendants, some of which we discuss in chapter 6, it would be a mistake to concentrate our fire entirely on them. Therefore, we will proceed in this chapter to address the role of state courts in civil cases as that role affects, and is in turn affected by, judicial federalism.

Most writers who doubt the ability and willingness of state judges to fairly adjudicate federal rights often focus on criminal cases. But some of the same critics typically argue that civil cases based on federal causes of action, even by willing plaintiffs, should rarely be litigated in state courts. Usually cited are the asserted need for uniformity in federal law, the unrealiability of state judges, and the need to protect at least certain types of federal interests.[4] Indeed, Congress has provided that certain matters, such as patent, copyright, and certain securities law actions, can only be litigated by private plaintiffs in federal court.[5] But there is a powerful countervailing tradition in favor of concurrent jurisdiction, permitting a plaintiff to choose a federal or state court in which to bring any action. Many federal

---

2. Thus, the federal civil rights laws can be criminally enforced by the U.S. Department of Justice under 18 U.S.C. §§ 241–242, but private enforcement of the federal constitutional and statutory rights covered by such laws, under 42 U.S.C. § 1983, far exceeds public action. See Martha Mendoza, *Civil Rights Cases Lowest on Federal Priority List*, Cincinnati Enquirer, March 21, 1994, p. A9 (in 96 percent of roughly 2,000 civil rights criminal cases referred each year to U.S. Attorneys, no action is taken).

3. With regard to Justice Holmes, see Compania General de Tabacos de Filipinas v. Collector, 275 U.S. 87, 100 (1927) (Holmes, J., dissenting) ("Taxes are what we pay for a civilized society.") With regard to criminal and civil caseloads, precise comparisons must be made with caution, since jurisdictions vary on how certain minor albeit voluminous matters (e.g., traffic tickets) are counted. That aside, more civil matters are litigated each year in federal and state courts. And, more pertinent for the matters considered by this chapter, the volume of such cases in state courts of course far exceeds the numbers of cases in federal court. Robert A. Carp & Ronald Stidham, Judicial Process in America 57–59, 75–76 (4th ed. 1998); Stumpf, *supra* note 1, at 66–71; William W. Schwarzer & Russell R. Wheeler, On the Federalization of the Administration of Civil and Criminal Justice 23 n.60 (Fed. Jud. Ctr. 1994).

4. E.g., Martin H. Redish & John E. Muench, *Adjudication of Federal Causes of Action in State Court*, 75 Mich. L. Rev. 311 (1976).

5. E.g., 28 U.S.C. §§ 1333(1) (admiralty), 1338(a) (patent and copyright), 1334 (bankruptcy); 15 U.S.C. § 78aa (Securities Exchange Act of 1934); 29 U.S.C. § 1132(e)(1) (Employment Retirement Income Security Act) (ERISA).

statutes expressly provide this option,[6] and recent self-studies by federal judges have argued that, to ameliorate the burgeoning caseloads of federal courts, many federal causes of action should be litigated concurrently with, or even exclusively in, state courts.[7]

In this chapter we explain the soundness of the countervailing tradition. It has been sometimes called the *new* forum shopping, not in the sense that civil plaintiffs have only recently begun litigating federal rights in state court, but that it has only begun to gain intellectual respectability. We first briefly address Supreme Court decisions that have construed most federal statutes to allow concurrent jurisdiction. We next argue that these decisions rightly empower plaintiffs to choose, and conclude that concurrent jurisdiction expands the opportunities for enforcement of federal rights without undermining the uniformity of federal law or other national interests and with several salubrious results.[8]

---

6. E.g., 15 U.S.C. § 77v(a) (Securities Act of 1933); 45 U.S.C. § 56 (Federal Employers' Liability Act) (FELA).

7. Report of the Federal Courts Study Committee 43–44 (1990) (recommending that certain ERISA actions be litigated in state court) (hereinafter Federal Courts Report); Judicial Conference of the United States, Long Range Plan for the Federal Courts 28–36 (1995) (arguing that Congress should not vest federal courts with jurisdiction to hear federal causes of action of disputes not involving rights under the U.S. Constitution, or matters deserving uniformity or where there is a paramount federal interest). Congress has on rare occasions provided for exclusive *state* jurisdiction. See the 1991 Telephone Consumer Protection Act, 47 U.S.C. § 227(b)(3), construed in Int'l Science & Tech. Inst., Inc. v. Ivacon Commm., Inc., 106 F.3d 1146 (4th Cir. 1997). See also Daniel Meador, *Federal Law in State Supreme Courts*, 3 Const. Commentary 347, 356 (1986) (arguing that actions under the Truth in Lending Act (TILA), 15 U.S.C. §§ 1601 *et seq.*, and the FELA, should be exclusively litigated in state court); Jon O. Newman, *Restructuring Federal Jurisdiction: Proposals to Preserve the Federal Judicial System*, 56 U. Chi. L. Rev. 761, 771 (1989) (similar proposal).

8. A related issue that we do not directly consider is whether Congress may *compel* state courts to adjudicate federal causes of action. On that point, see Howlett v. Rose, 496 U.S. 356 (1990) (generally, state courts may not refuse to entertain federal causes of action in the absence of a "valid excuse"); Testa v. Katt, 330 U.S. 386 (1947) (same). *But see* Alden v. Maine, 119 S.Ct. 2240 (1999) (Congress lacks power to subject nonconsenting states to suits on federal questions by private parties in their own courts, but reaffirming *Testa v. Katt* and *Howlett v. Rose*). See generally Richard H. Fallon, Daniel J. Meltzer & David L. Shapiro, Hart & Wechsler's The Federal Courts and the Federal System 469–478 (4th ed. 1996) (hereinafter Hart & Wechsler); Roderick M. Hills, Jr., *The Political Economy of Cooperative Federalism: Why State Autonomy Makes Sense and "Dual Sovereignty" Doesn't*, 96 Mich. L. Rev. 813, 927–933 (1998). To be sure, addressing the compulsion issue is informed by the policy issues addressed elsewhere in this chapter and throughout this book. E.g., Martin H. Redish & Steven G. Sklaver, *Federal Power to Commandeer State Courts: Implications for the Theory of Judicial Federalism*, 32 Ind. L. Rev. 71 (1998) (arguing that the Supremacy Clause requires even reluctant state courts to enforce federal causes of action, whether or not parity is accepted).

THE SUPREME COURT AND EXCLUSIVE FEDERAL JURISDICTION

As noted above, Congress has from time to time explicitly stated in a statute that a cause of action may only be filed in a federal court. Likewise, with a number of statutes, Congress has explicitly provided for concurrent jurisdiction. One must follow a more tortured path in outlining those statutes where courts have implied or inferred exclusivity. The journey starts with the leading case of *Claflin v. Houseman*,[9] which upheld state court jurisdiction of an action under the Bankrupt Act of 1867. *Claflin* is important for two reasons. First, it laid to rest any notion that state courts lacked the power to adjudicate federally created causes of action. The "general principle," *Claflin* held, was that "if exclusive jurisdiction be neither express nor implied, the state courts have concurrent jurisdiction whenever, by their own constitution, they are competent to take it." Second, the Court established a presumptive canon of construction to be applied when it faced a federal statute that is apparently silent on the issue of concurrent jurisdiction: The state court has "jurisdiction where it is not excluded by express provision, or by incompatibility in its exercise arising from the nature of the particular case."

As Professor Martin Redish has remarked, the application of the *Claflin* presumption in subsequent cases has not been "free from difficulty."[10] The initial part of the presumption is not the problem; it seems easy enough in most instances to determine if Congress has explicitly provided for exclusive jurisdiction only. *Claflin* sowed confusion when it also gave courts authority to find implied exclusivity without clarifying what factors should inform such a finding. The subsequent case law reflects this confusion and uncertainty. Without discussing *Claflin*, the Supreme Court in a number of cases found concurrent jurisdiction when a statute did not directly address the point. Likewise, in other cases, notably those involving the antitrust laws, the Court, with virtually no discussion of any kind, apparently invoked the implied exclusivity branch of *Claflin* and found exclusive jurisdiction.[11]

The first satisfactory discussion of *Claflin* appeared nearly a century later in *Charles Dowd Box Co. v. Courtney*.[12] There, the Court considered whether state courts had concurrent jurisdiction, in actions under section 301(a) of the Labor-Management Relations Act, for violation of a contract between an employer and a labor organization. The Court, in a unanimous opinion by Justice Harlan, initially observed that section 301(a) was silent on the issue of exclusivity: "[i]t provides that suits of the kind described 'may' be brought in the federal district courts, not that they must be." Then, pointing out that "exclusive federal court jurisdiction over cases arising under federal law has been the exception rather than the rule," the Court discussed *Claflin* and invoked the rebuttable presumption from

9. 93 U.S. 130 (1876).

10. Redish & Muench, *supra* note 4, at 316.

11. See Freeman v. Bee Machine Co., 319 U.S. 448, 451 n.6 (1943); General Inv. Co. v. Lake Shore & M.S. Ry., 260 U.S. 261, 287 (1922).

12. 368 U.S. 502 (1962).

that case. The Court found the presumption not rebutted, relying upon the legislative history of section 301(a), which contained references to suit in state court. The opinion is closed by a brief discussion of the contention that diversity and conflicts in labor law will result now that fifty state court systems, as well as (then) eleven federal circuits, will have jurisdiction over section 301(a) actions. The Court found no such problem. Diversity is "not necessarily [an] unhealthy prospect," it is a "usual consequence" of the existence of concurrent jurisdiction, and the Court stood ready to resolve any conflicts.

More recently, the Supreme Court has attempted to clarify the *Claflin* presumption. In *Gulf Offshore Co. v. Mobil Oil Corp.*,[13] a unanimous Court held that concurrent jurisdiction was permissible over claims arising under the Outer Continental Shelf Lands Act, and in so doing held that the presumption of concurrent jurisdiction can be rebutted by an explicit statutory directive, by unmistakable implication from legislative history, or by a clear incompatibility between state-court jurisdiction and federal interests. The Court added that: "The factors generally recommending exclusive federal-court jurisdiction over an area of federal law include the desirability of uniform interpretation, the expertise of federal judges in federal law, and the assumed greater hospitality of federal courts to peculiarly federal claims."

Likewise, in *Tafflin v. Levitt*,[14] the Court held that state courts had concurrent jurisdiction over civil Racketeer Influenced and Corrupt Organizations (RICO) actions, and in *Yellow Freight System, Inc. v. Donnelly*[15] held that there was concurrent jurisdiction over Title VII actions. In a concurring opinion in *Tafflin*, Justice Scalia that it should take an express action or clear statement by Congress to oust a state court of jurisdiction, and that the "implied exclusivity" branch of *Chaflin* and *Gulf Offshore* should be abandoned. Scalia's approach is not only easier to apply but, in our view, represents better policy.

On a number of occasions the Supreme Court has used a clear statement canon of construction before interpreting a statute to impose requirements upon the states. Clear statement rules, like any interpretive canon, serve a number of functions. They can provide a starting point in ascertaining the plain meaning of a statute, improve law-making by requiring Congress to be careful in drafting statutory language, and effectuate substantive background principles. A clear statement requirement is not neutral, and the crafter of such a canon should be explicit about, and ready to defend, the policy embodied in the rule.[16]

---

13. 453 U.S. 473 (1981).

14. 493 U.S. 455 (1990). The case involved the civil provisions of RICO, 18 U.S.C. § 1964(c).

15. 494 U.S. 820 (1990). The case involved Title VII of the 1964 Civil Rights Act, 42 U.S.C. § 2000e *et seq.*

16. See Cass Sunstein, *Interpreting Statutes in the Regulatory State*, 103 Harv. L. Rev. 405, 454–460 (1989); William E. Eskridge, Jr. & Philip P. Frickey, *Quasi-Constitutional Law: Clear Statement Rules as Constitutional Lawmaking*, 45 Vand. L. Rev. 593 (1992).

In the balance of this chapter we will defend a clear statement rule implementing the *Claflin* presumption. The rule is consistent with constitutional text and history, with the notion of giving plaintiffs freedom-of-forum choice, and with the systemic concerns of federal law. And, the rule will have a salutary effect on the law-making process and will not lead to harmful consequences for state courts.

THE UTILITY OF CONCURRENT JURISDICTION

The framers of the Constitution clearly envisioned the prospect of concurrent jurisdiction. Article III of the Constitution reflects the Madisonian Compromise, whereby Congress has the option to create lower federal courts. A corollary of this position is that state courts would and should be open to hear federal claims and federal causes of action. Review of state court decisions on such claims or actions could be brought, if need be, to the Supreme Court. Relatedly, state courts are bound to follow and apply federal law under the Supremacy Clause of the Constitution. Federal and state courts are not mutually exclusive sovereigns. Thus, concurrent jurisdiction is not simply a matter of congressional beneficence, but flows from the obligations imposed upon states by the Supremacy Clause. It is no surprise, then, that the *Claflin* Court's understanding of concurrent jurisdiction was the accepted rule even prior to that decision.[17]

LITIGANT CHOICE

Permitting a prospective plaintiff the choice of more than one forum in which to bring a lawsuit is thus a traditional, if oft-criticized, feature of the American legal landscape.[18] But whatever else might be said about forum-shopping, concurrent jurisdiction clearly serves the interests of plaintiffs in whose name, presumably, a federal cause of action is created in the first instance. Concurrent jurisdiction empowers plaintiffs by providing a choice of fora, given the chance that one court may be thought to be more hospitable or convenient than another.[19]

---

17. These now well-accepted propositions, it is true, have "not always appeared self-evident," Hart & Wechsler, *supra* note 8, at 450; see also Michael G. Collins, *Article III Cases, State Court Duties, and the Madisonian Compromise*, 1995 Wis. L. Rev. 39, but they are reflective of the twentieth-century caselaw.

18. George D. Brown, *The Ideologies of Forum Shopping—Why Doesn't a Conservative Court Protect Defendants?*, 71 N.C. L. Rev. 649 (1993); Kevin M. Clermont & Theodore Eisenberg, *Exorcising the Evil of Forum-Shopping*, 80 Cornell L. Rev. 1507 (1995); Gita F. Rothschild, *Forum Shopping*, 24 Litigation 40 (Spring 1998); Note, *Forum Shopping Reconsidered*, 103 Harv. L. Rev. 1677 (1990).

19. Gulf Offshore Co. v. Mobil Oil Corp., 453 U.S. 473, 483 n.12 (1981) ("Exclusive federal-court jurisdiction generally is unnecessary to protect the parties. The plaintiff may choose the available forum he prefers."); Erwin Chemerinsky, *Parity Reconsidered: Defining a Role for the Federal Judiciary*, 36 UCLA L. Rev. 233, 302–308 (1988) (allowing a litigant a choice of forum in cases raising federal claims maximizes opportunity for protecting constitutional rights, enhances litigants' autonomy, and enhances federalism).

Moreover, to the extent that a particular forum might be demonstrably unfair to a defendant, the disadvantaged party can remove the action to federal court if she feels that would ameliorate the unfairness.[20]

Despite its ubiquity, forum shopping in its many guises remains notoriously understudied by social scientists. Some studies have been done of the choices available to litigants with federal rights, and those studies might be read to undermine support for concurrent jurisdiction. Several studies have demonstrated that many attorneys, when they have the choice, prefer federal court over state court.[21] These studies are not without some persuasive force, and they suggest that federal courts, overall, possess a more positive reputation than state courts, a fact we do not dispute. But it is an unjustified leap from that fact to a rejection of the foundations of concurrent jurisdiction.

As Professors Fink and Tushnet observe, "[p]art of the distortion arises from the impact of particular experiences, but as the epistemologists tell us, 'For example' is not proof." Lawyers, and their clients, may not be as informed about the likelihood of success in state courts:

> Litigants probably are more concerned with the details of the conduct of a lawsuit than they are with grand abstractions about "federal interests," "liberty," or "federalism." These details involve such matters as the scope of discovery—federal discovery is broader than that

---

Professor Chemerinsky argues that the debate over federal and state court "parity" can never be empirically resolved, and that federal courts should focus upon the normative principle of litigant choice in shaping jurisdictional doctrine. Chemerinsky, *supra*, at 300–301. In response, Redish argues that a litigant-choice model can be interpreted to be a criticism of the concept of parity, since it permits plaintiffs to choose federal court over state court (an option that many current jurisdictional doctrines, such as abstention in its various forms, do not allow). Martin H. Redish, *Judicial Parity, Litigant Choice and Democratic Theory: A Comment on Federal Jurisdiction and Constitutional Rights*, 36 UCLA L. Rev. 329, 339–342 (1988).

We do not fully agree with either position. Unlike Chemerinsky, we argued in chapter 3 that empirical evidence can and should inform the debate over "parity," however one defines that term. Unlike Redish, we do not think a litigant choice model necessarily undercuts the concept of parity. Utilizing a presumption of concurrent jurisdiction necessarily assumes that state courts are competent to adjudicate federal statutory rights.

20. See 28 U.S.C. § 1441 (removal statute).

21. See Thomas B. Marvell, *The Rationales for Federal Question Jurisdiction: An Empirical Examination of Student Rights Litigation*, 1984 Wis. L. Rev. 1315 (survey of 267 attorneys involved in students rights cases); Neal Miller, *An Empirical Study of Forum Choices in Removal Cases Under Diversity and Federal Question Jurisdiction*, 41 Am. U. L. Rev. 369 (1992) (survey of 482 attorneys in cases removed from state to federal court); Kenneth Mitchell Mash, Uniformity in the Balance: An Examination of Section 1983 and Federal Jurisdiction 170–210 (unpublished Ph.D. dissertation, Penn State University, 1997) (survey of 103 attorneys who litigated cases under 42 U.S.C. § 1983, the principle civil rights statute). For an excellent review and summary of the literature by a contributor to it, see Victor E. Flango, *Litigant Choice Between State and Federal Courts*, 46 S.C. L. Rev. 961 (1995).

available in some state courts—the length of delay before trial in each court, and the location of the courthouse—state venue rules may force a trial to be held in a location remote from the attorney's office, which may be close to the federal district courthouse. These considerations have different effects in particular parts of the country.[22]

A likely explanation for the results of the studies is the reputation accorded attorneys who mostly work in federal court, and the diets of cases in the respective courts. With regard to attorney reputations, studies have shown that, especially in large cities, the bar is split into hemispheres, with the more prestigious group largely practicing in federal court. The diet of cases in federal courts typically involves fairly complex antitrust, securities, patent, discrimination, commercial, and civil rights disputes. On the average, more familiar and routine tort, contract, domestic relation, and other disputes with a narrower public impact are handled by state courts.[23] (Counterexamples of course come quickly to mind, such as social security disability benefits cases in federal court, and innovative tort and products liability cases that have emerged from state courts.) In sum, generalizations about court reputations lack explanatory power. Nevertheless, they are part of the lore of many lawyers and may account for the persistent support of diversity jurisdiction. While interesting and relevant, reputations and intuitions should not determine the propriety of concurrent jurisdiction.

The most serious problem with the reputational approach is that it invites the perpetuation of a self-fulfilling prophecy. Lawyers think that state courts are incompetent to deal with federal claims, and they go to federal court. State courts are less familiar with federal claims because the lawyers go to federal court, and so on. Finally, the reputational approach is static, a snapshot in time that does not allow for the evolution of the state court systems; a state court that is hostile or incompetent today or in the past will always be so.

---

22. Howard Fink and Mark V. Tushnet, Federal Jurisdiction: Policy and Practice 16–17 (1984).

More recent empirical suggests that litigants or interest groups seeking to enforce federal rights are increasingly turning to state court, even when their main locus of attention is federal court. See, e.g., Donald J. Farole, Jr., Interest Groups and Judicial Federalism: Organizational Litigation in State Judiciaries (1998) (comparative study of interest group litigation in five states in eminent domain (takings) and obscenity law).

23. On attorney reputation, see Edward O. Lauman & John P. Heinz, Chicago Lawyers: The Professions of the Bar (1982); John P. Heinz, Edward O. Laumann, Robert L. Nelson & Ethan Michelson, *The Changing Character of Lawyers' Work: Chicago in 1975 and 1995*, 32 Law & Soc'y Rev. 751 (1998) (hereinafter Heinz). On differences between the diet of cases in federal and state courts, see Herbert Kritzer et al., *Courts and Litigation Investment: Why Do Lawyers Spend More Time on Federal Cases?*, 9 Just. Sys. J. 7 (1984).

SYSTEMIC CONCERNS

As a number of writers have suggested,[24] the litigant choice model does not address how concurrent jurisdiction might affect other litigants or the content of federal law in general. The principal concern at this juncture is that concurrent jurisdiction will lead to a lack of uniformity in federal law. Uniformity is thought to be virtuous in almost every area of the law: it insures that like cases, and litigants, are treated alike. In the present context, disuniformity in the interpretation of federal law between federal and state courts can inhibit planning by lawyers (inside and outside of litigation), encourage litigation, and could eventually undermine respect for the legal system.[25]

To strive toward uniformity is one thing; to sacrifice concurrent jurisdiction on its altar is another. Even under a regime of exclusive federal jurisdiction, there will be frequent conflicts in the interpretation of federal law among the twelve circuit courts of appeals.[26] It seems doubtful that depriving state courts of concurrent jurisdiction will have much more than an incremental effect on the creation of these conflicts. Moreover, there may be short-term benefits to some disuniformity. It may permit an issue to "percolate" in lower federal and state courts, providing a broader base of views for the Supreme Court to consider when and if it decides to resolve the conflict.[27]

---

24. E.g., Richard A. Posner, The Federal Courts: Challenge and Reform 296 (1996) (litigant-choice model makes sense "provided the state court is competent to cope with the issues."); American Law Institute, Study of the Division of Jurisdiction Between State and Federal Courts 183 (1969) (uniformity interest "is more important than the wishes of the parties.").

25. Tafflin v. Levitt, 493 U.S. 455, 468 (1990) (White, J., concurring) (arguing that "improper interpretation of the Federal antitrust laws [by state courts] could have a disastrous effect on interstate commerce"). Justice Brennan has suggested that one of the reasons for the creation of general federal question jurisdiction for the federal courts in 1875 (now codified at 28 U.S.C. § 1331) was the desire for uniformity. Merrell Dow Pharmaceuticals, Inc. v. Thompson, 478 U.S. 804, 826 (1986) (Brennan, J., dissenting). Cf. Erwin Chemerinsky & Larry Kramer, *Defining the Role of the Federal Courts*, 1990 B.Y.U. L. Rev. 67, 84 (uniformity rationale for 28 U.S.C. § 1331 (the statute granting federal courts jurisdiction over any case that arises under federal law) undercut by fact that § 1331 did not provide for exclusive federal jurisdiction).

26. Arthur D. Hellman, *By Precedent Unbound: The Nature and Extent of Unresolved Intercircuit Conflict*, 56 U. Pitt. L. Rev. 693 (1995). For some empirical evidence, based on surveys of attorneys, that unresolved circuit conflicts on federal statutory issues (such as antitrust, labor, ERISA, and maritime law) do *not* inevitably lead to forum shopping or inhibit business or other activity, see Arthur D. Hellman, *Light on a Darkling Plain: Intercircuit Conflicts in the Perspective of Time and Experience*, 1998 Sup. Ct. Rev. 247, 266–302.

27. *Dowd Box*, 368 U.S. at 514, *quoted in Tafflin*, 495 U.S. at 467 ("[C]onflicts deriving from concurrent jurisdiction are not necessarily unhealthy."); Samuel Estreicher & John E. Sexton, Redefining the Supreme Court's Role: A Theory of Managing the Federal Judicial Process 48 (1986) (discussing benefits of percolation).

Judge Richard Posner has argued that the uniformity issue may be usefully examined from the perspective of interstate spillovers.[28] Posner contends that there should be a federal court available if there is a chance that a state court will externalize the costs of suit (i.e., hold for a local plaintiff as against an out-of-state defendant). He suggests, however, that many federal constitutional or statutory rights are apt not to involve externalities, or to involve them "tenuously." If that is true, then a federal system can tolerate some disuniformity that, for the most part, is confined to an individual state. Use of this analysis is helpful, though not dispositive, in evaluating the appropriateness of concurrent jurisdiction. Many federal causes of action are apt to have their benefits and burdens placed largely upon the residents of the forum state. Under the most-utilized federal civil rights statute, section 1983,[29] for example, a typical suit usually involves residents of one state.[30] On the other hand, some Title VII actions presumably involve defendant-employers with multistate operations. Similarly, some civil RICO defendants, especially those involved in the securities industry, engage in business across the nation.[31] The externality argument becomes most problematic with respect to actions brought under section 301 of the Labor-Management Relations Act, held to fall under concurrent jurisdiction in the *Dowd* case. But federal common law governs section 301 lawsuits brought in state court,[32] and the possibility of externalities is one factor that justifies creation of a federal common law in the first instance.[33]

An analogous argument suggests that concurrent jurisdiction is less problematic if the federal cause of action is similar to existing state law,[34] and if the federal action does not call for a "high level of analytical difficulty" for the judges and lawyers involved.[35] In either instance, the risk of an erroneous construction of federal law by a state court is lessened. Many federal causes of action have analogies in state law, or explicitly incorporate state law as a rule of decision. By the same token, some areas of exclusive federal jurisdiction (patent and admiralty

---

28. Posner, *supra* note 24, at 280–292.

29. 42 U.S.C. § 1983. Section 1983 actions are considered to be within the concurrent jurisdiction of state courts. See *infra* notes 47–49 and accompanying text.

30. Agency Holding Corp. v. Malley-Duff & Assoc., Inc., 483 U.S. 143, 154 (1987) ("[T]he typical § 1983 suit . . . most commonly involves a dispute wholly within one State.").

31. *Compare* Posner, *supra* note 24, at 295 (some securities fraud suits involve "small, local, closely-held corporations") *with* Agency Holding Corp. v. Malley-Duff & Assoc., Inc., 483 U.S. 143, 153 (1987) ("RICO cases commonly involve interstate transactions").

32. Local 174, Teamsters v. Lucas Flour Co., 369 U.S. 95, 102–104 (1962).

33. Posner, *supra* note 24, at 294. See also Redish & Muench, *supra* note 4, at 333–334 (arguing that *Dowd* was wrongly decided in light of use of federal common law in § 301 actions); Chemerinsky & Kramer, *supra* note 25, at 86 (federal judges are in the best position to develop federal common law but "this jurisdiction need not be exclusive").

34. Posner, *supra* note 24, at 295; Redish & Muench, *supra* note 4, at 334–335.

35. Posner, *supra* note 24, at 296. Here, Posner seems to be supporting the reputational argument against parity by inference.

come to mind) are thought to be exceptionally difficult for the bench and bar alike, and seem to have few analogies to state law. Still, the areas of federal law with little or no state law analogs would seem to be quite small. And while a significant portion of the litigating bar practices in only one court system, particularly in urban areas, but that is a far cry from saying that many lawyers exclusively practice in "federal" law as opposed to "state" law.[36]

Concerns over disuniformity and any possible state court decisions that depart significantly from settled federal law are largely ameliorated if the Supreme Court takes an active role in supervising those decisions through its certiorari jurisdiction. To be sure, the Supreme Court, given its other responsibilities, is not in a position to accept a huge volume of such cases. Arguably, however, the Court has performed its supervisory role in this context quite well, and the possibility of U.S. Supreme Court review surely focuses the attention of judges at the higher levels of the state court system. The Court can accept more cases from state courts if the perception arises that states are handling their concurrent jurisdiction poorly.[37]

Up to now, we have been looking at "the glass half empty," i.e., the concerns that presumptively argue against concurrent jurisdiction. But we can play offense as well as defense with the evidence. Perhaps the most obvious suggestion is that concurrent jurisdiction has the potential for reducing the increasingly burdensome caseload of the federal courts. Naturally, from the point of view of those of us who defend judicial federalism this would be a good development indeed. Likewise, routing federal causes of action through state courts on a more regular basis can do much to improve the quality of judging and litigating of such actions at that level. It will give state judges the opportunity to become more familiar with, and even contribute to, the development of federal law. If some state court systems are unable or unwilling to do that, presumably the bar in that state will vote with their wingtips (or in some parts of the country their Birkenstocks), by filing suit in federal court or, better still, demand improvements in the state court.

EMPIRICAL EVIDENCE

One's view of parity between federal and state court no doubt influences opinions on the desirability of concurrent jurisdiction.[38] Our views on that subject should be abundantly clear by now so they do not bear repeating here. But as we have suggested before, litigants' and attorneys' views of parity (no matter how well

36. Larry Kramer, *Diversity Jurisdiction*, 1990 B.Y.U. L. Rev. 97, 108–109. Nor is a specialized bar for exclusive federal jurisdiction cases something that should necessarily be encouraged. See Richard L. Revesz, *Specialized Courts and the Administrative Lawmaking System*, 138 U. Pa. L. Rev. 1111, 1164 (1990) (discussing dangers of an overspecialized bar); Rochelle Copper Dreyfuss, *Specialized Adjudication*, 1990 B.Y.U. L. Rev. 377, 424–425 (same). That said, the bar appears to be increasingly specialized overall, especially in large urban areas. Heinz, *supra* note 23.

37. See chapter 3 for more discussion of this point.

38. Hart & Wechsler, *supra* note 8, at 452.

or poorly grounded) inform their forum choice decisions on federal causes of action. For example, some attorneys might prefer a federal judge because she will handle all the motions in a case under her own individual calendar. Many, though not all, state courts operate under a master calendar, where different judges might rule on disputes in one case.[39] Yet some lawyers might prefer the less active case-management typical of state courts, and a state court might be preferred for reasons of geography, lack of delay, and home-court advantage.[40] Among other things, juries in state courts are usually drawn from a smaller area and, at least in urban areas, are likely to be more pro-plaintiff than those in federal court.[41] Finally, most states have adopted some version of the Federal Rules of Civil Procedure and the Federal Rules of Evidence, although some areas of different state procedure may be preferable for one or both parties.[42]

Critics of parity often level most of their fire at the treatment of criminal defendants in state courts. This is not counterintuitive. By their nature the rights of criminal defendants can often be countermajoritarian. That is, the fear of being a victim of crime can sometimes be presumed to overwhelm the sympathy of the public in general for strict adherence to constitutional procedures. This presumption can lead a state judge or jury to be hostile, or at least indifferent, to these rights. But however one comes out on the parity debate, it obviously has less applicability to the adjudication of most federal statutory causes of action, brought civilly by plaintiffs, than it does to federal constitutional rights of criminal defendants.[43] Many federal civil causes of action (like civil RICO) may seek to hold a private defendant liable. Others, like Title VII or the Age Discrimination in Employment Act (ADEA), might lead to a plaintiff being advantaged by appearing before a state court jury more balanced in terms of gender or ethnicity.[44] In short the theoretical or empirical discussions of parity focusing on the adjudication of federal constitutional rights in state criminal cases simply have less applicability when the person seeking to enforce a federal right is voluntarily in state court.

Acknowledging the limitations of any statistical inquiry, an empirical study of how state courts have dealt with federal causes of action over which they have

39. 1 Steven H. Steinglass, Section 1983 Litigation in State Courts § 7.2 (1998 ed.).

40. *Id.*, §§ 8.2–8.3.

41. *Id.*, § 7.3.

42. For example, some states do not have a rule similar to the notorious Federal Rule of Civil Procedure 11 (see Carl W. Tobias, *Rule 11 and Civil Rights Litigation*, 37 Buffalo L. Rev. 485 (1988–1989)), Steinglass, *supra* note 39, § 8.2(a); some states are less willing than federal courts to grant summary judgment motions, *id.*, § 8.2(d); and some states are more willing to certify class actions or permit interlocutory appeals, than are federal courts. *Id.*, §§ 8.8, 8.11. See also Susan N. Herman, *Beyond Parity: Section 1983 and the State Courts*, 54 Brooklyn L. Rev. 1057, 1100 (1989).

43. Of course, one can use some federal causes of action to adjudicate federal constitutional rights. E.g., 42 U.S.C. §§ 1983, 1985.

44. Cf. Arthur D. Hellman, *Case Selection in the Burger Court: A Preliminary Inquiry*, 60 Notre Dame L. Rev. 947, 994–995 (1985) (discussing egalitarian goals of Title VII).

concurrent jurisdiction might shed light on whether exclusive jurisdiction is a better choice. There is some impressionistic evidence that state courts have been competently handling causes of action similar to federal actions, such as suits under state antitrust[45] or securities[46] laws.

An empirical review of how states have handled section 1983 cases should be a good test of the thesis that state courts are competent to adjudicate federal causes of action. Unlike, say, most Title VII or civil RICO cases, section 1983 lawsuits are apt to be controversial, as they usually involve local governmental defendants for alleged violations of federal constitutional rights. Section 1983 was enacted by the Reconstruction Congress largely because state courts, particularly in the South, were unable or unwilling to protect the constitutional rights of the newly freed slaves.[47] While even critics of parity would probably agree that state courts have come some distance since then, one might still expect that of all federal causes of action, section 1983 would receive the most hostility in the states.

Indeed, one could make a persuasive argument that section 1983 actions are within the exclusive jurisdiction of the federal courts. Under modern doctrine, the *Gulf Offshore* test is called into play, because section 1983 itself is silent on the issue of concurrent jurisdiction. There are some fleeting references in the legislative history to the availability of concurrent jurisdiction,[48] but the principal thrust of section 1983 was to provide a federal court *alternative* to the inadequacies of state substantive and procedural law. Although the Supreme Court has frequently stated or assumed that there is concurrent jurisdiction over section 1983

45. See Herbert Hovenkamp, *The Indirect-Purchaser Rule and Cost-Plus Sales*, 103 Harv. L. Rev. 1717, 1719 (1990) (states have shown increased aggressiveness in antitrust enforcement) (hereinafter Hovenkamp, *Indirect Purchaser Rule*); David E. Rovella, *State AGs Look for New Targets*, Nat'l L. J., Jan. 26, 1998 (same); Herbert Hovenkamp, *State Antitrust in the Federal Scheme*, 58 Ind. L. J. 375, 384–385 (1983) (discussing why a plaintiff may wish to proceed under state, rather than federal, antitrust laws) (hereinafter Hovenkamp, *State Antitrust*). See also Joseph F. Zimmerman, *Interstate Cooperation: The Roles of the State Attorneys General*, 28 Publius: The Journal of Federalism 71 (Winter 1998).

46. Craig B. Brod, Note, *The Securities Exchange Act and the Rule of Exclusive Federal Jurisdiction*, 89 Yale L. J. 95, 111–113 & n.69 (1979) (state securities laws resemble their federal counterparts, and state opinions that have adjudicated federal law defenses "conform closely to those of federal courts"). See also Louis Loss, *The SEC Proxy Rules and State Law*, 73 Harv. L. Rev. 1249, 1274–1277 (1960) (arguing for concurrent jurisdiction of federal securities law causes of action); Romine v. CompuServe Corp., 160 F.3d 337, 342 (6th Cir. 1998) (Congress expressly providing for concurrent jurisdiction over 1933 Securities Act claims indicates that it did not fear "that [state] courts would inadequately protect plaintiff's rights.").

47. Patsy v. Florida Bd. of Regents, 457 U.S. 496, 502–507 (1982); Gene R. Nichol, *Federalism, State Courts, and Section* 1983, 73 Va. L. Rev. 959, 971–983 (1987).

48. *Patsy*, 457 U.S. at 506–507 (quoting remarks of several congressmen). See also Nichol, *supra* note 47, at 983 & n.144 (Congress had little concern with issue of concurrent jurisdiction); Herman, *supra* note 42, at 1072–1073.

actions,[49] it is not clear when the bench and bar first perceived that such actions were permitted to be filed in state court.

All of which is to say that even an agnostic on the issue of parity might think that relatively few section 1983 actions would be filed in state court, and those that were would be treated roughly in those courts. There is little empirical data, however, that might support or refute that point.[50] To fill that gap, we conducted a survey of section 1983 cases litigated in state courts in 1987. A computer search generated 117 published opinions from that year, of which 114 directly involved a section 1983 claim advanced by the plaintiff.[51] A number of variables were coded for each opinion, including: (1) the level of the court, either state supreme court, intermediate appellate court, or trial court; (2) the types of issues raised by the cause of action;[52] (3) which party or parties prevailed; (4) whether the case terminated in the trial court before or after a trial; and (5) whether and to what extent the courts cited Supreme Court or lower federal court opinions.

Table 4.1
Published State Courts Section 1983 Cases

1. LEVEL OF COURT	
State Supreme Court	37
Intermediate Appellate Court	73
Trial Court	4
Total	114

49. See Howlett v. Rose, 496 U.S. 356, 358 (1990); Felder v. Casey, 487 U.S. 131, 139 (1988); *Patsy*, 457 U.S. at 506–507; Maine v. Thiboutot, 448 U.S. 1, 3 n.1 (1980); Martinez v. California, 444 U.S. 277, 283 n.7 (1980).

50. There is some evidence, mainly impressions drawn from a doctrinal survey of cases, that state courts are increasingly hospitable to § 1983 claims. See Steinglass, *supra* note 39, §§ 2.5–2.7; Steven H. Steinglass, *The Emerging State Court § 1983 Action: A Procedural Review*, 38 U. Miami L. Rev. 381, 439 (1984) (after doctrinal and empirical survey of published state court § 1983 opinions from 1969 to 1983, concludes that "[m]ost state courts have accepted the obligation to enforce federal law through § 1983 and have been willing to look to the remedial attributes developed in federal court § 1983 litigation as a source of guidance.").

51. The WESTLAW search was as follows: ALLSTATES database: SY, DI (42+5 1983) & 42+5 1983/P (claim) (cause+2 action) & DATE (=1987). While this search does not capture every state court opinion that cites § 1983, it does include many, if not most, of the state court opinions where a § 1983 cause of action is directly ruled upon. A list of cases is available from the authors.

52. The categories utilized were traditional civil rights (involving one of the Bill of Rights or the Fourteenth Amendment); prisoners' rights; employment; housing; and others. For a use of similar categories in categorizing civil rights cases, see Theodore Eisenberg & Stewart Schwab, *The Reality of Constitutional Tort Litigation*, 72 Cornell L. Rev. 641, 661 (1987).

Table 4.1 (cont'd)

2. ISSUES RAISED	
Traditional Civil Rights	77
Prisoners' Rights	13
Employment	26
Housing	10
Total	126[a]
3. TRIAL COURT DISPOSITION	
In Favor of Plaintiff	
Pretrial: Summary Judgment	1
Trial: Judgment	19
Total	20
In Favor of Defendant	
Pretrial: Dismissal	31
Summary Judgment	41
Trial: Judgment	16
Total	88[b]
4. CITATION PATTERNS (PER DECISION)[c]	
(a) U.S. Supreme Court cases	
(b) U.S. Court of Appeals	3.12
(i) total	1.91
(ii) within circuit	.82
(c) U.S. District Court	
(i) total	.95
(ii) within circuit	.44

a. Total exceeds 114 since some cases fell into more than one category.
b. Total does not equal 114 since several cases involved interlocutory appeals.
c. Citations limited to § 1983 issue; includes citations found in concurring or dissenting opinions.

Some of the results of the survey are reported in Table 4.1. All but four of the opinions were from appellate courts, since state courts rarely publish trial court opinions. Issues involving the Bill of Rights, the Fourteenth Amendment, and employment matters dominated the agenda of plaintiffs bringing section 1983 actions. At the trial court level, defendants prevailed in over 80 percent of the cases, usually in a pretrial disposition, a rate of success that was usually affirmed on appeal.[53] Only thirteen of the cases were brought as pure section 1983 actions;

53. Of the twenty plaintiffs who prevailed at the trial level, seventeen were affirmed on appeal. Of the eighty-eight defendants who prevailed at the trial level, seventy were affirmed on appeal. This is consistent with the understanding that there are high rates of affirmance in state appellate courts. Stanton Wheeler, Bliss Cartwright, Robert A. Kagan &

the balance had state law claims joined as well, confirming the perception that this is a common practice in state court section 1983 litigation. Finally, the state decisions, on the average, cited nearly six federal court opinions dealing with section 1983. About half of that total were lower federal court opinions and of those, about 40 percent were from the federal circuit within which the state court sat.

Table 4.2
Results of Sample of Published Federal Appellate Court Section 1983 Cases in 1987

1. Issues Raised	
Traditional Civil Rights	10
Prisoners'	9
Employment	3
Housing	2
Total	24
2. Trial Court Disposition	
In Favor of Plaintiff	
Pretrial	0
Trial	2
Total	2
In Favor of Defendant	
Pretrial: Dismissal	10
Summary Judgment	6
Trial	1
Total	17
3. Citation Patterns	
(a) U.S. Supreme Court Cases	3.67
(b) U.S. Court of Appeals	
(i) total	4.75
(ii) within circuit	2.67
(c) U.S. District Court	
(i) total	.83
(ii) within circuit	.71

Lawrence M. Friedman, *Do the "Haves" Come Out Ahead? Winning and Losing in State Supreme Courts*, 1870–1970, 21 Law & Soc'y Rev. 403, 406–07 (1987); Margaret P.P. Mason, Note, *Courting Reversal: The Supervisory Role of State Supreme Courts*, 87 Yale L. J. 1191 (1978).

As a point of comparison, twenty federal appellate opinions from 1987 were also coded in a similar fashion.[54] The results of that survey are found in Table 4.2.

Comparing Tables 4.1 and 4.2 reveals that state courts are dealing with section 1983 much as are their federal counterparts. In both systems plaintiffs find it difficult but not impossible to prevail at the trial level,[55] though they meet with more success on appeal.[56] Pretrial dispositions, particularly in favor of defendants, are common in both systems. The citation rates indicate that state courts are aware of and follow federal law, particularly cases from the federal circuit in which they are located.[57] The latter point tends to undermine concerns about lack of uniformity. State judges are citing and presumably following the same appellate court decisions as do the states' federal district judges.

Any conclusions from relatively small samples of published opinions must be drawn with caution, given the uncertainties of whether published cases accurately reflect the vast number of unpublished dispositions of cases, particularly at the trial court level. Even with that caveat, the data from one year of state court adjudication of section 1983 cases reveal that those courts are competently dealing with civil rights cases. The data also support a more general presumption that state courts are competent to adjudicate federal causes of action.

THE COSTS OF CONCURRENT JURISDICTION

Any legal regime that presumptively permits federal causes of action to be brought in state courts is not without costs. We have previously addressed some of those concerns. Here we address two more: the possibility of overloading state courts with federal cases, and whether state courts in these circumstances should be forced to follow federal procedures.

---

54. The computer search was identical to that used for the state court search, see *supra* note 51, with a CTA database used. Only the first twenty opinions generated by that search were coded. A list of the cases is available from the authors.

55. For similar results from broad samples of federal court civil rights cases, see Eisenberg & Schwab, *supra* note 52, at 676–684; Theodore Eisenberg, *Litigation Models and Trial Outcomes in Civil Rights and Prisoner Cases*, 77 Geo. L. J. 1567, 1578–1580, 1588–1589 (1989).

56. For similar conclusions based on a broad sample of published federal appellate court constitutional tort cases, see Theodore Eisenberg & Stewart Schwab, *What Shapes Perceptions of the Federal Court System?*, 56 U. Chi. L. Rev. 501, 516–526 (1989).

57. That judges expressly cite precedent at all is some reflection of their thought processes and their desire to justify their decisions. Lawrence W. Friedman, Robert A. Kagan, Bliss Cartwright, & Stanton Wheeler, *State Supreme Courts: A Century of Style and Citation*, 33 Stan. L. Rev. 773, 792–795 (1981). Higher citation rates, especially of cases not from the citing court, are often associated with quality of the opinion. *Id.* at 803–804; Gregory A. Caldeira, *On the Reputation of State Supreme Courts*, 5 Pol. Behavior 83, 89 (1983). Cf. Tafflin v. Levitt, 493 U.S. 455, 465 (1990) (expressing confidence that state courts adjudicating civil RICO claims will be guided by federal court precedent).

State judges are sometimes heard to complain that their dockets are increasingly filled with cases that would otherwise be on the federal docket.[58] Statistics are difficult to come by, but no doubt there is some validity to the complaint. But it shouldn't be blown out of proportion. There is little chance that state sovereignty will be impaired by greater use of concurrent jurisdiction. The closest analogy is the current debate over the partial or complete abolition of the diversity jurisdiction of the federal courts.[59] State court judges have generally not opposed such proposals,[60] even though they would feel the brunt of increased caseloads. In fact, even the complete abolition of diversity jurisdiction would have relatively little effect on state court caseloads, adding perhaps ten or eleven cases on the average to the docket of state judges of courts of general jurisdiction.[61]

Federalism virtues are arguably served by an increase in concurrent jurisdiction. Such jurisdiction can invigorate state court protection of federal rights in general, and induce pressure (from local bars) to improve state court systems if the judges are thought not to be up to the task. While difficult to predict, the increases in state court dockets from greater use of state courts by plaintiffs pursuing federal causes of action will likely be minimal.

Whether state courts might be overburdened by federal causes of action will depend in part on the forum choices of litigants and their attorneys. It will also depend in part on whether Congress passes (or lets stand) statutes creating federal causes of action that provide for concurrent jurisdiction. For many years the conventional wisdom was that Congress would protect state interests, since the House and Senate are elected from the states themselves.[62] This portion is almost certainly overstated, since a variety of forces dilute the potency of a state's rights agenda in Congress.[63] But even if the political safeguards of federalism are weak,

58. Hills, *supra* note 8, at 930 (quoting Chief Judge Judith Kaye of the New York Court of Appeals).

59. Federal Courts Report, *supra* note 7, at 38–43 (outlining various proposals to limit or abolish diversity jurisdiction); Kramer, *supra* note 36, at 121–129 (same).

60. Kramer, *supra* note 36, at 98.

61. Victor E. Flango, *How Would the Abolition of Federal Diversity Jurisdiction Affect State Courts?*, 74 Judicature 35, 40–41 (1990). See also Kramer, *supra* note 36, at 109–117. *Cf.* Posner, *supra* note 24, at 290–291 (pointing out that effect could be different in different parts of the country).

62. See Jesse H. Choper, Judicial Review and the National Political Process (1980) and Herbert Wechsler, *The Political Safeguards of Federalism: The Role of the States in the Composition and Selection of the National Government*, 54 Colum. L. Rev. 543 (1954) for the two most prominent proponents of the theory. It was the basis for the majority opinion in Garcia v. San Antonio Metropolitan Transit Authority, 469 U.S. 528 (1985), which all but withdrew judicial oversight and review of arguments that Congress was harming state interests in a manner violative of the Tenth Amendment.

63. For excellent discussions of the burgeoning critical literature, see Elizabeth Garrett, *Enhancing the Political Safeguards of Federalism? The Unfunded Mandates Reform Act of 1995*, 45 U. Kan. L. Rev. 1113, 1118–1136 (1997) (discussing weakness of lobbies that argue in favor of states' rights); Larry Kramer, *Understanding Federalism*, 47

state courts are not apt to be victimized by the process. Jurisdictional issues, like those addressed here, are almost always low on Congress's agenda in any era.[64] Consider, too, that recent Congressional legislation that has federalized vast parts of criminal law has likely *reduced* the number of crimes that would otherwise occupy the state court docket.[65]

In two areas, preemption of state court procedure, and removal, a regime of greater concurrent jurisdiction, would require difficult policy issues to be addressed. Preemption of state procedures, when federal causes of action are litigated in the state forum, occurs when the state procedural rule interferes with or frustrates the substantive right created by the cause of action.[66] Preemption questions will of course increase if more federal actions are litigated in state courts. Not all will be easy to resolve.[67] Nevertheless, such doctrinal confusion seems a

---

Vand. L. Rev. 1485, 1503–1514, 1533–1542 (1994) (states *qua* states have little protection given the direct election of senators; relative weakness and diffusion of power within largely decentralized political parties usually make them poor candidates to protect federalism values); John C. Yoo, *The Judicial Safeguards of Federalism*, 70 S. Cal. L. Rev. 1311, 1321 (1997) ("Changes in culture, technology, and the economy have diluted regional and local identities in favor of politics that are national in scope and focus.").

64. While Congress amends or enacts jurisdictional statutes with some frequency, Michael E. Solimine & James L. Walker, *The Next Word: Congressional Response to Supreme Court Statutory Decisions*, 65 Temp. L. Rev. 425, 451 n.120 (1992), more generally it often ignores or leaves muddled the presence or absence of concurrent jurisdiction and a host of other procedural issues. Hart & Wechsler, *supra* note 8, at 829; Gregory E. Maggs, *Reducing the Costs of Statutory Ambiguity: Alternative Approaches and the Federal Courts Study Committee*, 29 Harv. J. Legis. 123 (1992). This means that Congress is unlikely to aggressively seek to increase or decrease the caseloads of state courts. For a rare counterexample, see the Securities Litigation Uniform Standards Act of 1998, Pub. L. No. 105–353, 112 Stat. 3227 (codified in 15 U.S.C.) (creating uniform federal law and exclusive federal jurisdiction for certain types of securities fraud class actions).

65. There is now a considerable and mostly critical literature on the federalization of crimes in the 1980s and 1990s that were traditionally left to enforcement by state authorities in state court. See American Bar Association, Criminal Justice Section Task Force, The Federalization of Criminal Law (1998); Posner, *supra* note 24, at 283–286; Steven D. Clymer, *Unequal Justice: The Federalization of Criminal Law*, 70 S. Cal. L. Rev. 643 (1997). But see Tom Stacy & Kim Dayton, *The Underfederalization of Crime*, 6 Cornell J. Law & Pub. Pol'y 247, 316 (1997) (arguing in favor of a greater federal presence in crime control, in part because state judges deal with a far higher percentage of criminal cases than federal judges).

66. Johnson v. Fankell, 520 U.S. 911 (1997); Felder v. Casey, 487 U.S. 131, 151 (1988).

67. For a survey of state procedures that might be subject to preemption, see Steinglass, *supra* note 39, §§ 12.1–14.4; Herman, *supra* note 42, at 1115–1134; Burt Neuborne, *Toward Procedural Parity in Constitutional Litigation*, 22 Wm. & Mary L. Rev. 725, 780–786 (1981).

For discussions of where the line ought to be drawn, when federal and state procedures do meaningfully differ, *compare* Redish & Sklaver, *supra* note 8, at 105 (rather than "ad hoc balancing," there should be "a strong presumption in favor of the use of federal procedures

small price to pay given the virtues of concurrent jurisdiction. The quantity of such questions is bound to decrease as more states adopt versions of federal rules of procedure and evidence.[68]

Another issue raised by concurrent jurisdiction is the removal of the federal action from state court to federal court by the defendant. Under current law, a federal cause of action brought in state court may be removed, subject to certain exceptions.[69] Thus, a section 1983 action filed in state court is removable. Because state courts are usually thought hospitable to civil rights defendants, a removal of such a suit is, on its face, ironic.[70] It makes good sense to retain this removal option, however, since it serves as an important safety valve to protect the

---

when a state court is called upon to adjudicate a federal cause of action.") (footnote omitted) with Vicki C. Jackson, *Printz and Testa: The Infrastructure of Federal Supremacy*, 32 Ind. L. Rev. 111, 127–136 (1998) (doubting that strong presumptive rule of Redish & Sklaver is called for, and pointing out benefits of procedural decentralization and state experimentation with procedural rules) and Ellen A. Peters, *Capacity and Respect: A Perspective on the Historic Role of the State Courts in the Federal System*, 73 N.Y.U. L. Rev. 1065, 1078–1080 (1998) (similar though briefer analysis).

68. See chapter 3 for further discussion of this point.

69. The principal statutory exceptions are found in 28 U.S.C. § 1445 (prohibiting, *inter alia*, the removal of FELA cases and private actions brought under the Violence Against Women Act (VAWA) of 1994). The statutory prohibition of removing these federal question cases presumably reflects, at least in part, a congressional judgment that state courts are up to the task of properly adjudicating these causes of action. Thus, the VAWA provision, 42 U.S.C. § 13981(e)(3), in effect creates mandatory concurrent jurisdiction over civil actions brought under that law. As one court commented:

> If Congress were truly concerned that state courts, judges, and juries were hostile to women and purposefully discriminating against them in the enforcement and application of law, the more natural response would have been to create exclusive federal jurisdiction over section 13981 claims, or, at the very least, only to allow concurrent jurisdiction in state courts that Congress concluded were not purposefully discriminating against women. Section 13981 instead permits its authorized causes of action to be brought in the very fora that the appellants must contend are hostile to the interests of women.

Brzonkala v. Virginia Polytechnic Institute, 169 F.3d 820, 886 (4th Cir. 1999) (en banc).

The principal judicially crafted exception is the application of the well-pleaded complaint rule to the removal context, which prevents removal of cases with federal issues embodied in defenses and counterclaims. See Rivet v. Regions Bank of Louisiana, 522 U.S. 470 (1998). This exception, too, is premised in part on confidence in state courts, and thus can be criticized on that basis by sceptics of parity. E.g., Larry W. Yackle, Reclaiming the Federal Courts 103–104 (1994).

70. 2 Steinglass, *supra* note 39, § 24.2(a). Cf. Herman, *supra* note 42, at 1084–1092 (arguing that removal of § 1983 actions should be prohibited).

defendant who thinks the state court an improper forum. If we are serious about maintaining the option of concurrent jurisdiction, it may make sense to consider modest restraints on the ability to remove.[71]

* * *

For all of these reasons we conclude that the current favorable attitude toward concurrent jurisdiction is justified. Perhaps the most prominent and controversial counterexample has been the Court's determination that the federal antitrust laws fall under the exclusive jurisdiction of the federal courts. In several cases, the Court has held (without citing the *Claflin* presumption) that private actions under the Sherman and Clayton Acts fall under the exclusive jurisdiction of the federal courts.[72] These decisions are suspect under the multipart test of *Gulf Offshore*. First, the jurisdictional grants state only that suit "may" be brought in a federal district court.[73] No language of exclusion is found in the statutes. Second, the legislative history of both acts seems to indicate a preference for concurrent jurisdiction.[74] Third, there are no persuasive incompatibility factors to prevent state

---

71. Richard Fallon and his coauthors list four jurisdictional options open to Congress: (1) exclusive state original jurisdiction, subject to appellate review by the Supreme Court; (2) exclusive federal jurisdiction; (3) concurrent federal and state jurisdiction, with state court decisions subject to Supreme Court review; and (4) concurrent state and federal jurisdiction, but with a right of state court defendants to remove to federal court. Hart & Wechsler, *supra* note 8, at 451. Congress has employed all of these options, but the last is the most common. Curiously, recent data shows that in removed federal question cases, the win rate (for plaintiffs in those cases) in federal court drops from an overall rate of 52 percent to 25 percent. Kevin M. Clermont & Theodore Eisenberg, *Do Case Outcomes Really Reveal Anything About the Legal System? Win Rates and Removal Jurisdiction*, 83 Cornell L. Rev. 581, 593–595 (1998). This result might suggest plaintiffs are bringing weaker cases in state court, or that federal judges are not as hospitable to federal claims as commonly thought. Neither explanation reflects poorly on state courts.

72. See cases cited *supra* note 11. See also Marrese v. American Academy of Orthopaedic Surgeons, 470 U.S. 373, 379-380 (1985) (citing, without discussion, earlier case for proposition that "federal antitrust claims are within the exclusive jurisdiction of the federal courts"); Village of Bolingbrook v. Citizens Utilities Co., 864 F.2d 481, 485 (7th Cir. 1988) (Easterbrook, J.) (suggesting that earlier cases are "ripe for reexamination" in light of *Gulf Offshore* and later cases).

73. The jurisdictional grant for the Sherman Act is the Act of July 2, 1890, ch. 647, § 7, 26 Stat. 209, 210. The grant for the Clayton Act (which empowered private plaintiffs to enforce the Sherman Act) is the Act of Oct. 15, 1914, ch. 323, §§ 4, 16, 38 Stat. 730, 731, 737. The latter law effectively supercceded the former, and its present version states that: "[A]ny person who shall be injured in his business or property by reason of anything forbidden in the antitrust laws may sue therefore in any district court of the United States." 15 U.S.C. § 15(a).

74. During the debates on the Sherman Act, a proposed amendment expressly providing for concurrent jurisdiction was defeated. One opponent of the measure, a supporter of concurrent jurisdiction, thought the amendment "useless and unnecessary." S. Doc. No. 147, 57th Cong., 2d Sess. 316 (1903). See generally Redish & Muench, *supra* note 4, at 316–317; Note, *Exclusive Jurisdiction of the Federal Courts in Private Civil Actions*,

courts from hearing such suits. As previously observed, many state courts are familiar with their own antitrust laws, most of which are modeled after the federal laws. State courts have also entertained federal antitrust defenses. Concerns of competence and the need for uniformity, especially given the opportunity for Court review, do not seem to be compelling.[75] However the *Gulf Offshore* criteria might be applied, application of a clear statement rule would require reversal of the earlier Court decisions.

This is not to say that exclusive federal jurisdiction over certain causes of action is never proper. For example, there seems little to be gained by permitting state courts to adjudicate admiralty, patent, or copyright actions. Those actions have long been solely litigated in federal courts, arguably have a greater need for uniformity, and for the most part lack significant analogies to state common law.[76] Similarly, it would be unwise to permit state courts to entertain bankruptcy matters. Given the existing and extensive system of specialized federal bankruptcy courts, it would be both unnecessary and disruptive to permit state courts to provide an alternative forum. Neither historical nor functional reasons, however, support the continued imposition of exclusive federal jurisdiction over other causes of action. The federal antitrust and securities laws are candidates for at least an experiment in concurrent jurisdiction.

---

70 Harv. L. Rev. 509, 510 n.13 (1957).

The legislative history of the Clayton Act is a bit more obtuse. There, Congress also rejected an amendment that would have expressly provided for concurrent jurisdiction. 51 Cong. Rec. 9664 (1914). Redish reads this rejection as an indication that Congress desired there to be exclusive jurisdiction. Redish & Muench, *supra* note 4, at 318. Another writer, reviewing the same materials, 51 Cong. Rec. at 9662–9664, disputes Redish's conclusion, attributing the defeat of the amendment to other issues raised by the proposal. Michael P. Kenny, *RICO and Federalism: A Case for Concurrent Jurisdiction*, 31 B.C. L. Rev. 239, 255 n.91 (1990). This exchange not only demonstrates the hazards of relying on legislative history to make decisions on concurrent jurisdiction, but also the dangers of deriving intent from rejected legislation.

75. Even under the current regime of exclusive jurisdiction, the Court has on occasion reviewed state court determinations of federal antitrust issues. See Hathorn v. Lovorn, 457 U.S. 255, 266 n.18 (1982) (giving examples). On the issue of competence, while antitrust law might be an area of a "high level of analytical difficulty," Posner, *supra* note 24, at 296, that state courts have adjudicated antitrust defenses as well as their own antitrust laws indicates that state courts are up to the task. On the need for uniformity, one might argue that states would be more likely to favor local plaintiffs at the expense of out-of-state defendants, or those with multistate operations. Posner, *supra* note 24, at 296; Hovenkamp, *Indirect-Purchaser Rule*, *supra* note 45, at 1719 n.17. This theoretical danger, however, has not been realized in practice under current antitrust laws, principally because most state courts have held that the defendant must have significant contacts with the forum state. See Hovenkamp, *State Antitrust, supra* note 45, at 399.

76. See Posner, *supra* note 24, at 286–287, 296. See also Florida Prepaid Postsecondary Ed. Exp. Bd. v. College Savings Bank, 119 S.Ct. 2199, 2212–2213 (1999) (Stevens, J., dissenting) (discussing how need for consistency and uniformity supports exclusive federal jurisdiction in patent cases).

Congress remains free to expressly state its desire for exclusive jurisdiction in the text of a statute, or to legislatively overturn a judicial finding of concurrent jurisdiction. Until then, the presumption of concurrent jurisdiction, implemented by a clear statement rule, serves the interests of the litigants and judicial personnel in the federal and state court systems. But beyond the narrower interests of the "consumers" of the judicial system, we believe it serves the wider interest of promoting state court competency and confidence in the local community's ability to develop the most populous set of legal concerns, the civil law cases. In the next chapter, we turn to a discussion of the performance of the state courts in handling causes of action which come from within, rather than without, the state court realm.

5

Federalism, Liberty, and State Constitutional Law

In previous chapters we have explored the possibility that state governments, and particularly state courts, are competent to play a meaningful role in the preservation of liberty. Most of that discussion has focused on state court adjudication of federal constitutional and statutory provisions. In this chapter, we address a different source of rights. We look now at state courts' interpretations of their own constitutions, acting independently of the federal constitution. It is often said that the U.S. Constitution establishes a "floor" of rights, below which the states may not go, but above which they are free to roam. This metaphor is simplistic and possibly misleading for many of the reasons discussed in chapter 2. However, for the sake of discussion, we assume that a citizen of a state must be provided all of the protections guaranteed by the federal government, and that states may interpret their own constitutions in any way that does not dilute those protections.

For the past two decades, some state courts have exercised what has been termed "the new judicial federalism." This refers to the practice of interpreting state constitutions in ways that expand and enhance the rights of the citizens of that state. At first blush, this would seem to be an example of federalism promoting liberty. But the phenomenon is too complex and ambiguous to allow such a facile conclusion. We address two of the major ambiguities in this chapter.

The first ambiguity relates to the actual performance of state courts. We consider the recent development of state constitutional law. The large literature on this topic, for the most part, advocates increased independence by state judiciaries in interpreting their own constitutions. One problem, however, is that state judges may not be keeping up with the literature, for empirical studies show that most state supreme courts simply follow federal constitutional law closely in cases involving individual rights. A case using the state constitution alone to sustain a rights claim is a comparatively rare event. If that pattern endures, what are the implications for the relationship of federalism to liberty? On the other hand, if state courts begin to act more independently, how does that affect the argument of some that most state courts cannot fully and fairly adjudicate *federal* constitutional law?

We then consider a second, related ambiguity. The U.S. Supreme Court can review decisions of state courts to the extent they turn on federal law. A decision based on a state constitution, even one that recognizes rights not guaranteed by the federal constitution, is not reviewable by the federal courts. But many state court decisions will discuss both federal and state case law and constitutional provisions, making it unclear whether and to what extent the case is deciding an issue of federal law.

The Supreme Court has chosen to resolve the ambiguity by assuming that a case is based on federal law, and hence is reviewable, unless the state court clearly indicates that the basis was state law. This default rule creates quite a divide in the legal community. Many of those who in the past relied on the leadership of the high court to defend liberties, are much less congenial to Supreme Court review in this context. The obvious fear is that a conservative Supreme Court will reverse more liberal decisions of state courts. Conversely, those who are generally comfortable with state court resolution of federal rights may view Supreme Court review of such cases as intrusive and unnecessary.

AMBIGUITIES OF STATE CONSTITUTIONAL LAW

In this part, we first address the recent development of state constitutional law, and note recent critiques that contend that the phenomenon is empirically overstated and normatively undesirable. We next consider two issues raised by the critiques: if there is a robust body of state constitutional law, does it suggest that state courts are also capable of guarding federal rights? And, conversely, if the recent criticisms of state constitutional law are correct, does that conclusion suggest that state courts cannot be fully trusted to adjudicate federal rights?

STATE CONSTITUTIONAL LAW, IN GENERAL

State courts have been interpreting their own constitutions, of course, as long as states have existed. We are here concerned with case law applying those provisions that protect individual rights, i.e., those similar (though not restricted) to those found in the federal Bill of Rights. Until about two decades ago, there were few such cases, and almost none that expanded rights beyond what was guaranteed in the First through Eighth Amendments of the Constitution. Several reasons probably account for this apparent restraint by state courts, among them the sometimes overlooked fact that the U.S. Supreme Court itself only began substantively expanding these rights in the latter part of this century.[1]

1. For an excellent overview, see G. Alan Tarr, Understanding State Constitutions 118 & n.108 (1998).

Times have changed. Since the 1970s, state courts (particularly the highest courts of the states) have issued hundreds of opinions interpreting their constitutions to protect rights beyond the federal minima.[2] No doubt, the increased interest by lawyers and litigants in state constitutional rights was fueled by the retrenchment of the Supreme Court in many rights disputes during the same period.[3] And helping to jumpstart the revival of state law on this topic was an influential law review article by U.S. Supreme Court Justice William Brennan, who suggested use of state courts as a "double source of protection" in response to the restrictive decisions of his own Court.[4] Because of federalism concerns and other institutional constraints, as he later argued, federal courts may "underenforce" certain constitutional values.[5] A "more responsible state court role," he suggested, should be met with "equal enthusiasm" by liberals and conservatives alike: the former because the decisions may increase rights protection, and the latter because responsibility for experimentation is being returned to the states. The academic community lavished attention on these developments, generating a literature rivaling in size, it almost seems, of that on federalism as a whole.[6]

The new judicial federalism was not without its critics. Some argued that the rise of state constitutional law was often little more than result-oriented jurisprudence, thinly disguised efforts to evade the more restrictive rights decisions of the Burger and Rehnquist Courts.[7] More recently, James Gardner and others have questioned the conceptual underpinnings of the entire enterprise. Writing in 1992, Gardner asserted that contrary to the claims of much of the conventional wisdom,

---

2. Jennifer Friesen, State Constitutional Law: Litigating Individual Rights, Claims and Defenses 2 (2d ed. 1996).

3. *Id.* at 3. Cf. Paul W. Kahn, *State Constitutionalism and the Problems of Fairness*, 30 Val. U. L. Rev. 459, 464 (1996) ("State constitutionalism represented a kind of forum shopping for liberals.").

4. William J. Brennan, Jr., *State Constitutions and the Protection of Individual Rights*, 90 Harv. L. Rev. 489, 503 (1977). A recent survey found this article ranked twenty-sixth on a list of the 100 most-cited law review articles. Fred R. Shapiro, *The Most-Cited Law Review Articles Revisited*, 71 Chi.-Kent L. Rev. 751, 768 (1996).

5. William J. Brennan, Jr., *The Bill of Rights and the States: The Revival of State Constitutions as Guardians of Individual Rights*, 61 N.Y.U. L. Rev. 535, 549–550 (1986). A similar argument was more recently advanced in Helen Hershkoff, *Positive Rights and State Constitutions: The Limits of Federal Rationality Review*, 112 Harv. L. Rev. 1131 (1999).

6. For a sampling of the enormous literature, see Friesen, *supra* note 2; Tarr, *supra* note 1; Robert F. Williams, State Constitutional Law: Cases and Materials (2d ed. 1993); Symposium, *The New Judicial Federalism: A New Generation*, 30 Val. U. L. Rev. 421 (1996); Symposium, *State Constitutional Commentary*, 59 Alb. L. Rev. 1539 (1996); Symposium, *The Emergence of State Constitutional Law*, 63 Tex. L. Rev. 959 (1985). Jennifer Friesen's recent, comprehensive bibliography of the topic (including both general discussions and state-specific articles and books) is over 100 pages long. Friesen, *supra* note 2, at 823–931.

7. E.g., Earl M. Maltz, *The Dark Side of State Court Activism*, 63 Tex. L. Rev. 995 (1985).

"state constitutional law today is a vast wasteland of confusing, conflicting, and essentially unintelligible pronouncements."[8] Gardner based this extraordinary conclusion on a survey of state supreme court decisions from seven states in 1990. He found that, with few exceptions, most of the decisions concerning individual rights followed federal courts case law (often referred to as "lockstep" analysis). Those few that did not, in his view, made little effort to justify departure from federal standards, especially given that the state constitutional provisions concerning rights usually tracked the federal counterpart. Gardner acknowledged but found unconvincing the usual reasons advanced to explain the apparent prevalence of lockstep analysis: that the application of the federal Bill of Rights to the states continued to retard the growth of state law; that ignorant lawyers and litigants often did little or nothing to advance alternative, state law arguments, even when available; and that a lack of historical information with regard to the drafting and meaning of each state constitution's rights provisions made principled departures from lockstep analysis difficult.[9] Rather, Gardner suggested, the poverty of state constitutional discourse had deeper roots: the relevant rights-protective provisions of most state constitutions were little different from each other, or from the U.S. Constitution. Moreover, there is little evidence that the attitude of citizens of each state toward rights (or of much else) is distinctive on a state law level. Thus, there is no distinctive state character on which a separate state constitutional jurisprudence could be predicated. He claimed that if such distinctive state culture even existed, it has been considerably undermined in this century by the ease of interstate travel and communications. For good or ill, most discussion of individual rights is addressed at a national level—all for the good, Gardner concluded, since true state distinctiveness could lead to an unhealthy balkanization of value formation in this country.[10]

---

8. James A. Gardner, *The Failed Discourse of State Constitutionalism*, 90 Mich. L. Rev. 761, 763 (1992).

9. *Id.* at 804–812. With regard to these explanations, Gardner argued that despite the incorporation excuse, nothing prevented state courts from taking the initiative in expanding the rights of criminal defendants under their own constitutions, *id.* at 806–807; that it is "absurd" to blame lawyers and law schools since most state courts have been lethargic in developing state constitutionalism, *id.* at 810; and that historical information about state constitutions is neither necessarily difficult to access, nor absolutely necessary to "create a rich constitutional discourse." *Id.* at 811.

10. *Id.* at 812–828. Writing contemporaneously, Paul Kahn reached largely similar conclusions. Like Gardner, Kahn argued that for the most part "public life is experienced in and through a national community," due to the mobility of citizens and the ubiquity of modern culture. These developments make it difficult to contend that there are unique cultures and characters for each state upon which the judges of that state could convincingly base a distinctive state constitutional jurisprudence. Paul W. Kahn, *Interpretation and Authority in State Constitutionalism*, 106 Harv. L. Rev. 1147 (1993).

TWO PROBLEMS WITH STATE CONSTITUTIONAL LAW

If state court decision-making on state constitutional law were hardy and robust (i.e., the critics were wrong), then would that demonstrate that federalism can promote liberty? Conversely, if the critics have the better of the argument, does that suggest that, consistent with the old school of thought (see chapters 1 and 2), federalism does not lead to greater protection of rights?

Take the first argument. Let us assume that state courts have, or at least can, develop in a principled fashion, a body of law protecting individual rights premised on their own constitutional provisions. This law would, on occasion, give greater protection to rights than that found in the federal constitution as interpreted by the Supreme Court. Those decisions beyond the minima of federal rights might be premised on different language in state constitutions, unique aspects of the framing and application of those provisions by state courts (even if they textually resemble their federal counterparts), the distinctive nature of the history of culture of the particular state, or some combination of the foregoing.

At first blush, this characterization of state processes would seem to bode well for the future of liberty under federalism in this country. Indeed, since these cases protect rights at a higher level than demanded by the federal constitution, it would seem to follow that state courts could be trusted to enforce *federal* constitutional rights as well. That is, the rise of state constitutional law arguably supports the concept of parity—that state judges and courts can, and will in general, fully and fairly adjudicate federal constitutional rights, a concept we explored in chapter 3.

The existence of an expansive, rights-protecting state constitutional law might seem to undermine unqualified attacks on parity. At the very least, there would seem to be some tension between the two lines of argument.[11] Most advocates of an expansive state constitutional law have not even acknowledged this tension, much less made an effort to resolve it.[12] One critic of parity, Larry W. Yackle, has recognized the tension and considered whether the rise of state constitutional law "proves that state courts are generally hospitable to personal liberty claims."[13] He

---

11. See, e.g., Barry Friedman, *Pas De Deux: The Supreme Court and the Habeas Courts*, 66 S. Cal. L. Rev. 2467, 2478 (1993) (noting tension); Barry Latzer, *Toward the Decentralization of Criminal Procedure: State Constitutional Law and Selective Disincorporation*, 87 J. Crim. L. & Criminology 63, 66, 95 (1996) (same). See also Louise Weinberg, Federal Courts: Cases and Comments on Judicial Federalism and Judicial Power 277 (1994) (briefly noting arguable tension between Neuborne's argument and Brennan's advocacy of state constitutional law).

12. Thus, as Paul Kahn has observed, Justice Brennan is a "puzzling" advocate of state constitutionalism, since he has been generally dismissive of state sovereignty in federalism disputes, and has been particularly critical of the concept of parity. Kahn, *supra* note 10, at 1147. For similar observations about Justice Brennan in this regard, see Kahn, *supra* note 3, at 465 and Earl M. Maltz, *False Prophet—Justice Brennan and the Theory of State Constitutional Law*, 15 Hastings Const. L. Q. 429 (1988).

13. Larry W. Yackle, Reclaiming the Federal Courts 12 n.3 (1994).

concludes that no such implication should be drawn. It stands to reason, he argues, that state courts would be giving "definitive treatment" to provisions of their own constitutions. Moreover, he suggests, "generous readings of state law do not necessarily signal equally generous readings of federal law." Reasons distinctive to each state may be explanatory. Thus, he continues, courts that have found property-tax funding schemes for public schools violative of state constitutions (despite their legality under federal constitutional law[14]) have "as much to do with logjams in local legislatures as with an enthusiasms for giving state constitutional provisions a capacious reading."

We do not find Yackle's effort to resolve the tension particularly persuasive. It is illogical to cabin a state judge's decision-making on state law from her jurisprudence with respect to the federal Constitution. In both cases, the litigants will follow similar practices in presenting the facts and law to the judge. In both cases, the judge will, presumably, follow similar paths of reaching and explaining a decision.[15] In both cases the operative provisions of the respective constitutions will be substantially identical.[16] And in many instances the decision based on state law will be just a countermajoritarian as one based on federal law.

Nor is Yackle's dismissal of the school funding cases entitled to much weight. Of these cases where plaintiffs have succeeded,[17] it could well be that institutional factors of the sort Yackle references, rather than a desire to protect liberty, accounts for the results.[18] Indeed, some have argued that the results have often been *majoritarian*—since many of the voters in each state prefers to see public schools

---

14. See San Antonio Independent School District v. Rodriguez, 411 U.S. 1 (1973) (property tax funding for public schools does not violate Equal Protection Clause of the Fourteenth Amendment).

15. Michael E. Solimine & James L. Walker, *State Court Protection of Federal Constitutional Rights*, 12 Harv. J. L. & Pub. Pol'y 127, 153 (1989).

16. One recent study reported that thirty-four of the fifty state constitutional provisions dealing with search and seizure were substantially identical to the Fourth Amendment, and thirty-four of the forty-five provisions dealing with double jeopardy were substantially identical to the Fifth Amendment. Other state analogs to other provisions of the Bill of Rights had lesser numbers substantially identical. Barry Latzer, *The Hidden Conservatism of the State Court "Revolution,"* 74 Judicature 190, 194 & n.19 (1991). See also Tarr, *supra* note 1, at 12 ("over time state bills of rights have come to resemble more closely the federal Bill of Rights [though] important differences remain.") (footnote omitted).

17. Kahn, *supra* note 3, at 467 n.31 (comprehensive citation of cases, indicating that there has been such litigation in about one-half of the states, and plaintiffs have prevailed to some degree in about one-half of those cases).

18. *Id.* at 468 (arguing that differences among states in results are not due to differences in text or history of relevant provisions in state constitutions, but rather "successful litigation has more been the product, not the cause, of a political consensus that the schools need fundamental change").

better funded.[19] But that conclusion may be too facile. State supreme courts that have struck down property tax financing have typically left the difficult remedial issues to state legislators. And it is not by any means clear that all citizens in a state prefer the results (e.g., voters in more well-to-do school districts may be adversely impacted by more equitable funding schemes), or that the decisions have, in fact, led to more equitable funding of schools.[20] Then, too, the complexities of the substantive and remedial issues raised by these cases resemble the sort of institutional, public law litigation that has been a mainstay of the federal courts since the Warren era. So depending on which parts of the school funding litigation story we wish to consult, some of it does suggest, pace Yackle, that state courts are capable of enforcing liberties identical or similar to those found in the federal Constitution.

Now let us consider the implications for federalism and liberty if the critics of state constitutionalism are correct. Recall that Gardner and others asserted that the much heralded rise of state constitutional law regarding individual rights was overstated, as most state courts kept to the federal path. Gardner drew this conclusion from a modest empirical study—but an avalanche of data from other researches covering many more cases shows that he is right. Despite the considerable hoopla afforded a few decisions from a few states, the vast majority

19. George D. Brown, *Binding Advisory Opinions: A Federal Courts Perspective on the State School Finance Decisions*, 35 B.C. L. Rev. 543, 554 (1994).

20. See Dorothy A. Brown, *The Invisibility Factor: The Limits of Public Choice Theory and Public Institutions*, 74 Wash. U. L. Q. 179 (1996) (case study of school finance litigation in New Jersey showing that different parts of the state were affected in different ways by legislative response to state supreme court decision); Michael Heise, *State Constitutional Litigation, Educational Finance, and Legal Impact: An Empirical Analysis*, 63 U. Cin. L. Rev. 1735 (1995) (despite three decades of school finance litigation, it is not clear if court decisions have led to more equitable spending per student or more spending overall); Michael Heise, *Equal Educational Opportunity, Hollow Victories, and the Demise of School Finance Equity Theory: An Empirical Perspective and Alternative Explanation*, 32 Ga. L. Rev. 543 (1998) (similar analysis). Cf. William A. Fischel, *How Serrano Caused Proposition 13*, 12 J. L. & Pol. 607 (1996) (arguing that current poor fiscal conditions of California public schools was due to property tax rollbacks after passage of Proposition 13, which itself was in part a response to the school finance decision of California Supreme Court, which restricted ability of local schools to raise funds through property taxes); Douglas S. Reed, *Twenty-Five Years After Rodriguez: School Finance Litigation and the Impact of the New Judicial Federalism*, 32 Law & Soc'y Rev. 175 (1998) (more favorable assessment of school finance litigation).

of state courts follows federal law when construing the liberty-protective provisions of their own constitutions,[21] and indeed it is still relatively rare for a state court to rely exclusively on state law at all.[22]

What accounts for the widespread prevalence of lockstep analysis? Recall that Gardner was dismissive of the standard reasons advanced—e.g., the impact of the incorporation of the Bill of Rights, textual similarities between the liberty provisions of federal and state constitutions, and the failure of lawyers to advance arguments premised on state law. Too dismissive, we think. The high degree of rapport between the language of the federal Bill of Rights and its state counterparts alone probably drives a good bit of the lockstep. It seems difficult (though of course not impossible) for a state judge to depart from federal law when the constitutional texts share so much common ground. On matters of criminal procedure especially, no doubt the desire to permit federal and local law enforcement officials to operate under parallel rules has played a part.[23] And uninformed lawyering can adversely affect the decision-making and opinion-writing process of state judges (or any judge), who may not all have the time or desire to sample the extensive academic literature exhorting them to depart from federal law.[24]

But the deeper rationales advanced by Gardner and others resonate as well. It was questioned whether state constitutional text and history were different enough from the federal organs, or from each other, to truly support or justify a separate state constitutionalism. There is some support for this skepticism. Whatever may have been true in the past, in this century it is, of course, unrealistic to contend that each state has a completely distinctive political or social culture, especially one that

---

21. See Michael Esler, *State Supreme Court Commitment to State Law*, 78 Judicature 25, 28 (1994) (study of state supreme court decisions from 1981 to 1986 on self-incrimination issues showed, *inter alia*, that 78 percent of decisions were based on federal law); Latzer, *supra* note 16, at 192 (study of criminal procedure decisions of state supreme courts from late 1960s to 1989, based exclusively on state law, showed *inter alia* that 68 percent followed position taken by federal law).

22. See Craig F. Emmert & Carol Ann Traut, *State Supreme Court Courts, State Constitutions, and Judicial Policymaking*, 16 Jus. Sys. J. 16, 42–44 (1992) (about 80 % of state supreme court decisions from 1981 to 1985 concerning criminal justice and other liberty issues, involving analogous state and federal constitutional provisions, were resolved on basis of federal law); Paul Kramer, Waiting For Godot?—The New Judicial Federalism 1987–1992: Reality or Hoax? (Sept. 1996) (presented at annual meeting of American Political Science Association) (replicating Emmert & Traut study for 1987–1992, showing that about 70 percent of state supreme courts relied on federal law even when presented with choice). See generally Tarr, *supra* note 1, at 167–168 (discussing empirical studies).

23. Esler, *supra* note 21, at 31; Shirley S. Abrahamson, *Criminal Law and State Constitutions: The Emergence of State Constitutional Law*, 63 Tex. L. Rev. 1141, 1178 (1985); James W. Diehm, *New Federalism and Constitutional Criminal Procedure: Are We Repeating the Mistakes of the Past?*, 55 Md. L. Rev. 223, 248–250 (1996).

24. Jennifer Friesen, *State Courts as Sources of Constitutional Law: How to Become Independently Wealthy*, 72 Notre Dame L. Rev. 1065, 1071 & n.17 (1997).

differs in important ways from national culture.[25] Consider the considerable ethnic, racial, and economic diversity found within large states like New York, Texas, or California. Critics of Gardner relied largely on unpersuasive anecdotal examples to contend that state distinctiveness, as it pertained to state constitutionalism, was possible.[26] This having been said, it is also clear that in our view the differences between and among the states, and groups of states, are an important fact in achieving the goals of federalism. As we discuss further in chapters 1, 2, and 7, homogeneity in a country as large as the United States is not normatively desirable, and hardly empirically possible. A national culture does not trump local differences.

Then, too, the liberty-protective provision of state constitutions share many more similarities than differences with each other and with the U.S. Constitution.[27]

---

25. The seminal work in this area is Daniel J. Elazar, American Federalism: A View From the States chs. 4–5 (3d ed. 1984), who posited that states belonged to one of three political subcultures: individualistic, moralistic, and traditionalist. He did not suggest that each state was distinctive from the other forty-nine. Elazar's categories probably overgeneralized to begin with, and certainly today the "political culture of any given state or locality consists of a synthesis of all three subcultures with different accents in the mixture from place to place." Larry Kramer, *Understanding Federalism*, 47 Vand. L. Rev. 1485, 1559 (1994).

26. E.g., Neil H. Cogan, *Moses and Modernism*, 92 Mich. L. Rev. 1347, 1356–1358 (1993) (essay review); Randall T. Shepard, *The Maturing Nature of State Constitution Jurisprudence*, 30 Val. U. L. Rev. 421, 436–440 (1996). As Gardner has observed, one can easily find counterexamples in those states that are sometimes asserted to have a distinctive culture pertinent to state constitutionalism. James A. Gardner, *What Is a State Constitution?*, 24 Rutgers L. J. 1025, 1028 n.12 (1993). For evidence of regional variation in state supreme court enforcement of state constitutional rights, see Staci L. Beavers & Jeffrey S. Walz, *Modeling Judicial Federalism: Predictors of State Court Protections of Defendants' Rights Under State Constitutions, 1969–1989*, 28 Publius: The Journal of Federalism 43 (Spring 1998).

For an argument conceding that the fifty states are generally not different enough from each other to justify the creation of fifty unique bodies of state constitutional law, but contending that since the more-or-less similar constitutions of the states are different from the *federal* constitution, there is justification for the development of a "trans-state constitutional theory," see Daniel B. Rodriguez, *State Constitutional Theory and Its Prospects*, 28 N. Mex. L. Rev. 271, 300–302 (1998).

27. On the similarities of constitutions, see Gardner, *supra* note 26, at 1034, 1054; Kahn, *supra* note 10, at 1148; Tarr, *supra* note 1, at 11–28. Robert Schapiro argues that the issue of the distinctiveness (or lack thereof) of each state's polity can be distinguished from the issue of each state possessing or generating an independent constitutional tradition. The latter can be "constituted not by the beliefs of the population of the state, but rather by the ideals defined by the [state] constitution itself. These constitutional aspirations will likely overlap with the values of the citizens, but the two are not coextensive." Robert A. Schapiro, *Identity and Interpretation in State Constitutional Law*, 84 Va. L. Rev. 389, 393 (1998). Schapiro's point is not without value, but the weakness we see in his argument is the difficulty for each state's judges to determine an independent constitutional aspiration, apart from her state's community. The task is not apt to be easy, as Schapiro seems to concede.

We find it unnecessary to embrace Gardner's fear of balkanization if a truly disparate state constitutionalism flourished. The adjudication of most individual rights would generate few interstate externalities,[28] and lack of uniformity on these issues, we think, would not prove calamitous to the national political culture. We could point to those few states that have developed a distinctive jurisprudence concerning the privacy-protective provisions of their constitutions, which lack explicit counterparts in most other constitutions. Nonetheless, we think Gardner and other critics are right to conclude that, on the whole, a truly distinctive state constitutionalism on liberty issues has not developed, at least yet.

What does the dominance of lockstep analysis by state courts mean for the protection of liberty? Most advocates of an activist state constitutionalism would no doubt argue that the lockstep reduces the protection from two arenas, to one—the federal courts. We draw a different conclusion. To state the obvious, the lockstep means that state courts are *following* federal case law—a happy development, one might think, for the critics of parity.[29] To be sure, one can quarrel with substance of protection given liberties and individual rights by federal courts. But that debate is separate, we think, from the allocation of power among courts in a federal system. A distinctive state constitutionalism can mean increased liberty to the beneficiaries of those rights fortunate enough to be in those states. That circumstance being the exception, not the rule, however, does not suggest that liberties are at risk in a federal system. Federalism bodes well for liberty as long as state courts enforce federally derived rights.

THE AMBIGUITIES OF SUPREME COURT REVIEW

It is a commonplace to restate the primacy of the U.S. Supreme Court's role to review issues of federal law from state courts. This role is premised by the accepted notions that the Supreme Court does and should be the principal and final expositor of federal law, as derived from the text and history of Article III of the Constitution, as well as on the need for national uniformity of federal law.[30] In contrast, it is generally accepted that the Supreme Court has no authority to review

---

28. For further discussion of this point see chapter 4.

29. Cf. Gardner, *supra* note 26, at 1054 (state court adjudication of identical state constitutional provisions can "institutionalize a monitoring process whereby state courts 'shadow' federal court rulings"). Relatedly, simply because state courts are not exceeding the federal floor does not mean federalism is not protective of or adding to liberty. Assuming one could determine an optimal level of liberty protection in a federal system, there is no systemic reason why the floor established by the federal courts is not already at that level. If that's the case, state courts should not be compelled, without more, to exceed the floor.

30. See Richard H. Fallon, Daniel J. Meltzer & David L. Shapiro, Hart & Wechsler's The Federal Courts and the Federal System 491–509 (4th ed. 1996) (general discussion of the history of Supreme Court review of state court decisions) (hereinafter Hart & Wechsler); Michigan v. Long, 463 U.S. 1032, 1040 (1983) (discussing need for uniformity).

state court decisions based adequately and independently on state law,[31] including individual rights and liberty decisions. Problems arise when the state court decision is ambiguous as to its groundings in state law, federal law, or some combination of the two. We review the Supreme Court's struggles to interpret such cases, and consider the implications of the Supreme Court's jurisprudence for the adjudication of liberty cases in the states.

MICHIGAN V. LONG: ANTECEDENTS AND AFTERMATH

The Supreme Court case that has dominated discourse on the Court's review of state judiciaries in this regard is *Michigan v. Long*.[32] There, the Supreme Court reviewed a decision of the Michigan Supreme Court that held a certain police search to be unlawful. The lower court relied exclusively on federal law, but for two citations to the Michigan Constitution, and ended its opinion by stating that the search "was proscribed by the Fourth Amendment" and by the analogous provision of the state constitution. The majority opinion by Justice O'Connor found wanting the Court's previous interpretative rules to cope with similarly ambiguous state court opinions,[33] and adopted a rule that the adequacy and independence of any state ground must be "clear from the face of the opinion."[34] Such a default rule was justified, the Court explained, by the desire to avoid advisory opinions, to refrain from the "intrusive practice" of requiring state courts to clarify their opinions, but also to maintain the uniformity of federal law. The Court found no plain statement

31. The present language of the statute permitting Supreme Court review of state court decisions, 28 U.S.C. § 1257(a), seems to limit such review to issues arising under federal law. While the language of that provision and its predecessor statutes has been informed by the text and history of Article III, see Hart & Wechsler, *supra* note 30, at 8–9, 18–19, 592–594 (general discussion), it has been persuasively argued that, rightly understood, there is no barrier derived from Article III that prevents the Supreme Court from reviewing even the state law decisions of state courts. The barrier is better viewed as a prudential one, based on respect for state autonomy when a state court interprets its own law. Richard A. Matasar & Gregory S. Bruch, *Procedural Common Law, Federal Jurisdiction Policy, and the Abandonment of the Adequate and Independent State Grounds Doctrine*, 86 Colum. L. Rev. 1291, 1294–1322, 1358–1367 (1986); Solimine & Walker, *supra* note 15, at 157 & n.129 (citing other authorities reaching same conclusion). For a thorough discussion of the history of § 1257, see Edward Hartnett, *Why Is the Supreme Court of the United States Protecting State Judges From Popular Democracy?*, 75 Tex. L. Rev. 907 (1997).

32. 463 U.S. 1032 (1983).

33. *Id.* at 1038–1039. The Court described the confusing and inconsistent nature of past efforts to deal with ambiguities in state court opinions. In past cases, the Court had variously held that an ambiguous opinion below would be assumed *not* to be based on federal law; vacated or continued a case to obtain a clarification; or independently examined state law to determine the manner in which the state court was using federal law. *Id.* The Court found that all of these methods were for various reasons unsatisfactory. *Id.* at 1039–1040.

34. *Id.* at 1041.

from the Michigan court, since it only utilized federal case law in reaching its decision.

Justice Stevens opened his vigorous dissent by arguing that the jurisdictional issues presented were "far more important" than the merits of the unlawful search and seizure claim.[35] Acknowledging that the Court had in the past employed different methods to determine the purported independence of a state law, Justice Stevens contended that, in the face of ambiguity, a presumption *against* jurisdiction was more appropriate.[36] The primary reason for this position advanced by the dissent was that it was unnecessary for the Supreme Court to spend scarce resources policing those instances when a "state court [has] interpreted federal rights too broadly and 'overprotected' the citizen." Such review was inappropriate since, in his view, the "primary role" of the Supreme Court was "to make sure that persons who seek to *vindicate* federal rights have been fairly heard." The asserted need for uniformity in federal law, he added, was "truly an ungovernable engine," since the "same need is no less present" when the state ground is adequate and independent.

In recent Terms Justice Ginsburg has, like Justice Stevens, argued that *Michigan v. Long* is problematic and should be overruled.[37] She has not expressly adopted Justice Stevens's position that review of "overenforced" federal rights by state courts is inappropriate. Rather she has emphasized the ability of states to serve as laboratories of experimentation,[38] and suggested that the Court use a jurisdictional presumption "that encourages States to explore different means to secure respect for individual rights in modern times."[39] Nor is she confident that

---

35. 463 U.S. at 1065–1070 (Stevens, J., dissenting).

36. *Id.* at 1066–1067. For an argument (not advanced by Justice Stevens) that the intent of the framers of § 1257 was not to allow state officers to review their own state courts' judgments, but was intended for aggrieved private parties, see Hartnett, *supra* note 31.

37. Arizona v. Evans, 514 U.S. 1, 31–34 (1995) (Ginsburg, J., joined by Stevens, J., dissenting); Ohio v. Robinette, 519 U.S. 33, 42–45 (1996) (Ginsburg, J., concurring). See also Pennsylvania v. LaBron, 518 U.S. 938, 950 (1996) (Stevens, J., joined by Ginsburg, J., dissenting).

38. Arizona v. Evans, 514 U.S. 1, 30 (Ginsburg, J., dissenting). Justice Ginsburg referenced the familiar passage from Justice Brandeis:

> It is one of the happy incidents of the federal system that a single courageous State may, if its citizens choose, serve as a laboratory; and try novel social and economic experiments without risk to the rest of the country.

New State Ice Co. v. Liebman, 285 U.S. 262, 311 (1932) (Brandeis, J., dissenting). Cited in Arizona v. Evans, 514 U.S. at 30 (Ginsburg, J., dissenting).

For an argument that the "laboratories" metaphor in the context of state courts is unobjectionable as a descriptive device, but does not itself justify state court overexpansion of federal rights, see James A. Gardner, *The "State-as-Laboratories" Metaphor in State Constitutional Law*, 30 Val. U. L. Rev. 475 (1996).

39. Arizona v. Evans, 514 U.S. 1, 30 (Ginsburg, J., dissenting).

the plain statement rule is easy to comply with. In one case she sternly lectured the state court "to be clear about its ultimate reliance on state law," and to "speak with the clarity that [the court] sought to require of its State's police officers [on the merits of the case]."[40] The balance of the Court has been unmoved by this opposition and has reaffirmed the plain statement rule.

THE IMPACT OF *MICHIGAN v. LONG*

Coming as it did, just as the idea of increased state court reliance on their own constitutions began to flower, it was no shock that *Michigan v. Long* generated considerable academic commentary.[41] Some argued that the new plain statement rule unnecessarily expanded federal jurisdiction and was a thinly veiled attempt to chill the expansion of rights by state courts.[42] Others supported the decision, arguing that it preserved the need for uniformity in federal law and could encourage an intersystem dialogue on the scope of rights between different levels of court.[43] Likewise, some argued that the plain statement rule would be a disincentive for state courts to expand rights under their own constitutions, as it would purportedly be difficult to comply with, and expose a forthright state court to the displeasure of the electorate.[44] Others contended that the rule would encourage state courts to develop their own law, since those courts would, presumably, be motivated to consider whether they should rely on federal or state law.[45] Finally, consider the impact of the plain statement rule on the issue of parity.

40. Ohio v. Robinette, 519 U.S. 33, 44–45 (1996) (Ginsburg, J., concurring).

41. For collection of the literature, see Hart & Wechsler, *supra* note 30, at 543 & n.12; Ann Althouse, *How to Build a Separate Sphere: Federal Courts and State Power*, 100 Harv. L. Rev. 1485, 1493 n.45 (1987).

42. E.g., Ronald K.L. Collins, *Reliance on State Constitutions—The Montana Disaster*, 63 Tex. L. Rev. 1095 (1985). In this regard, it is worth noting that the Court applied the plain statement rule in the context of federal habeas corpus in Harris v. Reed, 489 U.S. 255 (1989). The Court held that a federal court could proceed to hear a habeas petition unless the state court opinion under review plainly stated that it was based on independent state law grounds. *Id.* at 260–265. Justice Stevens concurred, noting that in his view the application of *Long* here was not problematic, since habeas petitions only seek review of alleged underenforcement of federal rights by state courts. *Id.* at 267 (Stevens, J., concurring). This has the effect of helping criminal defendants, a result not usually associated with the *Long* case. See Howard P. Fink et al., Federal Courts in the 21st Century: Cases and Materials 889 (1996) (Justices showed "admirable consistency" in *Long* and *Harris*). See also Martin H. Redish, Federal Jurisdiction: Tensions in the Allocation of Judicial Power 279 (2d ed. 1990) (logically *Harris* applies on direct review of a state criminal conviction by the Supreme Court).

43. E.g., Laurence Tribe, American Constitutional Law 165–166 (2d ed. 1988); Redish, *supra* note 42, at 266–267; Althouse, *supra* note 41, at 1509.

44. E.g., Latzer, *supra* note 16, at 196 n.33; Esler, *supra* note 21, at 30.

45. E.g., Gardner, *supra* note 8, at 775–776; Kahn, *supra* note 10, at 1167. Cf. Arizona v. Evans, 514 U.S. 1, 8 (1995) (after *Michigan v. Long*, a state court "is freer [to depart from federal law] because it is disabused of its erroneous view of what the United

Critics of parity might, pace Justice Stevens, desire an expansive Supreme Court reviewing role to ensure that state courts are complying with federal law. Those sympathetic with the concept of parity might view such a role as unnecessary and interfering with state functions.[46]

When the dust has settled, we side with the supporters of *Michigan v. Long*. To support this conclusion, let us consider at some greater length the objections to the plain statement rule advanced by Justice Stevens and others.[47] Those objections fall into two, interrelated categories: should the Supreme Court review at all a state court decision that purportedly overenforces federal rights? And, if so, is the interpretative rule employed by the Court a sound one to deal with ambiguously worded state court decisions?

The concept that state court overenforcement of federal rights should be free of Supreme Court review does not survive close examination. Even the term overenforcement is problematic. Individual rights are crucial in a free society, but they are not the only language of constitutional discourse. One of the things that the critics of parity and others seem to ignore is that the denial of a claim based on individual rights does not always add up to an injustice. As we developed in chapter 2, any discussion of rights must include other compelling constitutional and personal values.[48] Any invocation of "rights" by one person, or one group, affects and perhaps diminishes other individual or collective interests, broadly conceived.[49] A simple example will illustrate this point. In the famous case of *Calif. Board of Regents v. Bakke*,[50] both sides were claiming an equal protection right. Would an application of Justice Stevens's position have precluded the review of Bakke's victory on the California Supreme Court? Should it? And what about the state of California agency that appealed the lower court ruling? Was it not representing a

---

States Constitution requires").

46. See Thomas E. Baker, *The Ambiguous Independent and Adequate State Ground in Criminal Cases: Federalism Along a Mobius Strip*, 19 Ga. L. Rev. 799, 823–824, 828 (1985) (discussing parity issue and *Long*); Solimine & Walker, *supra* note 15, at 159–160 (same).

47. We are thus primarily concerned with the "independence" prong of the "adequate and independent" state ground doctrine. See Hart & Wechsler, *supra* note 30, at 524–528 (distinguishing the concepts); Matasar & Bruch, *supra* note 31, at 1293 n.2 (same).

48. Hart & Wechsler, *supra* note 30, at 537. It is difficult to disentangle rights from government powers. They are conceptually interdependent, so it is problematic to defend the overenforcement of rights in the abstract without considering competing governmental concerns. For discussion of this point, *see* Richard H. Fallon, Jr., *Individual Rights and the Powers of Government*, 27 Ga. L. Rev. 343 (1993); Barry Friedman, *Trumping Rights*, 27 Ga. L. Rev. 435 (1993), and chapter 2.

49. Robert N. Clinton, Richard A. Matasar, & Michael G. Collins, Federal Courts: Theory and Practice 1393 (1996); Maltz, *supra* note 7, at 1009–1010.

50. Calif. Bd. of Regents v. Bakke, 438 U.S. 265 (1978), *aff'd in part, rev'd in part*, 533 P.2d 1152 (Cal. 1976).

completely different set of interests contrary to those of citizen Alan Bakke and his supporters?[51]

While a fetish should not be made out of uniformity, there is something to be said for national convergence on high-profile issues like affirmative action, gay rights,[52] and even flag burning.[53] The fact that such decisions are rendered by state courts that happen to find for the party asserting the federal rights should not, itself, disable the Supreme Court from reviewing the case. More generally, we think that fostering ultimate appellate review of any decision on federal law is no insult to state courts, and is simply an unremarkable characteristic of a hierarchal system of courts. Such review ensures that state judges are following federal law, and deflects critics of parity who contend that the Supreme Court is not up to the institutional task of monitoring the adjudication of federal law in state courts. There is some evidence to confirm the predictions of the critics of *Michigan v. Long* that the Supreme Court would take an increasingly aggressive stand against rights-enforcing state court decisions.[54] But what is more remarkable is, even after *Long*, Supreme Court review of state courts in the aggregate is relatively rare (historically, about twenty-five cases per term, and the number has been declining as has the Court's overall docket).[55] Given that actual Supreme Court review is a relatively rare event, perhaps it is surprising that there is not much more evidence of state courts misinterpreting federal law on a much more frequent basis.[56]

---

51. Hart & Wechsler, *supra* note 30, at 537. Fallon and his coauthors also observe that Justice Stevens' position should logically extend to prevent "review of 'Lochner-style' overenforcement of supposed federal limits on the states' power to enact social legislation." *Id.* at 536. See also Fink, *supra* note 42, at 890 (similar reference to *Lochner*). The reference to *Lochner* should be treated carefully, since in that case it was the U.S. Supreme Court, not the New York Court of Appeals, that enforced the substantive due process rights of the employer in question. Lochner v. New York, 69 N.E. 373 (N.Y. 1904), *rev'd*, 198 U.S. 45 (1905). Thus, the Supreme Court could have reviewed the actual *Lochner* case even under Justice Stevens's position. For a discussion of modern *Lochner*-style litigation in state courts, see Tarr, *supra* note 1, at 147; Peter J. Galie, *State Courts and Economic Rights*, 496 Annals Am. Acad. Pol. & Soc. Sci. 76 (March 1988).

52. E.g., Romer v. Evans, 882 P.2d 1335 (Colo. 1994) (struck down statewide anti-gay rights initiative), *aff'd*, 517 U.S. 620 (1996).

53. E.g., Johnson v. Texas, 755 S.W.2d 92 (Tex. Ct. Crim. App. 1988) (overturned conviction for flag burning on First Amendment grounds), *aff'd sub. nom* Texas v. Johnson, 491 U.S. 397 (1989).

54. Richard A. Brisbin, Jr. & John C. Kilwein, *U.S. Supreme Court Review of State High Court Decisions*, 78 Judicature 33, 37 (1994) (Rehnquist Court more likely to review liberal state supreme court decisions on criminal procedure issues than prior Courts (Table 2)).

55. We calculate this data from information in *id.* at 34 (Table 1).

56. No doubt, the *threat* of reversal by the Supreme Court plays a role in state court adherence to federal law, as well as the norms of following precedent and the clarity of Court opinions. See John C. Kilwein & Richard A. Brisbin, Jr., *Policy Convergence in a Federal Judicial System: The Application of Intensified Scrutiny Doctrines by State Supreme Courts*, 41 Am. J. Pol. Sci. 122, 131–133 (1997). See generally Evan H. Caminker,

It is true that the plain statement rule encroaches to some degree on the vigor of the separate and independent state ground doctrine. This might lead, some say, to the Supreme Court rendering more advisory opinions, since presumably a state court on remand after reversal can come to the same result on state law grounds. Justices Stevens and Ginsburg have reminded us of this occurring.[57] Aside from their anecdotal examples, it is not clear how often this occurs. More importantly, it cannot be said that a case before the Supreme Court is in a classic advisory posture, since both sides are vigorously in opposition (though, concededly, the state court disposition on remand may moot that federal issue).[58] The possibility of a change in position by a state court after remand ameliorates any intrusive effect the plain statement rule has on the state decision-making process.[59]

If some variant of Supreme Court review is justifiable, what standard of review is optimal? At first, it is difficult to take seriously some critics' assertions that the plain statement rule makes for difficult compliance. Either the state court states plainly that its decision is based on state law, or it doesn't. The real problem is state courts not making plain statements when the opportunity is apparently available to them,[60] or continuing to use ambiguously phrased statements of reliance on state law, even in the face of the *Long* rule. Put another way, is this evidence that the required plain statement is either difficult to comply with, or difficult to interpret once made?

Consider two examples, both cases from state supreme courts upholding the contentions of defendants that they were subject to unlawful searches and seizure. In one case, the Pennsylvania Supreme Court discussed federal case law but also referenced the state's "jurisprudence of the automobile exception" to the Fourth Amendment warrant requirement.[61] The Supreme Court held that this was not a plain statement, since the state court relied on federal law, and the state opinions it also cited were, themselves, based on federal law. In the other case, the Ohio Supreme Court exclusively discussed federal case law, but stated that its result was premised on both the U.S. and Ohio Constitutions.[62] Without dissent on that issue,

---

Precedent and Prediction: The Forward-Looking Aspects of Inferior Court Decisionmaking, 73 Tex. L. Rev. 1 (1994); Donald H. Zeigler, *Gazing Into the Crystal Ball: Reflections on the Standards State Judges Should Use to Ascertain Federal Law*, 40 Wm. & Mary L. Rev. 1143 (1999).

57. Arizona v. Evans, 514 U.S. 1, 32 (1995) (Ginsburg & Stevens, JJ., dissenting); Pennsylvania v. Labron, 518 U.S. 938, 951 (1996) (Stevens & Ginsburg, JJ., dissenting).

58. Matasar & Bruch, *supra* note 31, at 1303–1304, 1369–1370.

59. Hart & Wechsler, *supra* note 30, at 544.

Relatedly, *Long* has not appeared to chill (indeed, it may facilitate) a dialogue between state courts and the Supreme Court on the scope of federal rights. Redish, *supra* note 42, at 267. For some evidence of such a dialogue taking place after *Long*, see Solimine & Walker, *supra* note 15, at 160 & n.148.

60. Felicia A. Rosenfeld, Note, *Fulfilling the Goals of Michigan v. Long: The State Court Reaction*, 56 Ford. L. Rev. 1041 (1988). This study cries out for an update.

61. Pennsylvania v. LaBron, 518 U.S. 938 (1996) (per curiam).

62. Ohio v. Robinette, 519 U.S. 33 (1996).

the Supreme Court found this not to be a clear statement since it spoke of the state constitution in only general terms. Understandably, Justice Ginsburg lamented in a concurring opinion that the Ohio court had not spoken more clearly.

Both cases illustrate the difficulty of making and interpreting a plain statement when the state constitutional provision is substantially identical to the federal provision.[63] What accounts for the difficulties? Some have argued that the demands of the plain statement requirement might cause state judges to forego expanding state constitutional rights, since they cannot have the "cover" of referring to federal law without risking Supreme Court review. To believe that any state judge engages in this sort of convoluted strategic behavior requires more empirical support than now available. It is doubtful that interested publics in each state parse opinions as closely as these critics believe. And there is little evidence that state judges have been specifically punished at the polls for expanding state constitutional rights.[64]

A more reasonable explanation, we think, is that neither the lawyers nor the judges are yet fully socialized to the heady idea that they may argue cases and write opinions, respectively, without reference to the federal Constitution. Furthermore, judges on a collegial court, must write not only for themselves but also to satisfy a majority of the members, thus further decreasing the likelihood of a bold departure from "lockstep" analysis with the federal Constitution. This is particularly true when courts are asked to construe closely analogous, or even identically worded, provisions of their own state constitutions. In these situations, a state court could clearly say that, despite any similarities, it is nonetheless developing and applying a jurisprudence of its own state constitution, no matter what federal law may hold.[65]

But in practice courts have been reluctant to do so. It is possible, of course, that the reluctance of state courts to clearly declare an independent state grounding for

63. This was true in the two cases discussed in the previous paragraph. Cf. U.S. Const., amend. IV *with* Ohio Const., art. I, § 14 *and* Pa. Const., art. I, § 8. The Ohio provision has long been interpreted virtually identically to the Fourth Amendment. State v. Geraldo, 429 N.E.2d 141 (Ohio 1981). The jurisprudence of the Pennsylvania provision in this regard is less clear. Pennsylvania v. LaBron, 518 U.S. 938, 943–951 (1996) (Stevens, J., dissenting); Bruce Ledewitz, *The Role of Lower State Courts in Adopting State Law to Changed Federal Interpretations*, 67 Temp. L. Rev. 1003 (1994) (extensive discussion of Pa. Const. art. I, § 8).

64. Lindl v. Murphy, 96 F.3d 856, 864 (7th Cir. 1996) (en banc) (Easterbrook, J.), *rev'd on other grounds*, 521 U.S. 320 (1997). But see Gerald F. Uelman, *Crocodiles in the Bathtub: Maintaining the Independence of State Supreme Courts in an Era of Judicial Politicization*, 72 Notre Dame L. Rev. 1133 (1997) (arguing that elections for state supreme court justices are becoming more contentious in part due to increased reliance on state constitutional law); Paul D. Carrington, *Judicial Independence and Democratic Accountability in Highest State Courts*, 61 Law & Contemp. Prob. 79, 99–107 (Summer 1998) (same).

65. Ohio v. Robinette, 519 U.S. 33, 44 (1996) (Ginsburg, J., concurring) (giving example of such a plain statement); Friesen, *supra* note 2, at 56 (listing model plain statements).

their decisions is simply a fear of departing from settled federal law. Or it could be reflective of a belief that there is not a principled basis, given the interpretive history of the state constitution or the culture of the state, to justify such a departure. But we believe that the most important reason is that these cases are not seen as conflicts between state and federal interests by the judges. Thus, the reluctance of many state supreme courts to develop state constitutional law after *Michigan v. Long* is probably driven more by the dynamics of the process of state court review, and the multiplicity of interests in a particular case, than by the putative infirmities of the *Long* rule.

The assertion that *Long*'s plain statement rule has chilled state court decision-making could well benefit from more empirical work. From what we know now, however, we think the impact of the case has probably been overstated, and to the extent that state constitutionalism has not flourished as much as desired by some, it is due to other factors, like those explored earlier in this chapter. We concede that plain statement rules of interpretation are premised, explicitly or implicitly, on substantive norms. We think the norms implicit in *Michigan v. Long*—uniformity in federal law while permitting state court departure from the federal floor—are sound ones.

6

Special Problems for Judicial Federalism: Race, the Death Penalty, and Habeas Corpus

One result of mounting a defense of judicial federalism is a tendency to gloss over problems that such a system may either facilitate or even partially cause. We hope to remedy that situation by discussing three important problem areas that are sometimes associated with judicial federalism.

Throughout American history, African-Americans and other racial and ethnic minorities have been subjected to discrimination and unfairness by many state courts. Today that legacy of injustice is intertwined with two other developments arguably flowing from it. One is the increasing use of the death penalty, administered almost entirely in the state system, and which is used disproportionately against nonwhite defendants. The second is the narrowing, both doctrinally and statutorily, of the availability of habeas corpus relief in federal courts. To many, federal habeas corpus has been a necessary corrective to the injustices (i.e., violations of federal law) meted out to minority defendants in state criminal proceedings in general, and to death penalty defendants in particular.

The major point of this chapter is not to defend state courts against their past sins. But we think the exaggeration of the record of state courts that is often made, especially compared to the performance of federal courts,[1] is both unfair and, in the long run, counterproductive. In the first place, state courts are, at most, complicit

---

1. The studies of racial and gender bias have examined both federal and state courts. For a summary of that literature as it relates to federal courts, see Richard H. Fallon, Daniel J. Meltzer & David L. Shapiro, Hart & Wechsler's The Federal Courts and the Federal System 60nn. 197–198 (4th ed. 1996) (hereinafter Hart & Wechsler); Todd David Peterson, *Studying the Impact of Race and Ethnicity in the Federal Courts*, 64 Geo. Wash. L. Rev. 173 (1996).

in racial and ethnic prejudice. Racism in the United States is systemic and the state courts are part of that system. But judges do not arrest and prosecute. State judges have hardly been innocent bystanders, but their role has clearly been secondary to that of other actors in the justice system. Judges, of course, do have a responsibility to see that defendants are treated fairly and are well represented, a task at which they have frequently failed at in the past.[2] But the data show no pattern of racism or prejudice that can be attributed to the fact that the judges are state judges or that is facilitated because their courts operate independently of the federal system. We turn now to a discussion of prejudice in the state courts.

RACE AND THE JUDGES

The federal rights and other liberties of the freed slaves after the Civil War were considerably limited after Reconstruction, especially, though not only, in the South. There are many examples of this shameful legacy, and a considerable number are due to the abject failure of state courts and judges to protect those rights, particularly in criminal proceedings.[3] Along many points of the criminal justice system—as victim, witness, detainee, defendant, sentencee, prisoner, etc.—black Americans were subject to many forms of overt and subtle discrimination by private groups, by substantive law, and within the court system itself.[4] Unfortunately, there continue to be modern examples of such discrimination, even if they are carried on in more subtle and less violent forms than in the early part of this century. For example, there is considerable anecdotal and some empirical evidence demonstrating that people of color are more likely to be detained (for that reason alone) by police at traffic stops or for other forms of questioning.[5] And a disproportionate percentage of the increasing prisoner population are made up of African-Americans, a circumstance attributed by some in part to the discriminatory impact of sentencing laws.[6]

---

2. Stephen B. Bright, *Counsel for the Poor: The Death Sentence Not for the Worst Crime but for the Worst Lawyer*, 103 Yale L. J. 1835, 1855–1857 (1994) (describing the role of state judges in appointing counsel for indigent defendants in death penalty cases).

3. In the balance of this chapter, we focus almost exclusively on the rights of African-Americans in the criminal justice system. This has also been the focus of most of the literature, and in so doing we recognize that we are slighting the use of the *civil* litigation process in state courts by blacks, and hardships visited by state courts upon women, and other racial and ethnic minorities in both criminal and civil cases.

4. For an excellent overview of the deprivations suffered by black Americans in this regard, see Randall Kennedy, Race, Crime, and the Law 29–135 (1997).

5. Kennedy, *supra* note 4, at 136–167 (discussing anecdotal and empirical evidence); Tracey Maclin, *Race and the Fourth Amendment*, 51 Vand. L. Rev. 333, 344–354 (1998) (same); David A. Sklansky, *Traffic Stops, Minority Motorists, and the Future of the Fourth Amendment*, 1997 Sup. Ct. Rev. 271, 312–314 (same). See generally Pamela S. Karlan, *Race, Rights, and Remedies in Criminal Adjudication*, 96 Mich. L. Rev. 2001 (1998).

6. Michael Tonry, Malign Neglect: Race, Crime and Punishment in America (1995); Samuel R. Gross, *Crime, Politics, and Race*, 20 Harv. J. L. & Pub. Pol'y 405 (1997).

Not surprisingly, many African-Americans are not fully trusting of the fairness of the criminal justice system in general or of state courts in particular. Perhaps the most noticeable (if overblown) manifestation of this suspicion was the reaction of many black Americans to the acquittal of O.J. Simpson in the trial for the murder of his wife. Many blacks, it seemed, believed him guilty but nonetheless rejoiced at his having "beat the system."[7] More troubling to us, sober and careful empirical analysis shows that with regard to all cases, the prevailing opinion among African-Americans is that the criminal justice system is skewed in favor of whites.[8]

Such suspicions, of course, are reasonable, given the evidence. But the question, perennially, is "what is to be done"? Recent debate seems to have created two camps. One would attempt to achieve fairness by accentuating the power of African-Americans in the criminal justice system. Thus, for example, juries could be required to closely represent the demographic makeup of the local community. And, at least in certain cases, black jurors would be permitted to or even encouraged to engage in "jury nullification"—the acquittal of a defendant to correct perceived societal injustices—even when the law and facts would seem to call for a conviction.[9] An opposing camp freely acknowledges the perceived problems with the present system but proposes radically different reforms. This camp considers the *underenforcement* of criminal law (i.e., black-on-black crime) to be as great an affront to African-Americans as the denial of liberties to black criminal defendants. The second camp would take steps to purge the system of attentiveness to race rather than accentuate it. For example, it rejects jury nullification or quotas while arguing that peremptory challenges (which historically permitted the attorneys to remove a number of potential jurors for any reason, and often disproportionately removed black jurors) be entirely abolished.[10]

Can judicial federalism inform this debate? At first blush, an affirmative answer is doubtful. As we already observed, actors in the state court systems have for the

7. Kennedy, *supra* note 4, at 25; Christo Lassiter, *The O.J. Simpson Verdict: A Lesson in Black and White*, 1 Mich. J. of Race & Law 69 (1996).

8. For a summary of this literature, see Scot Wortley, John Hagan, & Ross Macmillan, *Just Des(s)erts? The Racial Polarization of Criminal Injustice*, 31 Law & Soc'y Rev. 637, 646–651 (1997). See also Linda Greenhouse, *47 % in Poll View Legal System as Unfair to Poor and Minorities*, N.Y. Times, Feb. 24, 1999, p. A12.

9. E.g., Albert W. Alschuler, *Racial Quotas and the Jury*, 44 Duke L. J. 704 (1995); Paul Butler, *Racially Based Jury Nullification: Black Power in the Criminal Justice System*, 105 Yale L. J. 677 (1995). See generally Paul Butler, *Affirmative Action and the Criminal Law*, 68 U. Colo. L. Rev. 841 (1997).

10. E.g., Kennedy, *supra* note 4, at 295–310 (sharply criticizing advocates of jury nullification by blacks, in part because it is premised on and would institutionalize a static view of poor race relations); John J. DiIulio, Jr., *White Lies About Black Crime*, 118 Pub. Int. 30 (Winter 1995) (arguing that view that most blacks differ fundamentally from whites in their views on crime and punishment is a myth); Thomas J. Nolan, *Racism in the Criminal Justice System: Problems and Suggestions*, 20 Harv. J. L. & Pub. Pol'y 417 (1997). See generally Nicholas Lemann, *Justice for Blacks?*, N.Y. Rev. Books 25 (March 5, 1998).

most part been the source of racial prejudice rather than its cure.[11] So, it might seem, many of the reforms suggested above should take place by federal mandate—either by Congressional legislation or by Supreme Court doctrine. Indeed, it might be said that another edition of the Warren Court criminal procedure revolution is needed, as that epoch is widely viewed today as being a crusade on behalf of black criminal defendants.[12]

For several reasons, we think judicial federalism is a large part of solving the problem, rather than its cause as is often assumed. The vast majority of criminal litigation in the United States takes place at the state and local level, not in the federal system.[13] Of necessity, then, many of the reforms can and should take place at the state level. Racism comes in a wide variety of guises, all of which are informed by local custom, culture, and practice. The racism of New Orleans is not the racism of Chicago or Boise. Whatever skepticism one may have about the ability of states to experiment generally, i.e., to be laboratories, that virtue can be put to good use regarding criminal procedure. Whatever reforms are necessary should be tailored to fit local conditions and circumstances. And as we indicated earlier, we think state courts in general and state judges in particular can be trusted to undertake the role of reformers.[14]

---

11. Cf. Kennedy, *supra* note 4, at 49–58 (describing various congressional proposals to protect blacks' rights in criminal cases in late 1800s and early 1900s as being attacked and defeated on state's rights grounds).

12. Sklansky, *supra* note 5, at 316 ("It is almost commonplace by now that much of the Court's criminal procedure jurisprudence during the middle part of this century was a form of race jurisprudence, prompted largely by the treatment of black suspects and black defendants in the South.") (footnote omitted); William J. Stuntz, *The Uneasy Relationship Between Criminal Procedure and Criminal Justice*, 107 Yale L. J. 1, 5 (1997) (similar comment).

13. Indeed, despite the increasing federalization by Congressional statutes of crimes traditionally relegated to state control, in the 1990s state criminal caseloads have burgeoned while federal criminal caseloads have not appreciably increased. Tom Stacy & Kim Dayton, *The Underfederalization of Crime*, 6 Cornell J. L. & Pub. Pol'y 247, 251–258, 311–316 (1997).

14. For an argument that for the reasons stated in the text a second criminal procedure revolution is unnecessary, see Barry Latzer, *Toward the Decentralization of Criminal Procedure: State Constitutional Law and Selective Disincorporation*, 87 J. Crim. L. & Criminology 63 (1996). Ironically, perhaps, states have apparently engaged in relatively little experimentation with regard to criminal procedure. The mandates of federal constitutional norms, by incorporation under the Fourteenth Amendment, gives them little leeway to do so. *Id.* at 122–124 (advocating selective disincorporation of certain federal constitutional rules in order to permit experimentation). To date, states have mostly adopted versions of the Federal Rules of Criminal Procedure. Jerold Israel, *Federal Criminal Procedure as a Model for the States*, 543 Annals Am. Acad. Pol. & Soc. Sci. 130 (Jan. 1996). However, state constitutions can serve as an independent basis for developing criminal procedure. See in general chapter 5, and in particular Nina Morrison, Note, *Curing "Constitutional Amnesia": Criminal Procedure Under State Constitutions*, 73 N.Y.U. L. Rev. 880 (1998); Special Project, *The Continuing Evolution of Criminal Constitutional Law*

Throughout this book we have focused on state judges themselves, so it is appropriate to consider here how the state judiciary itself can contribute to racial nondiscrimination in state criminal proceedings. The demographics and conduct of state judges no doubt plays an important (if understudied) role in fostering the integrity of the criminal justice system.[15] For that reason, some have suggested that the race problem in state criminal justice systems can be ameliorated, in part, by increasing the number of African-American judges on the state bench.[16]

Why and how would that amelioration take place? Some have argued that black judges to varying degrees bring different backgrounds and expertise to bear as compared to their white counterparts. Ultimately, the argument runs, black judges will render fairer justice, especially (though not only) to black litigants.[17] There is something to this but we think the rationale is overstated. There is considerable evidence that most if not all black judges act in ways similar to their white counterparts. Anecdotal accounts of black judges indicate that they are hardly monolithic on their role orientation; many acknowledge on a high level of generality the benefits of a diverse bench (as do we) but suggest it does not logically follow that there is some special African-American type of judging. Empirical studies have likewise shown little if any differences between the decision-making of black judges and their white counterparts.[18]

---

in State Courts, 47 Vand. L. Rev. 795 (1994).

15. Kennedy, *supra* note 4, at ix (judges, followed closely by prosecutors "are the officials upon whom society most relies to protect the integrity of criminal law").

16. E.g., Kennedy, *supra* note 4, at 389 (hopefully referring to the "changing demographics of the bench, bar, and police department"); Sherrilyn A. Ifill, *Judging the Judges: Racial Diversity, Impartiality and Representation on State Trial Courts*, 39 B.C. L. Rev. 95 (1997) (explicitly calling for more black judges to be selected).

17. E.g., A. Leon Higginbotham, *Seeking Pluralism in Judicial Systems: The American Experience and the South African Challenge*, 42 Duke L. J. 1028, 1033 1041 (1993); Ifill, *supra* note 16, at 119–120.

18. For views of black judges themselves, *see* Julian Abele Cook, Jr., *Dream Makers: Black Judges on Justice*, 94 Mich. L. Rev. 1479, 1491–1493 (1996) (book review) (black judges themselves are divided on whether they have a unique rule beyond increasing diversity and the appearance of fairness). Another author, reviewing the same book as did Judge Cook, emphasized what he thinks are the unique contributions African-Americans bring to judging, and the differences are "the product of reason, not group bias or resentment." Andrew E. Taslitz, *An African-American Sense of Fact: The O.J. Trial and Black Judges on Justice*, 7 B.U. Pub. Int. L. J. 219, 247 (1998). "However," the author continues,

> Black-White differences should not be exaggerated. The African-American sense of fact should be viewed as a variation on an American sense of fact. Both Black and White Americans share in the many commonalities of American culture. While Blacks might give relatively more emphasis to situation than to character, character matters to Blacks and Whites. Many media images and religious messages of good and bad character will be shared. Although Blacks may be more sensitive than Whites to the dangers of stereotyping, both share an American commitment to the ideal of individualized justice. While blacks are more skeptical than Whites of the police, Whites also abhor police perjury and incompetence and are increasingly more aware of the problem, thanks to a media

To us, this is an indication that black judges (like most judges, we hope) on the whole take seriously their charge to serve as impartial decision-makers, irrespective of the race or other characteristics of the litigants before them. Largely for this reason, we are dubious of another rationale often advanced to increase the numbers of black judges, namely, that they are and should be representative of the African-American community. This argument, to be sure, has considerable support in the literature and provided the basis for the Supreme Court holding that state judicial elections are subject to regulation under the Voting Rights Act.[19] It is argued that judges, like other elected officials in the legislative and executive branches, should "represent the communities they serve by reflecting community values in their discretionary decision making."[20]

In our view, the representation model makes a poor fit for state judiciaries. For one thing, the model applies awkwardly at best to state judges who are *not* elected

---

somewhat more sensitive to the occasional failings of our men and women in blue. While blacks better understand the inequality in access to fact-finding resources bred by racism, both Blacks and Whites accept aspirational notions of equal opportunity to present a case to unbiased fact-finders. Cases like O.J. stand out because the differences were highlighted in a case charged with evidence of racist police abuses. In many other cases, however, Blacks and Whites talk across and learn from their differences. Everyday, throughout America, racially mixed juries reach unanimous verdicts. From difference-in-dialogue comes commonality in belief. And the jurors who leave these experiences learn to respect and cherish both the differences and the common ground. (*Id.* at 247–248) (footnotes omitted)

For studies showing that generally that black judges on state courts do not render decisions differently from their white counterparts, see Malcolm D. Holmes, et al., *Judges' Ethnicity and Minority Sentencing: Evidence Concerning Hispanics*, 74 Social Sci. Q. 496 (1993); Cassia Spohn, *The Sentencing Decisions of Black and White Judges: Expected and Unexpected Similarities*, 24 Law & Soc'y Rev. 1197 (1990). Similar results have been reached with studies of black federal judges, though the relatively small number (to date) of such judges suggest caution in interpreting the results. See Orley Ashenfelter, Theodore Eisenberg, & Stewart J. Schwab, *Politics and the Judiciary: The Influence of Judicial Background on Case Outcomes*, 24 J. Legal Stud. 257, 275–281 (1995); Gregory C. Sisk, Michael Heise, & Andrew P. Morriss, *Charting the Influences on the Judicial Mind: An Empirical Study of Judicial Reasoning*, 73 N.Y. U. L. Rev. 1377, 1954–1959 (1998). But see Kevin L. Lyles, The Gatekeepers: Federal District Courts in the Political Process 223–246 (1997) (survey of federal district judges found differences in attitudes toward judicial role between black, white, and Latino judges); Nancy Crowe, The Impact of Gender and Race on the U.S. Courts of Appeals: 1981–1996 (1999) (Ph.D. dissertation, University of Chicago).

19. By its terms, the Voting Rights Act applies to elected representatives. 42 U.S.C. § 1973(b)(1994). In Chisom v. Roemer, 501 U.S. 380 (1991), the Supreme Court held that elected state judges fell under that definition. For a summary of subsequent litigation, see Anna M. Scuggs, Jean-Claude Mazzola, & Mary E. Zaug, *Recent Voting Rights Act Challenges to Judicial Elections*, 79 Judicature 34 (1995).

20. Ifill, *supra* note 16, at 105. Ifill goes on to argue that there should be "both individual and structural impartiality for judges," *id.* (footnote omitted), and that such a mandate should be effected to increase the numbers of African-American judges. *Id.* at 119–148.

or who only face retention elections (i.e., they run against themselves). Since the Jacksonian era, most state judges have been elected, but there has been a trend in the latter part of this century toward judicial merit selection. As we detailed in chapter 3, modern judicial elections are poor examples of representative democracy. They are characterized by low salience among voters, a virtual absence of meaningful debate on issues, low voter turnout, and frequent, uncontested incumbent victories. To the extent voting takes place at all, it relies heavily on cues such as partisan affiliation and name recognition.[21] The cynic might say that these are characteristics of elections, for *non*judicial offices, as well. There's something to that, but the difference is one of degree; almost all judicial elections (in contrast to nonjudicial races) exhibit these characteristics.

However, we do think there is one strong justification for seeking an increase in black judges. It will increase the *perception* of fairness of procedure in the courtroom. Not only will more African-American defendants face a black judge in court, but the sight of black judges presiding over the trials of and sentencing of white defendants can have a salutary effect on the African-American community (and other Americans). We are nowhere near a color blind society, but such a change in perception would go a long way toward ameliorating the palpable and understandable hostility many African-Americans and other minorities feel toward the criminal justice system in the states.[22] To some degree, of course, the perception argument traffics in its own stereotypes. It might imply, similar to the arguments we rejected above, that only black judges can be fair to black litigants. Like it or not, many people might believe it, and that perception must be taken seriously as a motivating factor in seeking to increase the role of nonwhites in the state judicial systems.

How can we best seek to have more black judges on state courts? There is no doubt that currently among the states there are disproportionately few black judges, well under the proportion of African-Americans in the total population of the country as a whole and especially of the large cities.[23] For previously stated

---

21. Further discussion of and support for the propositions made in the text are in Richard L. Hasen, *"High Court Wrongly Elected": A Public Choice Model of Judging and Its Implications for the Voting Rights Act*, 75 N.C. L. Rev. 1305, 1318–1319 (1997); Steven P. Croley, *The Majoritarian Difficulty: Elective Judiciaries and the Rule of Law*, 62 U. Chi. L. Rev. 689, 730–739 (1995), and in references in chapter 3. For an explicit argument, drawing in part on social science evidence, that judges are not representatives, see Michael E. Solimine & Susan E. Wheatley, *Rethinking Feminist Judging*, 70 Ind. L. J. 891, 912–915 (1995).

22. See Cook, *supra* note 18, at 1481–1482 (black jurists increase respect by black participants in the judicial process); Higginbotham, *supra* note 17, at 1034–1035 (unrepresentative judiciary affects perceptions).

23. See Harry P. Stumpf, American Judicial Politics 160 (2d ed. 1998) (reporting that as of 1991, less than 3 percent of all state judges were black); Ifill, *supra* note 16, at 95 (reporting similar figures). African-Americans make up about 12 percent of the population. Stumpf, *supra*, at 224.

reasons, it is also well under the proportion of African-Americans who are defendants in the criminal justice system or who are imprisoned.

One way to increase these numbers has been to pursue litigation under the Voting Rights Act to, in effect, racially gerrymander electoral districts for judges to insure that more blacks are elected to those posts. Whatever the merits or demerits of that strategy for other state offices (who, in our view, are more properly deemed representative), we think that it is a cure worse than the disease for judges. The notion that judges should not simply serve narrow constituencies is underscored by the tradition in most states of the jurisdiction of a judge's court being coterminous with the electoral basis of the court. Racial gerrymandering severely undermines that goal by, for example, electing a judge from one small part of a city while simultaneously permitting the judge to hear cases from litigants all over the city. The litigants who are not from the small district might find it curious and divisive that they had no chance to vote (and others did) for this putatively impartial judge of their rights. True, geographic and population realities almost always make some districting required for nearly all elected offices, including judgeships. But the other branches of government do not hold themselves out as impartial arbitrators of the law and facts, treating all litigants as equals.[24]

Our skepticism toward quota-like efforts to increase black judges is underscored by the history of racial discrimination in the composition of juries. As many have correctly pointed out, the jury is analogous to a judge herself, being (in theory) an impartial institution treating all those who come before it equally and without prejudice.[25] In 1986 the Supreme Court in *Batson v. Kentucky*[26] held that potential black jurors could not be automatically excluded from the jury pool (by way of a

---

24. For further discussion of the argument in the text, see Solimine & Wheatley, *supra* note 20, at 915. While the post-*Chisom* litigation has been extensive, see note 19 *supra*, success by plaintiffs in fully contested litigation has been rare. This is due in part to the receptivity of courts to the argument that "linkage"—the identity of the jurisdictional and electoral bases of judges—is a state interest that can outweigh evidence of vote dilution. E.g., Cousin v. Sundquist, 145 F.3d 818, 821–822 (6th Cir. 1998) (citing cases), *cert. denied,* 119 S.Ct. 1026 (1999); Milwaukee Branch of the NAACP v. Thompson, 116 F.3d 1194, 1200–1201 (7th Cir. 1997) (Easterbrook, J.) (same), *cert. denied,* 522 U.S. 1076 (1998). And the possibility of a court-ordered or voluntarily assumed remedy of a racially gerrymandered judicial district is doubtful given the Supreme Court's extreme skepticism of such remedies in general, starting with Shaw v. Reno, 509 U.S. 630 (1993). Stumpf, *supra* note 23, at 163 (acknowledging this point).

The linkage argument has not gone uncriticized. Richard Hasen, *supra* note 21, argues that given the low salience of judicial elections among voters, nonlinkage will not raise perceptions of unfairness to nonrepresented litigants. Sherrilyn Ifill, *supra* note 16, argues that linkage myopically assumes that state judges are not true representatives and do not represent community values (i.e., linkage wrongly assumes a robust model of impartial judging).

25. Ifill, *supra* note 16, at 120–124; Solimine & Wheatley, *supra* note 21, at 915 n.174.

26. 476 U.S. 79 (1986).

peremptory challenge) on the basis of race. The party exercising the challenge must advance a race-neutral reason. In the post-*Batson* world, how do we ensure that juries are more diversely composed? Some call for quotas to insure that each jury is composed of a certain number of members of racial and ethnic groups. It has been persuasively argued, however, that such quotas depend upon and might even improperly encourage stereotypical thinking by the designated juror(s). There is no guarantee that such juries would be seen as more legitimate; the opposite might well be true. Moreover, the idea has very difficult issues of implementation. Better that peremptory challenges be abolished altogether, and greater efforts be made to assemble jury pools and select juries in individual cases on a nondiscriminatory basis.[27]

Similar reasoning should inform increasing the number of black judges. In our view, the better approach is to take nondiscriminatory steps to insure that there will be more black judges. Those states that follow merit selection can take steps to ensure that more minority lawyers are considered in the pool. Those states that elect their judges must make efforts to seek black candidates. The latter path is no doubt the more difficult one, since almost invariably black lawyers must ingratiate themselves with the local political party organization that must support the candidate in the primary and general election. In contrast, in most merit selection states the black lawyer need only impress the smaller group who run the appointment process.[28] It is no surprise, then, that data to date shows that the numbers of black judges seem to be higher (or at least do no worse) in states with judicial merit selection as opposed to those with contested elections.[29] No doubt,

---

27. For the argument in favor of jury quotas, see Alschuler, *supra* note 9. For an extended argument against, see Kennedy *supra* note 4, at 240–245.

28. For a candid acknowledgment of the difficulties facing black lawyers in this regard, see Milwaukee Branch of the NAACP v. Thompson, 116 F.3d 1194, 1198 (7th Cir. 1997) (Easterbrook, J.), *cert. denied*, 522 U.S. 1076 (1998). The until recently historic low numbers of blacks in the legal profession (less than 4 % as of 1996, Ifill, *supra* note 16, at 96 n.7) no doubt plays a large role in the paucity of black judges. Sherrilyn Ifill disputes that theory, *id.*, apparently arguing that racism has played a large part since in the past few years women lawyers, unlike blacks, have achieved far more rapid gains as members of the judiciary. Her point is undermined by the fact that women make up a much greater percentage of the legal profession than do blacks. Stumpf, *supra* note 23, at 224 (27 % of profession expected to be female by 2000).

29. Croley, *supra* note 21, at 784–786. Other avenues to increase the number of black judges, such as cumulative voting, could be explored. E.g., Cousin v. Sundquist, 145 F.3d 818, 829–831 (6th Cir. 1998) (considering but rejecting cumulative voting for judges as a potential remedy for Voting Rights Act violations, in part because it would require all judicial candidates to run against each other, and would encourage racial bloc voting and thus reduce the perception of colorblind justice), *cert. denied*, 119 S.Ct. 1026 (1999). See generally Ronald V. Chapman, Comment, *Judicial Roulette: Alternatives to Single-Member Districts as a Legal and Political Solution to Voting-Rights Challenges to At-Large Judicial Elections*, 48 SMU L. Rev. 457 (1995).

the easier road would be the one of racially gerrymandered judicial districts. But that road would come at a high cost to the impartiality of the state judiciary.

THE DEATH PENALTY AND STATE JUDICIARIES

The imposition of a death sentence as a penalty for crime by the federal and state governments in this country raises enormously complex and important issues of substantive law, criminal procedure, morality, and ethics, almost all of which are beyond the scope of the present volume. What we focus on here are the many criticisms of the death penalty, almost all of which do not reflect well on state courts. The most persistent and documented criticism has been that the penalty has been applied in a racially discriminatory way. That is, among other things, black criminal defendants are more likely to be sentenced to death as compared to their white counterparts.[30] And while the Supreme Court in the 1970s began subjecting the penalty itself and its attendant procedures in state courts to scrutiny under the Eighth Amendment,[31] since then, it is often said, a majority of the Court has in effect "deregulated" the process and permitted the state great latitude in the court procedures they follow when considering whether to impose these penalties. Concern with these procedures, and related concern with the adequacy of defense counsel (almost always appointed) and other issues led the American Bar Association in 1997 to call for a moratorium in the states on the imposition of the penalty.[32] Finally, it is often said that state judges find it particularly difficult to fairly adjudicate the rights of defendants in these cases. Support for (or opposition to) the death penalty has become a high-profile issue in the 1980s and 1990s in elections in general and judicial elections in particular. In that environment, it is often difficult for a state judge facing election to make rulings that may allow a defendant to avoid the penalty, given possible retribution at the polls. As proof, the electoral defeats of three California Supreme Court justices in 1986 are often cited, widely attributed to the votes of these jurists to set aside death penalties upon appellate review.[33]

---

30. The leading work in this area has been done by law professor David Baldus and his colleagues. A brief but helpful review of the work of Baldus and other researchers on the issue is found in Kennedy, *supra* note 4, at 330–331 & nn.51–52.

31. In Furman v. Georgia, 408 U.S. 238 (1972) the Supreme Court first held that state imposition of the death penalty must be subjected to scrutiny under the Eighth Amendment to the Constitution, and in so doing struck down all state statutes at the time. In response to *Furman*, numerous states began rewriting and reapplying their death penalty statutes, and the Court first began to review those statutes in a trilogy of cases decided in 1976, most notably Gregg v. Georgia, 428 U.S. 153 (1976).

32. The deregulation metaphor is taken from Robert Weisberg, *Deregulating Death*, 1983 Sup. Ct. Rev. 305. The ABA's action is discussed in Symposium, *The ABA's Proposal Moratorium on the Death Penalty*, 61 Law & Contemp. Prob. 1 (Autumn 1998).

33. On the death penalty issue in state judicial elections in general, and the 1986 California experience in particular, see Croley, *supra* note 21, at 737–738; Scott D. Weiner, Note, *Popular Justice: State Judicial Elections and Procedural Due Process*, 31 Harv. C.R.-

For over three decades, all executions in this nation have been administered by states. (Federal death penalty statutes were reenacted starting in the late 1980s, and since then several federal defendants have been sentenced to death, but as of 1999 no executions of those individuals had taken place.) It is no surprise, then, that virtually all proposals to reform death penalty litigation (short of outright abolition) have been directed at the states, and usually involve actions taken at the federal level, by Congress or the federal courts. For example, with regard to the disparate impact of the penalty on African-Americans, a Racial Justice Act proposed in Congress in the late 1980s and early 1990s would have permitted the introduction of statistical evidence, in both federal and state courts, to demonstrate that prosecutors and other state officials were administering the death penalty in a racially discriminatory manner. (It didn't pass.)[34] But on this and other death penalty issues, we think state political institutions, including state courts, can and have a productive role to play. Judicial federalism has the potential to ameliorate rather than exacerbate problems associated with death penalty litigation.

Put another way, viewing some of these issues from the perspective of judicial federalism can inform both the descriptive and prescriptive analysis. Virtually all of the scholarly discussion of the death penalty has been of purportedly national trends, and thus has treated all states, and state courts, more-or-less alike. In a similar view, Franklin Zimring has opined that the "political science of capital punishment" is a "vast and neglected topic."[35] He points out that a few Southern states (mainly Texas, Alabama, Georgia, and Florida) account for many of the rising tide of executions in the 1980s and 1990s. Some thirty-eight states have death penalty statutes on the books, but only a few states by the late 1990s were actively executing prisoners. The low or absent rate of executions in states outside the South, Zimring speculates, may be attributable in part to ambivalence of public officials in vigorously imposing the penalty, even among those who publicly support it.[36] An alternative explanation, of course, is that skillful lawyers and sympathetic federal and state judges have in many cases delayed or thwarted

C.L. L. Rev. 187, 198–200 (1996).

34. For a discussion of the proposed Racial Justice Act and other death penalty reforms, see Kennedy, *supra* note 4, at 340–348. The various versions of the Racial Justice Act would have in effect overruled the Supreme Court's decision in McCleskey v. Kemp, 481 U.S. 279 (1987). That case made it virtually impossible for a state capital prisoner seeking federal habeas corpus relief to demonstrate that the death penalty was being administered in a racially discriminatory manner in a particular state. Statistics showing such circumstances were not enough, the Court held. Rather, the prisoner must demonstrate that state prosecutors or other officials *intended* to discriminate against racial minorities, a much more difficult evidentiary burden. See generally Evan Tsen Lee & Ashutoh Bhagwat, *The McCleskey Puzzle: Remedying Prosecutorial Discrimination Against Black Victims in Capital Sentencing*, 1998 Sup. Ct. Rev. 145.

35. Franklin E. Zimring, *The Wages of Ambivalence: On the Context and Prospect of New York's Death Penalty*, 44 Buff. L. Rev. 303, 303 (1996).

36. *Id.* at 303–304.

entirely the imposition of the penalty.[37] Perhaps both theories have explanatory force, especially outside of the South.

Consider again the issue of race discrimination and the penalty. As observed above, respected social science studies have strongly suggested that blacks accused of capital crimes are more likely to be sentenced to death as compared to similarly situated white defendants. But almost all of the studies are based on data on one state, usually in the South,[38] and they have not gone uncontested on substance. Critics argue that many of the alleged disparities are due to the prior record, type of offense, and other characteristics of the accused, and that most death penalties are accessed for offenses for which both the defendant and the victim are of the same race.[39] Moreover, it is worth noting that polls indicate that majorities of both blacks and whites support the death penalty.[40]

Extended consideration of the discrimination studies and the poll numbers are beyond our scope. But federalism concerns usually play a secondary role in the literature. Proponents of the discrimination studies rarely pause to consider whether data from one or a small group of states should be extrapolated to all jurisdictions. Nationwide polls will obscure regional and state differences. And, the states can individually respond to the discrimination concerns. In 1998, for example, Kentucky became the first state to enact its own Racial Justice Act. Like the unenacted federal proposal, it will require prosecutors under certain circumstances to demonstrate that their decisions to seek a death penalty in a particular case are free from racial basis.[41] One state is just that, but it demonstrates that state

---

37. Daniel D. Polsby, *Recontextualizing the Context of the Death Penalty*, 44 Buff. L. Rev. 527, 532–533 (1996).

38. The leading study by Baldus, *supra* note 30, was of Georgia. More recently, Baldus has moved north in his study of death penalty litigation, and found racial bias in the administration of the death penalty in Philadelphia. David Baldus, George Woodworth, David Zuckerman, Neil Alan Weiner, & Barbara Broffitt, *Racial Discrimination and the Death Penalty in the Post-Furman Era: An Empirical and Legal Overview, With Recent Findings From Philadelphia*, 83 Cornell L. Rev. 1638 (1998) (hereinafter Baldus).

39. E.g., Reuben M. Greenberg, *Race, the Criminal Justice System, and Community-Oriented Policing*, 20 Harv. J. L. & Pub. Pol'y 397, 397–399 (1997); John C. McAdams, *Racial Disparity and Death Penalty*, 61 Law & Contemp. Prob. 153 (Autumn 1998); Stanley Rothman & Stephen Powers, *Execution by Quota?*, 116 Pub. Int. 3 (Summer 1994).

40. John J. DiIulio, Jr., *The Question of Black Crime*, 117 Pub. Int. 3 (Fall 1994); McAdams, *supra* note 39, at 167.

41. David E. Rovella, *"Race Pervades Death Penalty,"* Nat'l L. J. June 8, 1998, at A20. Similar proposals have been under consideration in other state legislatures. E.g., H.B.828, 122nd General Assembly, Ohio, 1998 (permitting the presentation of evidence at the sentencing hearing in capital cases to show that the death penalty has been imposed in a demographically disparate manner). State institutions (courts and legislatures) can thus, in effect, overrule the *McCleskey* case (*supra* note 34) for their own jurisdictions, since the latter case is regarded as an interpretation of the federal habeas corpus statute and not one of federal constitutional law. Even if *McCleskey* turns to some degree on constitutional considerations, state institutions can still develop law above the federal floor of rights, as we describe in chapter 5. For examples of developments in several states on this issue, see

institutions are capable of response on issues thought by most to be wholly in the federal domain.

Consider, too, the substantive law on the death penalty developed by the Supreme Court since the mid-1970s. The deregulation metaphor has some explanatory force. The Court has more frequently upheld state court imposition of death penalties in recent years, though this was a period when the Reagan administration also began arguing in favor of the penalty.[42] And federal court review of such sentences will no doubt be further restricted after the statutory changes in 1996 to the federal habeas corpus statute (discussed below). While the Court's doctrine usually does not speak explicitly in these terms, there is little doubt that the recent cases often deferring to death penalty procedures in state courts give considerable weight to federalism values: the autonomy of states, the possible benefits of experimentation, and the like. One's evaluation of this doctrine depends heavily on the confidence one has in state courts to fairly police the death penalty process, largely free from federal court oversight.[43] Even on the high-profile issue of the death penalty, there is some evidence that some state courts are worthy of that confidence. Several state supreme courts (including, perhaps surprisingly, Georgia and Mississippi) have begun to develop principles drawn from state constitutional law to oversee death penalty litigation on their courts, beyond that demanded by federal law for their courts. For example, several of these courts have held that they will conduct more intensive appellate review of trial court decisions on whether to change venue of capital cases (i.e., hold the trial in another part of the state) to secure more unbiased jurors.[44]

State court death penalty adjudication can even inform the development of federal law itself. As Justice John Paul Stevens has suggested, various state courts can approach and resolve, in different ways, issues left open by the Supreme Court's cases. The Court does not have to review every such case, when asked, and can allow the issue to percolate in the lower courts. Federal courts, and particularly the Supreme Court, may need to eventually provide a uniform answer to the issue but, in the meantime, that answer will be better resolved if the various lower courts consider it beforehand.[45]

Baldus, *supra* note 38, at 1736–1738.

42. Tracey E. George & Lee Epstein, *On the Nature of Supreme Court Decision Making*, 86 Am. Pol. Sci. Rev. 323, 329–330 (1992) (statistical analysis of Supreme Court death penalty decisions from 1971 to 1988).

43. In this paragraph we draw heavily on Louis D. Bilionis, *Legitimating Death*, 91 Mich. L. Rev. 1643 (1993).

44. *Id.* at 1682–1690. These developments have even been acknowledged by the harshest critics of state court performance in death penalty cases. See Stephen B. Bright & Patrick J. Kennan, *Judges and the Politics of Death: Deciding Between the Bill of Rights and the Next Election in Capital Cases*, 75 B.U. L. Rev. 759, 829–830 (1995).

45. Brown v. Texas, 522 U.S. 940, 942-943(1998) (statement by Stevens, J., joined by Souter, Ginsburg, & Breyer, JJ., respecting the denial of certiorari) (case concerned whether state can prohibit the accused from presenting truthful evidence on eligibility for parole in sentencing phase of capital case). Stevens also referred to the percolation in lower

Finally, consider the behavior of state judges in capital cases. It is often stated that given the high profile of the death penalty in elections in general, and judicial elections in particular, it must be difficult for elected state judges to protect countermajoritarian rights in those cases.[46] Stephen Bright's careful study of this problem documents the pressures many state judges no doubt feel, and provides many examples of electoral campaigns dominated by that issue. He also points out that thirty-two states have both the death penalty and judicial elections, and that judicial reticence is also manifested by inadequate supervision of appointment of counsel for indigents, and excessive deference to prosecutors in various rulings during trial.[47] Bright's study consists mainly of anecdotal examples, but it seems supported by empirical studies of state supreme court decision-making. Those studies indicate that justices in states with competitive judicial elections were more likely to uphold death sentences.[48] This evidence is sobering, and no doubt it is reflective of electoral pressure in state *trial* judges as well. The death penalty may just be such an inflammatory issue, one on which there has been so much demagoguery, that it poses an unfortunate exception to our generalization that state judges are not bullied by majoritarian pressures.

Still, we do not think the picture is completely bleak. State judges, on the death penalty and other issues, at all levels no doubt feel electoral pressures but do not necessarily succumb to them. After all, it was their opposition to death penalty sentences that got Rose Bird and her colleagues in trouble on the California Supreme Court. And even then it took a huge amount of interest group activity and money to defeat them at the polls.[49] Moreover, more recent empirical studies have found no substantial systemwide evidence that state judicial methods affect case outcomes. These same studies confirm the commonsense intuition that other variables, such as prosecutorial discretion to seek the death penalty, can influence the process through which capital cases come before state judges and juries.[50] Thus,

---

federal and state courts of the issue of racial bias in peremptory challenges, an issue only resolved by the Court in 1986. *Id.* at 356–357; note 26 *supra*.

46. E.g., Harris v. Alabama, 513 U.S. 504, 519-521 (1995) (Stevens, J., dissenting).

47. Bright & Kennan, *supra* note 44, at 760–767. Over 99 percent of death row inmates are indigent. Brad Synder, Note, *Disparate Impact on Death Row: M.L.B. and the Indigent's Right to Counsel at Capital State Postconviction Hearings*, 107 Yale L. J. 2211, 2238 (1998).

48. E.g., Paul R. Brace & Melinda Gann Hall, *The Interplay of Preferences, Case Facts, Context, and Rules in the Politics of Judicial Choice*, 59 J. Pol. 1206, 1221–1222 (1997). The study only examined the work of eight state supreme courts, but the authors earlier defended their methodology, and suggested that their study was still relevant in explaining judicial behavior in the other states. Paul R. Brace & Melinda Gann Hall, *Studying Courts Comparatively: The View From the States*, 48 Pol. Res. Q. 5, 14 (1995).

49. Weiner, *supra* note 33, at 199.

50. John Blume & Theodore Eisenberg, *Judicial Politics, Death Penalty Appeals, and Case Selection: An Empirical Study*, 72 S. Cal. L. Rev. 465 (1999). This study used a different and somewhat broader array of data than the those of the Brace and Hall studies, note 48 *supra*. The Blume and Eisenberg study examined appeals of death penalty cases for

for example, California is generally not classified as a state with partisan judicial elections, yet as we noted death penalty politics has played a major role in the retention elections for its highest court. Likewise, California has a large death row, but its state prosecutors seek the death penalty at a lower rate than other states that have frequent executions. Here, too, the death penalty process in the states would benefit from more empirical study.

Decisions by state judges to uphold death sentences must also depend ultimately on the facts of the case and the legal precedents at hand, as in all other matters. As long as the United States remains the rare exception in a world sick of the death penalty,[51] American judges still have to follow the law as it is written. Indeed, conservative critics (using their own anecdotal examples) decry "liberal" federal and state judges overturning or reducing death sentences.[52] Liberal critics of state judges in this regard probably make a better case, but even they have not demonstrated that state judges systematically disregard federal rights in capital cases.

HABEAS CORPUS AND STATE JUDICIARIES

A final conundrum facing both critics and supporters of parity is the existence and scope of federal habeas corpus relief. Litigants in state court cases that raise federal issues generally have one chance to prevail; the result in trial court can usually be appealed up the state court ladder, with the chance that the U.S. Supreme Court might review the case thereafter. Federal habeas corpus is the exception: it enables the defendant convicted in state court (but not a losing prosecutor) another sequential avenue of relief, by asking a federal trial judge to

---

twenty-six states from 1995 to 1997 (about 800 cases), which states accounted for 97 % of state prisoners under death sentences as of 1996. It also considered data from the FBI and the Bureau of Justice Statistics to estimate how often state prosecutors in those states sought the death penalty for murders (as opposed to a lesser penalty).

51. The United States is the only economically developed democratic nation in the world to maintain the death penalty for ordinary crimes. It is also, importantly, the only nation where political subdivisions are divided on the imposition of the death penalty, or for that matter where they can be divided on it. Currently thirty-five states allow the death penalty and fifteen do not. Bright & Kennan, *supra* note 44. As we already observed, many states allow the death penalty but have not executed anyone since the penalty was re-instated by the state legislature in response to *Furman*.

Each of us, to varying degrees, finds the death penalty as presently administered problematic on utilitarian, ethical, and religious grounds, though neither of us would necessarily oppose its use in all circumstances. Like Randall Kennedy, Kennedy, *supra* note 4, at 345 n.*, we can critique the death penalty process without necessarily staking out a definitive position on whether the penalty should exist at all.

52. E.g., Max Boot, Out of Order: Arrogance, Corruption and Incompetence on the Bench 55–60 (1998).

grant her a writ ordering a retrial or other relief based on violations of federal law that attended her conviction.[53]

Recent doctrinal and statutory developments in the availability of federal habeas relief have implications for parity and related issues. We already briefly surveyed some of those developments in chapter 3. Of constitutional origins,[54] federal judges have long had some authority to issue a writ of habeas corpus for a prisoner in *federal* custody; Congress expanded the writ in 1867 to include prisoners in *state* custody. But for many decades the latter writ was rarely granted, since with few exceptions courts held that it was only exercisable in narrow circumstances, such as when the convicting state court completely lacked jurisdiction to hear the case. The Warren Court brought that narrow view to an end in *Brown v. Allen*,[55] which held that the writ could also be granted if the conviction was obtained as a result of violations of federal law. The doctrinal revolution in criminal procedure by the Court of course provided more substantive reasons for state prisoners to attempt to obtain habeas relief, and the Court also ameliorated procedural obstacles to habeas review.[56]

In the 1960s and 1970s this expansive view of habeas had its supporters, but it also came under increasing attack in the academy,[57] from state attorneys generals,

---

53. Most states also provide some mechanism for postconviction relief in *state* courts, after the defendant has exhausted her direct appeals. This is yet another way for state courts to correct errors in applying federal law. See generally 1 James S. Liebman & Randy Hertz, Federal Habeas Corpus Practice and Procedure 137–189 (2d ed. 1994); Frank J. Remington, *State Prisoner Access to Post-Conviction Relief—Lessening Role for Federal Courts: An Increasingly Important Role for State Courts*, 44 Ohio St. L. J. 287 (1983); Frank J. Remington, *Post-Conviction Review—What State Trial Courts Can Do to Reduce Problems*, 72 Judicature 53 (1988). This is an area deserving of further scholarly attention, especially empirical study. In the balance of this chapter, we are referring exclusively to habeas corpus relief available in a *federal* court.

54. Reference to habeas corpus is found in the U.S. Const., art. I, § 9, cl.2 (limiting circumstances in which Congress can suspend the writ). Statutory codification of federal court power to issue the writ is found in 28 U.S.C. §§ 2241–2255.

55. 344 U.S. 443 (1953).

56. Most notably in Fay v. Noia, 372 U.S. 391 (1963) (holding that federal court could consider habeas petition even when claims had not been properly presented to state courts, as long as prisoner had not "deliberately bypassed" state procedures).

57. The leading critics were Paul M. Bator, *Finality in Criminal Law and Federal Habeas Corpus for State Prisoners*, 76 Harv. L. Rev. 441 (1963) (arguing that intent of framers of 1867 expansion of habeas was limited to gross violations of process in state court) and Henry J. Friendly, *Is Innocence Irrelevant? Collateral Attacks on Criminal Judgments*, 38 U. Chi. L. Rev. 142 (1970) (arguing that habeas relief should generally be restricted to those state prisoners who could make a "colorable showing of innocence"). Both Bator (a Harvard law school professor) and Friendly (a judge on the U.S. Court of Appeals for the Second Circuit) were leading exponents of the Legal Process school, which we discussed in chapter 3. Bator's article was published shortly before *Fay v. Noia*, *supra* note 56, was decided. It was relied upon in the dissent in *Fay*, 372 U.S. at 449 n.1, 451 nn. 4 & 6, 457 n.12 (Harlan, J., dissenting), but dismissed by Justice Brennan for the majority

and in Congress.[58] The Burger and Rehnquist Courts, while leaving *Brown v. Allen* intact, gradually restricted or overruled Warren Court precedents, and placed greater barriers to obtaining habeas relief.[59] The courts paid increasing fidelity to the costs of exercising habeas relief: the value of finality of state court convictions, as it pertains to the retributive and deterrent functions of criminal law, the quality of state court judging, and the balance of federalism.[60]

There is little doubt that, intentionally or not, the increasing criticism of a liberal habeas regime and the restrictive decisions of the Burger and Rehnquist Courts had synergistic effects. The synergy culminated in Congress's election-year passage of the Antiterrorism and Effective Death Penalty Act of 1996 (AEDPA). With regard to habeas, the AEDPA, for the first time, provides for a statute of limitations (of one year) for the bringing of habeas petitions after the exhaustion of state remedies; requires, under certain circumstances, the prompt resolution of heretofore protracted resolution of habeas petitions in death penalty cases; and provides that habeas relief can only be awarded when a state court not merely misapplies federal constitutional law, but rather was contrary to "clearly established Federal law," as determined by the Supreme Court.[61] Already, critics of the statute are predicting

---

in a footnote. *Id.* at 421 n.30. Bator's article later became the citation of choice as the Court began to adopt his worldview on habeas. E.g., Calderon v. Thompson, 523 U.S. 538, 555 (1998); Stone v. Powell, 428 U.S. 465, 475 n.7, 498 n.35 (1976). Writing in 1981, Bator remarked that his article had "the strange history of being pronounced dead almost as soon as it was written, only to enjoy a mysterious recent resurrection." Paul M. Bator, *The State Courts and Federal Constitutional Litigation*, 22 Wm. & Mary L. Rev. 605, 613 (1981) (footnote omitted) (citing *Stone v. Powell*).

58. The efforts of state attorneys generals (e.g., by filing amicus briefs) and of the Republican administrations in the 1980s and 1990s (e.g., by calling for various restrictions and supporting proposals in Congress) to restrict habeas relief is well described in Katy J. Harriger, *The Federalism Debate in the Transformation of Federal Habeas Corpus Law*, 27 Publius: The Journal of Federalism 1, 9–20 (Summer 1997), and Larry W. Yackle, *The Habeas Hagioscope*, 66 S. Cal. L. Rev. 2331, 2349–2373 (1993).

59. E.g., Wainwright v. Sykes, 433 U.S. 72 (1977) (limiting ability to entertain claims procedurally defaulted in state court); Stone v. Powell, 428 U.S. 465 (1976) (violations of exclusionary rule not cognizable in habeas); McCleskey v. Zant, 499 U.S. 467 (1991) (limiting federal court consideration of successive habeas petitions); Teague v. Lane, 489 U.S. 288 (1989) (limiting retroactive application of new constitutional rules to aid habeas petitioners). For a comprehensive overview and critique of the history of habeas and its application in and since the Warren Court, see Hart & Wechsler, *supra* note 1, at 1337–1461; Larry W. Yackle, Reclaiming the Federal Courts 151–211 (1994) (hereinafter Yackle, Reclaiming). For general overviews, see James S. Liebman & Randy Hertz, Federal Habeas Corpus Practice and Procedure (2 vols., 2d ed. 1994); Larry W. Yackle, Federal Courts 417–476 (1999).

60. E.g., Calderon v. Thompson, 523 U.S. 538, 554-555 (1998) (citing numerous cases).

61. The principal provisions of the Act, Pub. L. 104–132, 110 Stat. 1214 (1996), concerning habeas relief for state prisoners are codified as amendments to 28 U.S.C. § 2244 (successive petitions), § 2254 (application of new substantive rules), §§ 2261–2266 (special

that it will sharply reduce the already restricted availability of habeas relief, and thus further reduce the vindication of federal rights in state criminal proceedings.[62] We think this is alarmist and unsustainable. Most likely, the affect of the AEDPA in most cases will be marginal. Broadly speaking, it does little more than codify the doctrinal restrictions on habeas relief developed by the Burger and Rehnquist Courts, and is likely to be so interpreted by courts. The AEDPA was an example of symbolic, election-year politics. Supported by President Clinton and most Democratic and Republican members of Congress, it was largely meant to burnish the legislators' crime-fighting credentials for voters back home.[63]

Empirical studies of the case of habeas corpus shed some light on these issues. After *Brown v. Allen* and other Warren Court decisions were rendered, the number of habeas petitions from state prisoners soared from 560 in 1950, to 4,845 in 1965, and 9,063 in 1970. The filings began to level off after that increase, though it reached a high of 11,980 in 1994. Nor were these increases a mere function of the burgeoning numbers of state prisoners; the rate of petitions per state prisoner varied from 0.37 percent, 2.55 percent, 5.13 percent, and 1.30 percent in the years just mentioned, respectively.[64] Despite (or perhaps because of) these increased filings, studies have consistently shown that only very small percentages of these petitions are found meritorious. In the 1970s, studies demonstrated that only 3–4 percent of petitions were granted by federal district judges.[65] These conclusions were confirmed and augmented by studies conducted in the 1990s by researchers at the National Center for State Courts (NCSC). One study closely examined the contents and disposition of several thousand habeas petitions from four states (Alabama, New York, California, and Texas), filed in both state and federal courts. This study found, among other things, that federal courts granted barely 1 percent of the petitions filed. The percentage granted by state courts was near 10 percent,

---

habeas procedures in death penalty cases). A detailed discussion of the AEDPA is beyond the scope of the present work. There is already a burgeoning literature on point, e.g., Hart & Wechsler, *supra* note 1, 1999 Supp. at 159–185; Evan Tsen Lee, *Section 2254(d) of the New Habeas Statute: An (Opinionated) User's Manual*, 51 Vand. L. Rev. 103 (1998); Larry W. Yackle, *A Primer on the New Habeas Corpus Statute*, 44 Buff. L. Rev. 381 (1996).

62. E.g., Stephen B. Bright, *Is Fairness Irrelevant? The Evisceration of Federal Habeas Corpus Review and Limits on the Ability of State Courts to Protect Fundamental Rights*, 54 Wash. & Lee L. Rev. 1 (1997).

63. This more benign vision of the AEDPA is taken by two harsh critics of the substantive provisions in Mark Tushnet & Larry Yackle, *Symbolic Statutes and Real Laws: The Pathologies of the Antiterrorism and Effective Death Penalty Act and the Prison Litigation Reform Act*, 47 Duke L. J. 1 (1997).

64. Data collected in Hart & Wechsler, *supra* note 1, at 1363.

65. See Paul H. Robinson, An Empirical Study of Federal Habeas Corpus Review of State Court Judgments 23 (Federal Justice Research Program, Office for Improvements in the Administration of Justice) (1979); Richard Faust, Tina J. Rubenstein, & Larry W. Yackle, *The Great Writ in Action: Empirical Light on the Federal Habeas Corpus Debate*, 18 N.Y.U. Rev. L. & Soc. Change 649, 681 (1991); David L. Shapiro, *Federal Habeas Corpus: A Study in Massachusetts*, 87 Harv. L. Rev. 321, 333 (1973).

though was due almost entirely to a relatively large number granted by judges in New York.[66] A similar study by NCSC researchers examined a random sample of federal court disposition of habeas petitions in nine states in 1992, which states produce about half of the petitions filed each year. It found, too, that but 1 percent of the petitions were granted.[67]

To be sure, many reasons account for this spectacularly high level of rejection of habeas claims. The vast majority of petitioners are not represented by attorneys (there being no constitutional right to such representation). In one sense, filing a habeas petition becomes a "no-cost" effort by a prisoner. It is possible, perhaps even likely, that some of the petitions would be granted if they were not in handwritten form and otherwise poorly presented. Whether this would change the final outcome of any case is impossible to know. But, the alleged federal constitutional errors advanced in many of the petitions are not squarely rejected, since many petitions are rejected for procedural infirmities (e.g., failure to exhaust state court remedies). Still, given the overall rejection rate, it is difficult to escape the conclusion that "state courts are doing a good job in protecting federal constitutional rights [thus] weak[ening] the argument that federal review is a necessary safeguard against errors made in state courts."[68] As we argued in chapter 3, surely there would be a much higher rate of granting (and perhaps filing) of petitions if in fact state courts were systematically trampling on federal rights.

A somewhat different picture emerges from the habeas petitions filed in cases where the death penalty was imposed. The NCSC studies just mentioned found that up to 15 percent of habeas petitions were granted in such cases.[69] Other research, however, has uncovered considerably higher rates. In the early 1990s James Liebman reported, from a survey of published and unpublished federal court opinions, that habeas petitions were granted in 40 percent of capital cases reviewed (after the restoration of the death penalty) between 1976 and 1991.[70] More recently Liebman has extended this study up to 1995 and finds that overall 38.5 percent of such petitions have been granted.[71]

Differing research techniques can account for some of the divergent conclusions of these studies, and it is true that any figure must be evaluated cautiously, since

---

66. Victor E. Flango, Habeas Corpus in State and Federal Courts ch. 6 (National Center for State Courts 1994).

67. Roger A. Hanson & Henry W.K. Daley, Federal Habeas Corpus Review: Challenging State Court Criminal Convictions 17 (U.S. Dep't of Justice, Bureau of Justice Statistics 1995).

68. Flango, *supra* note 66, at 89, 91.

69. *Id.* at 81–88.

70. As reported in James S. Liebman, *More Than "Slightly Retro": The Rehnquist Court's Rout of Habeas Corpus Jurisdiction in Teague v. Lane*, 18 N.Y.U. Rev. L. & Soc. Change 537, 541 n.15 (1991).

71. James S. Liebman & William F. Ryan, *"Some Effectual Power": The Quantity and Quality of Decisionmaking That Article III and the Supremacy Clause Demand of the Federal Courts*, 98 Colum. L. Rev. 696, 864–865 n. 802 (1998).

the inability of state prosecutors to "appeal" acquittals (or convictions on noncapital grounds) inevitably effects the data set.[72] Nonetheless, a higher rate of constitutional error in capital cases (as revealed by habeas) is not shocking. Such cases are likely to be pursued more diligently by the petitioner and supportive interest groups, and indeed considered more carefully by federal judges. Moreover, as we described above, the heavier regulation of the state court death penalty process by Supreme Court doctrine no doubt creates additional opportunities for error creation even by conscientious state judges, not distracted by electoral concerns. The potential for error is greater for state judges that are so distracted.

What, then, do we make of the current habeas regime? Proposals to simply abolish federal habeas corpus for state prisoners have been seriously advanced, on the basis that it is both unnecessary and invasive of the interests of states to manage their criminal proceedings free from federal oversight.[73] We do not support such a radical step, and so conclude for several reasons. First, the generally tiny rate of granting of petitions is supportive of state court adjudication, much more so than critics of parity are willing to acknowledge. But the fact remains that there are errors revealed and corrected by the habeas process, and the error rate is much higher in capital cases. If habeas were abandoned, then the only opportunity for review by a federal court would be direct review by the Supreme Court. That is an appropriate and compelling opportunity that should be available in our system, one that we have supported in chapter 5 and elsewhere in this book. Given the large number of cases seeking review in the Court, and the few that it grants review, realistically very few cases will be considered on direct appeal. In most civil cases, we think, that is not necessarily unfortunate. But criminal cases of course potentially place the liberty and life of the defendant at issue. In those cases, it is not inappropriate to have federal courts via habeas take a second look at those dispositions, at least in some circumstances. The availability of direct review, as we argued in chapter 5, serves as a useful reminder to state judges that incorrect

---

72. The NCSC studies utilized only a sample of cases from selected jurisdictions, while the Liebman study examines all accessible federal court decisions during the period in question. (The fact that he was understandably unable to guarantee that he captured *every* habeas decision by a federal judge probably skews his data, since those sort of decisions were probably denials of frivolous petitions.) And, the studies code the cases in different ways. See the exchange among Flango, Liebman and others reported in Randall Samborn, *Habeas Corpus Statistics Reveal Caseload Is Light*, Nat'l L. J., Oct. 17, 1994 at A19.

The skewing effect on data of the asymmetrical nature of habeas petitions is addressed in Kent S. Schiedegger, *Habeas Corpus, Relitigation, and the Legislative Power*, 98 Colum. L. Rev. 888, 940–941 (1998). Schiedegger has conducted his own study of this issue, and has come up with figures similar to those of the NCSC studies. *Id.* at 942–943. Liebman discounts this study, in part because it was based on a sample from a single year. Liebman & Ryan, *supra* note 71, at 865 n.802.

73. E.g., U.S. Department of Justice, Office of Legal Policy, Federal Habeas Corpus: Review of State Judgments 56-59 (1988).

applications of federal law are subject to reversal. The same rationale holds for habeas cases.[74]

Second, it appears that despite the high number of filings, the disposition of most habeas petitions has not been especially burdensome on federal courts nor, we presume, on states attorneys generals who typically must respond to such claims. Most petitions are disposed of fairly rapidly on a paper record, without hearings being convened or other undue demands on federal court resources. The petitions that do take considerable time and resources, by all parties, are death penalty cases, particularly successive petitions in those cases. The AEDPA, as we saw, was intended to specifically ameliorate that problem.

Finally, we concede the actual and symbolic costs associated with habeas review. In some circumstances a federal judge will order a state prisoner, perhaps convicted of the most heinous of crimes, released to be retried. Given that the order may take place years after the conviction, the passage of time may make retrial impossible. This scenario weakens the virtue of bringing closure and finality to litigation, and undermines the interest of a state in the integrity of its criminal process, surely the most visible function (along with public education, perhaps) of local government in a federal system. So there are costs, but they should not be overstated. Very few petitions are, in fact, granted. That cuts both ways. It can mean that the current habeas regime works, or that the whole system is (nearly) a colossal waste. There's some truth to both conclusions, we think, but ultimately the benefits, outlined above, outweigh the costs. Indeed, it is striking that recent surveys show that both federal *and* state judges support the continued existence of at least some form of federal habeas corpus. For example, one study (of a concededly relatively small sample of judges) showed that 76 percent of the federal judges and 54 percent of the state judges supported federal habeas corpus.[75]

---

74. Yackle, Reclaiming, *supra* note 58, at 162 (using this rationalc to justify habeas in the face of a low rate of the granting of petitions).

75. Christopher E. Smith & Darwin L. Burke, *Judges' Views on Habeas Corpus: A Comparison of State and Federal Judges*, 22 Okla. City U. L. Rev. 1125, 1138 (1997). The authors surveyed a sample of 100 federal judges and 100 intermediate appellate state judges, both from states that generate high numbers of habeas petitions. Usable responses were obtained from forty-seven state judges and forty-three federal judges. *Id.* at 131–133. To our knowledge, this is the only systematic survey of judges in this issue. Anecdotal support of habeas by state judges can be found. E.g., Stanley Mosk, *States' Rights—and Wrongs*, 72 N.Y.U. L. Rev. 552, 552–555 (1997) (California Supreme Court justice).

Another, related reason we support some availability of federal habeas relief is the jurisdictional redundancy theory advanced by Robert Cover. He argued that habeas could be justified, in part, on the basis that it in effect creates a mechanism for a helpful dialogue between state courts and federal courts on the existence and scope of federal constitutional rights. State judges, he argued, will tend to have more practical (and often narrow) perspectives on the need for and application of such rights, while federal judges would tend to have a more "utopian" and more-rights protective perspective. Both perspectives can and should inform the optimal development of rights. Robert M. Cover & T. Alexander Aleinikoff, *Dialectical Federalism: Habeas Corpus and the Court*, 86 Yale L. J. 1035

Presumably, the latter judges concluded that the costs of habeas did not outweigh the benefits. The conclusion of such interested parties is entitled to weight.

If some sort of federal habeas corpus regime is appropriate, what, then, should be the precise scope of habeas review? That is a difficult and complicated question. A scholarly literature has developed, especially in light of the general doctrinal restrictions on habeas in the past two decades, on what that role should be. One school would restrict habeas relief to only those cases where there is a demonstrable flaw in the state court *process*, when the defendant did not have a full and fair opportunity to present her federal constitutional defense. Substantive decisions by state judges on those issues would not be revisited, unless the process was flawed. Another school would accept the premise of the process model, but adds that review is possible if the claim is made that the adjudication resulted in the conviction of an innocent person. Still another school would permit habeas to the extent it is necessary to deter the violation of federal rights, which would require a careful balancing of the benefits of such relief and the institutional and societal costs with respect to particular rights. Finally, various schools advocate a relatively broad availability of habeas relief, though there is disagreement on *how* full the scope of review should be, and how difficult the procedural prerequisites should be for petitioners.[76]

As stated, the complexity of these arguments, combined with the recent and heretofore largely unexamined effect of the AEDPA, dissuades us from drawing definitive conclusions here on which school is "best." Indeed, any such facile conclusion is virtually impossible, since there is considerable overlap among the schools described above. And, the doctrinal and (now) statutory development of habeas review is best seen as a dynamic process, dependent on, among other things, changes in substantive criminal procedure, the perceived need for a corrective mechanism for state court adjudication, and the availability of other remedies against state actors for violations of federal rights.[77] Generally, our overall confidence in state courts causes us to lean toward the process models. But we hesitate to fully embrace that model, given that it would prevent review of substantive decisions. That sort of review should exist, at least in some narrow

(1997); Robert M. Cover, *The Uses of Jurisdictional Redundancy: Interest, Ideology, and Innovation*, 22 Wm. & Mary L. Rev. 639 (1981). Cover's model is an appealing one, but (like any other model) it does not perfectfully reflect actual practice. It seems doubtful that all state and federal judges possess the different perspectives he posits. Hart & Wechsler, *supra* note 1, at 1359 n.5. The dialogue of necessity is more like a monologue, since in individual cases the state judge cannot talk back. And, the dialogue can take place with direct review as well. For an example, *see* note 45 *supra*.

76. The enormous literature on these issues is helpfully summarized in Hart & Wechsler, *supra* note 1, at 1356–1360; and Evan Tsen Lee, *The Theories of Federal Habeas Corpus*, 72 Wash. U. L. Q. 151 (1994).

77. These points are carefully developed in Barry Friedman, *Habeas and Hubris*, 45 Vand. L. Rev. 797 (1992), Ann Woolhandler, *Demodeling Habeas*, 45 Stan. L. Rev. 575 (1993); Joseph L. Hoffman & Lauren K. Robel, *Federal Court Supervision of State Criminal Justice Administration*, 543 Annals Am. Acad. Pol. & Soc. Sci. 154 (Jan. 1996).

circumstances. There are, inevitably it seems, certain types of criminal cases in state courts that call for a limited federal presence via habeas. A generation ago it may have been involving African-American defendants in Southern courts. Today, it may be death penalty litigation. Tomorrow, it may be something else entirely. If we are to have federal habeas corpus, the due process model is an excellent place to start. In many instances, it is probably a good place to finish. But current habeas review, constricted though it is said to be, probably as a practical matter falls somewhere in the middle of the spectrum of models we summarized above. We are not convinced that the current regime, though it has no guiding and consistent principle of justification, has been such a failure that it should be discarded.[78]

* * *

We have looked at three problems in the justice system where judicial federalism plays a leading role. In each of these problems we recognized shortcomings of the state systems, but in none did we find sufficient justification for criticizing the system of judicial federalism.

Judicial federalism, contrary to an oft-cited opinion, is not a handmaiden to racial prejudice. The problem of race is four centuries old in America and is not the product of a power-sharing arrangement. Although the sickness of racism

---

78. Judge Richard Posner agrees with virtually all of our reasons that habeas corpus review, should it exist at all, should be narrow, but he, like us, is unclear on how "narrow" it should be. Richard A. Posner, The Federal Courts: Challenge and Reform 297–299 (1996). Jordon Steiker has recently sketched out several reforms which, we think, are largely consistent with our process-oriented vision of habeas. Concerned with what he calls the "procedural fetishism" of recent habeas doctrine, and the arguably inefficient and burdensome process of direct, state post-conviction, and federal habeas review, he argues that some of the procedures can be streamlined or eliminated. For example, he argues, state death-row inmates could be permitted to go directly to federal appellate courts after exhaustion of direct review in state courts. Part of this proposal would involve federal district judges determining (in a particular case) whether constitutionally adequate fact-finding took place. His proposals would accelerate review of death penalty cases, which have garnered particular attention by conservative critics of the current habeas regime. Jordon Steiker, *Restructuring Post-Conviction Review of Federal Constitutional Claims Raised by State Prisoners: Confronting the New Face of Excessive Proceduralism*, 1998 U. Chi. Legal Forum 315. Somewhat similar proposals were earlier advanced in Daniel J. Meador, *Straightening Out Federal Review of State Criminal Cases*, 44 Ohio St. L. J. 273 (1983).

Another spin on these sort of proposals would permit a federal decision-maker (e.g., a federal district judge, or a three-judge district court, or the U.S. Department of Justice) to certify that a particular state's history and procedures are constitutionally adequate enough, so that habeas petitions from that state can enjoy (from the state's perspective) only a modest process-oriented review. The AEDPA, in a similar fashion, provides certain restrictions on granting habeas relief in death penalty cases when, and only when, the state has established a mechanism for the provision of competent counsel in state post-conviction proceedings. 28 U.S.C. §§ 2261–2266. Federal judges determine if the state has met these requirements. E.g., Calderon v. Ashmus, 523 U.S. 740 (1998) (federal district judge should determine states' compliance in habeas proceeding itself).

implicates federal constitutional rights belonging to all Americans, which need to be vigorously enforced by the federal government, its manifestations are diverse and local. We must ultimately look there for its cure.

The death penalty as well is a local and regional phenomenon. Those who oppose its use recognize that the states can serve as examples to each other in this regard. States that do not impose the death penalty can serve as examples of abolition for states that do have capital punishment statutes on the books, though admittedly that process has appeared to work in the reverse in the past two decades. Meanwhile, no one federal solution is likely to be forthcoming. Tragically, the gas chambers and gurneys of the state prisons are truly laboratories in our federal judicial system.

Finally, the right of habeas corpus remains an important part of the common law landscape. It serves the same purpose it did hundreds of years ago in restraining the hand of the government in its dealings with its people. The fact that it is not successful in overturning the decisions of state courts to any great degree, we believe is strong evidence of the existence of a fair and impartial state judicial system in general.

7

Judicial Federalism: Power, Ideology, and Community

Up to this point we have been making the case for the necessity, equality, and competence of the state judicial systems as part of a "harmonious and consistent whole"[1] with the federal system. In this, the concluding chapter, we first review the positions and evidence adduced so far, we seek then to analyze them in the context of a nation of states, where legal matters are often intense and ubiquitous, and then turn to a discussion of the ideological dimensions of the argument. We conclude by looking at the entire case for judicial federalism in the context of effective public policy decisions.

THE PLACE OF RIGHTS IN AMERICAN JUDICIAL FEDERALISM

We do not think the structure and function of judicial federalism is an inherent threat to individual liberties. However, we recognize that one of the premises upon which that belief is based is controversial. We speak of the premise that rights can vary from place to place, a proposition we find no more alarming or threatening than the statement that rights can vary from time to time, in other words that rights evolve.

In our analysis, not every right is applied, or should be applied, at a sufficiently high level of generality to require it to be observed and enforced in exactly the same way, everywhere, simultaneously. Even the most important of civil liberties, the right to speak freely, may have different applications and manifestations in different jurisdictions. The federal courts have recognized this in the area of obscenity by allowing different community standards as to the definition of obscenity, and therefore different rights to publish in different communities.[2] Of course if one were to argue, as did the late justices Douglas and Black, that the

1. The Federalist No. 82 (Alexander Hamilton).
2. Miller v. California, 413 U.S. 15 (1973).

right to speak and publish was absolute, then these variations would not be permissible. But once some limitation on speech is allowed, whether it be obscenity, or libel, or slander, or even advertising, then it makes sense that varying communities and/or governments may want to apply those limitations according to a variable schedule.[3]

Similar arguments can be made for the rights of litigants in civil cases such as the rules for recovery of damages in cases of torts or contracts. Certainly the rights of parents or children may differ as may the substance of criminal law (if not much of the procedure due to the federalization of same during much of the 1960s). In other words, wherever there has not been developed a clear and unmistakable national consensus, an American right, if you will, then there is no urgent need for uniformity throughout the jurisdictions on the practical disposition of rights claims.

One does not have to look far for examples of these broad national consensus. At long last, and despite Supreme Court betrayal, legislative gridlock, and executive passivity for four generations, there is a clear and unmistakable national consensus that one may not be legally kept apart in public life because of race. Separation by race inherently violates the meaning of equal protection of the law. For any state judicial system to experiment with some form of separation would surely be met with something close to universal condemnation. On the other hand, the Supreme Court's pursuance of a color blind society obviously hampers state and local quests for remedial procedures under affirmative action plans.[4] Whatever one thinks of affirmative action, there may be many different circumstances throughout the land that would benefit from experimentation and local judicial scrutiny. So, there may be a national consensus on the ideal, but the details are yet to be filled in.

This is not to say that national solutions to rights on a federation are unneeded. As we have described elsewhere in this volume, economic analysis of federalism suggests that each state can optimally define its own rights, especially when there is little chance of interstate spillovers (externalities), and when people have relative freedom to enter and exit different jurisdictions.[5] However, this paradigm did not work well for combating racial discrimination in schools. There was little action

---

3. The position of justices Douglas and Black on obscenity is found in their dissenting opinion in Roth v. United States, 354 U.S. 476 (1957). Some variations in libel law among the states were permitted by Gertz v. Robert Welch, Inc., 418 U.S. 323 (1974).

4. See, e.g., Richmond v. J.A. Croson Co., 488 U.S. 469, 522–527 (1989) (Scalia, J., concurring) (extended discussion about evils of state and local government in promoting affirmative action). For another perspective on this point, see Daniel P. Tokaji & Mark D. Rosenbaum, *Promoting Equality by Protecting Local Power: A Neo-Federalist Challenge to State Affirmative Action Bars*, 10 Stan. L. & Pol'y Rev. 129 (1999).

5. A helpful summary of this general approach (though not focusing on rights as such) is William W. Bratton & Joseph A. McCahery, *The New Economics of Jurisdictional Competition: Devolutionary Federalism in a Second-Best World*, 86 Geo. L. J. 201 (1997). For a discussion of such an economic analysis that does focus on rights, see David L. Shapiro, Federalism: A Dialogue 94–96 (1995).

in the states until the federal government acted via the U.S. Supreme Court's decision in *Brown v. Board of Education*[6] in 1954. Perhaps the conditions for a robust competitive federalism in this regard have not always obtained in the past. And perhaps on particularly contentious and perhaps unique issues, norms can only be changed through federal action.

Finally, states create rights. Before there was an Americans with Disabilities Act in 1990, many states had adopted measures to secure opportunities for people with disabilities to participate fully in society.[7] In the eyes of many, these measures

---

6. 347 U.S. 483 (1954). It is worth noting, however, that one of the four cases consolidated under the *Brown* decision came from a *state* court, the Supreme Court of Delaware, which held for the plaintiffs. Gebhart v. Belton, 91 A.2d 137 (Del. 1952), *aff'd*, 347 U.S. 483 (1954). The cases from the other states (Kansas, South Carolina, and Virginia) were litigated in federal courts, and those found for the defendants, and thus were reversed by the Supreme Court. The author of the lower court decision in Delaware, which also held for the plaintiff, Belton v. Gebhart, 87 A.2d 862 (Del. Ct. Chancery 1952), was Chancellor Collins J. Seitz, who would later serve on the U.S. Court of Appeals for the Third Circuit.

As David Shapiro has suggested, perhaps even *Brown* itself is not truly the paradigmatic example of state hostility to federal rights, as is commonly thought:

> the ultimate collapse of state-imposed segregation in the South and the emergence of black citizens as a social and political force that has surely transformed that region of the country "was not simply a consequence of superior federal strength in a contest with a number of recalcitrant states." Rather, it "marked a major change in the attitudes of the dominant groups in those states," and an upsetting of established customs that would have been far harder to accomplish simply by the issuance of decrees from a centralized source. The existence of diffused power, in other words, may have prolonged the struggle, but it has also contributed to the durability of the ultimate outcome—a durability that can only be further strengthened as black Americans begin to play a major role (as they surely have) in state and local institutions. Federalism, in other words, has served both to impede and ultimately to promote the progress on this front.

Shapiro, *supra* note 5, at 105 (footnotes omitted) (quoting Daniel J. Elazar, American Federalism: A View From the States 13–14 (3d ed. 1984)).

7. Stephen L. Percy, *ADA, Disability Rights, and Evolving Regulatory Federalism*, 23 Publius: The Journal of Federalism 87, 91 (Fall 1993). There is some dispute over the record of the states, prior to the passage of the ADA, with regard to the rights of persons covered by the act. The debate is being played out, appropriately enough, in the context of judicial federalism. The Eleventh Amendment to the U.S. Constitution has been interpreted to prevent a plaintiff from suing a state (as opposed to a political subdivision, or a state official) in federal court. Congress can abrogate this immunity by legislating under its power through Section 5 of the Fourteenth Amendment. Seminole Tribe of Florida v. Florida, 517 U.S. 44 (1996). However, there apparently must be some evidence that states have not been protecting rights before Congress may properly exercise its Section 5 power to "enforce" the Fourteenth Amendment. City of Boerne v. Flores, 521 U.S. 507 (1997); Florida Prepaid Postsecondary Ed. Exp. Bd. v. College Savings Bank, 119 S.Ct. 2199 (1999). The ADA was passed under Section 5, and the legislative history of the act is replete with examples (though many are quite old) of state governments discriminating against persons with disabilities. The scope and strength of that evidence is subject to varying interpretations, and may eventually be addressed (in the context of Eleventh Amendment abrogation) by the

did not go far enough. But more importantly, it appeared an easier task to convince one federal legislature than to work in fifty different statehouses. Much the same story can be written concerning equal rights for women, the protection of children, and the protection of the environment. Federal action took place after at least some state initiatives on point. The states, for example, over the last several years have become leaders in the fight to create enhanced protections for personal privacy, using provisions of the various state constitutions, and depending on the culture of the particular states involved.[8] The fact that some, if not many, of the rights created by the states eventually become national norms should not, perversely, be used as an argument against differential rights throughout the country.

Considering the judicial systems as a whole, we believe it is demeaning and inaccurate to assert a lack of adequate talent in the state and local judicial arena. The same pool of legal talent is available to fill the positions of trust in the state and local systems as is available to the federal system. Most federal judges and prosecutors are from the communities in which they serve, or are at least close by, and whatever gaps in education and training that once existed are certainly now narrowed. There was a time, we recognize, when some state and local judicial officers were woefully unprepared, and even unable, to exercise the judicial function. But the standardization of legal education and the increased educational requirements for state and local judicial officers has vastly improved that picture.[9]

Of course the question remains, educational standards aside, is there any reason that we should expect inequity from the state and local courts? Of primary concern to many is the possibility of what is sometimes called the majoritarian pressures on elected judges. We dealt with this at some length in chapter 3. But it remains to say this much: the majority, by definition, is neither the lunatic fringe nor is it powerful special interest groups. Too many times in making the majoritarian critique of the state and local systems, examples are used that do not reflect the will of the majority in the states. The racist campaign to impeach Earl Warren (a federal officer with life tenure) has even been used to show the danger of majoritarian pressure.[10] Yet there is no evidence that there ever was any widespread sentiment in the country to take action against the chief justice. Similarly, the campaign to

---

Supreme Court. The issues are reviewed in S. Elizabeth Wilborn Malloy, *Whose Federalism?*, 32 Ind. L. Rev. 45 (1998).

8. Timothy O. Lenz, *"Rights Talk" About Privacy in State Courts*, 60 Alb. L. Rev. 1613 (1997).

9. James G. Apple, *Judicial Education Changes Direction*, State-Federal Judicial Observer 4 (March 1994).

10. Actually, the impeachment movement against Earl Warren was largely a Southern phenomenon. Various resolutions were introduced in Congress without effect. The impeachment sentiment against Justice William O. Douglas had a broader base and was fueled by charges of immorality as much as by decisions he had rendered. See Ed Cray, Chief Justice: A Biography of Earl Warren (1997).

remove Justice Rose Bird in California was highly partisan (i.e., narrow), and the product of major interest groups who wanted her out and who spent huge sums of money to accomplish their task.[11]

But Justice Bird was not ultimately removed because of the unpopularity of her opinions with the general public. Nor is there any evidence that she changed her opinions for fear of being removed. The point being that the basic flaws in the electoral system are not to be laid at the doorstep of the judicial system. There is little systemic evidence that the election of judges is compromising the fairness or inventiveness of the state and local systems.

There are some dangers lurking here. Recent studies have shown that the amount of money spent by state judicial candidates is increasing dramatically, and this is leading to an increase in the size of contributions being made to these campaigns by interested parties.[12] Even if nothing is expected from these contributions, an admittedly unlikely situation, the appearance of impropriety is unmistakable. Without an ability to limit these contributions, or reduce the cost of running for the court, the danger to the system will persist. But we insist that most of the reservations about an elected judiciary are overdrawn, and they actually reflect a culture that traditionally has been suspicious of the general population when it comes to courts and rights.[13]

Unless there are earth-shaking constitutional changes in our future, the overwhelming majority of law work in the nation will remain with the state and local judicial systems. We are still a nation of delegated federal powers and reserved state powers. As the recent *Lopez* case illustrates, the Supreme Court will likely continue to see that this structure is rigorously guarded.[14] Yet, depending on how one measures it, probably 90 to 95 percent of the law work in the nation takes place in the state judicial systems.[15]

This does not mean that there are not immense pressures put on the state systems because of federal actions and interests. This is not something new. As Harold Laski pointed out many years ago, the states are simply not equipped to

---

11. John H. Culver & John T. Wold, *Rose Bird and the Politics of Judicial Accountability in California*, 70 Judicature 81, 81–89 (1986). See also chapter 6 at note 49.

12. See chapter 3 at note 40.

13. For a provocative and entertaining summary of antipopulist and populist rhetoric, *see* Richard D. Parker, Here the People Rule 114 (1994) for a working definition of populism: "For what is behind populism *is* the idea of political liberty: liberty to be shared among all, not simply by the 'better' people; liberty whose realization demands exercise and requires energy; liberty to shape, then reshape, society." (Emphasis in original.)

14. United States v. Lopez, 514 U.S. 549 (1995) (ruling provision of Gun Free School Zones Act of 1990 beyond Congressional authority under the Commerce Clause). For discussions of the *Lopez* decision, see David B. Kopel & Glenn H. Reynolds, *Taking Federalism Seriously: Lopez and the Partial Birth Abortion Ban Act*, 30 Conn. L. Rev. 59 (1998); Steven G. Calabresi, *A Government of Limited and Enumerated Powers: In Defense of United States v. Lopez*, 94 Mich. L. Rev. 752 (1995).

15. See Brian J. Ostrom & Neal B. Kauder, Examining the Work of the State Courts (1993); chapter 4 at note 3.

deal with global forces the way that the federal government is. In today's terms that means that states are clearly less able to negotiate with multinational corporations, or position themselves in a global economy. But this ought not have a major impact on the judicial systems. On them, some of the pressures are not determined by global forces but rather by conscious, and we believe ill-thought out, policy decisions at the national level. Premier among all of them is the misbegotten federal War on Drugs.[16] This failed national policy has done more harm to the state judicial systems than all other federal actions combined. It has led to a distortion of resources, a corruption of the legal profession (and much of the police), and a surrender of initiative on the part of the state. Some states are actually spending more on prisons than on colleges.[17] The pattern of incarceration of nonviolent drug offenders is a fiscal time bomb for the states. In response to federal policy, some jurisdictions are exiling state drug cases to the federal government, sending cases that are plainly in the jurisdiction of the state to the federal courts for adjudication and sentencing.

The argument on which the national drug policy is based is the same one that all major federal policies are based: the idea that the narcotics problem is an international problem and therefore needs the resources of the federal judicial system to deal with it. Clearly, much of the criminal activity in narcotics involves the transportation of contraband among the several states. But most often, the people who are transporting the drugs are not international nor even national criminals. They are hired help who are basically committing a crime against a *state*. There are some signs that the population of some states are beginning to wonder whether they should not reclaim their jurisdiction over this crime. Some politicians who have made a high profile of accepting the federal model of drug control have suffered electoral disappointments, while other states have begun to experiment with a softer attitude on drugs.[18]

---

16. See Dirk Chase Eldredge, Ending the War on Drugs: A Solution for America, a Conservative Republican Calls for an End to Prohibition (1998).

17. "An analysis of New York state budgets showed the state has increased spending on prisons in the last decade by nearly as much as it has decreased spending on higher education." Liz Leyden, *Study Contrasts N.Y. Prison, Education Priorities*, Washington Post, Nov. 30, 1998. *See generally* Timothy Egan, *The War on Crack Retreats, Still Taking Prisoners*, N.Y. Times, Feb. 28, 1999, at A1.

18. Perhaps the best illustration is the rather surprising loss of antidrug crusader Dan Lungren in the California Gubernatorial race in 1998. *See* Mark Z. Barabak, *California and the West; Lungren Is Left Pondering What Might Have Been*, Los Angeles Times, Dec. 28, 1998, p. 3. For a call for moderation on the subject by Republicans see Scott Holleran, *Who Stands Up for Individual Rights Today? Not Republicans*, Arizona Republic, Nov. 30, 1998, p. B5. Several states approved ballot measures in November 1998 that permit the medical use of marijuana for certain patients. The measures in Alaska, Arizona, Oregon, and Washington State could take effect quickly. Those in Nevada, Colorado, and the District of Columbia face legal and administrative delays. The federal government still regards marijuana as illegal.

Two other areas where states are beginning to exercise legal initiative are the issues of domestic relations and assisted suicide. In the first area we have the example of the state courts of Hawaii exploring the legitimation of the unions of gay men and of lesbians on equal terms with heterosexual unions. In the second we have several states considering and adopting laws facilitating the ability of a person to end his or her life when he or she no longer wishes to suffer through a debilitating illness. In neither of these cases would a national standard be appropriate or justifiable.[19] Yet in both there was pressure from the national government to conform to one; the Defense of Marriage Act passed by Congress and famously signed late at night by President Clinton during the 1996 presidential election, and the interference of the federal Drug Enforcement Agency with those states that seek to facilitate drug-assisted suicide. Clearly this over reaching by the federal government is not based on any worry about abuse of liberty by states.

As we point out in chapter 6 and elsewhere, it is important to stay ever mindful of the many injustices that occur in our state judicial system. For example, states sometimes imprison innocent people for long periods of time.[20] It is of little comfort that these injustices were eventually exposed. And the judges and juries who may have been complicit or at least negligent in these cases are part of the state judicial systems. There is also evidence to support the claim that in the most serious of all criminal cases at the state level the representation afforded to defendants on trial for their lives is also sorely inadequate.[21] We cannot overlook these, and other, failures. But we also recognize that the vast majority of failures is due not so much to a lack of principles, or rectitude, as it is to a lack of resources and information. By allocating more resources, and encouraging more, not less, popular involvement in the state and local judicial systems, fewer miscarriages of justice will take place. Simply put, the people of the states are not the problem, they are the solution.

---

19. For an argument drawn from economic analysis that the states should determine marriage validity without federal interference, given the lack of externalities and the mobility of persons seeking to be married, see Michael E. Solimine, *Competitive Federalism and Interstate Recognition of Marriage*, 32 Creighton L. Rev. 83 (1998). For an argument supporting on federalism grounds the Supreme Court's decision in Washington v. Glucksberg, 521 U.S. 702 (1997), in refraining from imposing a national solution in right-to-die cases, see Michael C. Dorf, *The Supreme Court, 1997 Term—Foreward: The Limits of Socratic Deliberation*, 112 Harv. L. Rev. 4, 62–65 (1998). See also *Glucksberg*, 521 U.S. at 735 (pointing out that holding "permits this debate to continue" presumably meaning within and amongst states).

20. Alex Rodriguez, *Freed from Death Row; Wrongfully Convicted Speak Against Capital Punishment*, Chicago Sun-Times, Nov. 15, 1998, p. 15. Cf. Paul G. Cassel, *The Guilty and the "Innocent": An Examination of Alleged Cases of Wrongful Conviction From False Confessions*, 22 Harv. J. L. & Pub. Pol'y 523 (1999).

21. Chapter 6 at notes 2 & 47.

We are a litigious people, and if the writings of De Tocqueville are any guide, we always have been.[22] On the one hand this has caused some consternation, perhaps deservedly so, as critics claim there has been a "death of common sense" in our country.[23] We have far more attorneys than any other society and the airwaves are filled with representations (and severe misrepresentations) of outrageous verdicts in civil cases. As in every issue, legal or otherwise, there is an alternative view. Litigiousness is also a belief that every person deserves justice, a day in court. It is a reflection of the faith of the American people in the rule of law. Contingency fees of millions, now in some tobacco suits fractional billions of dollars, may be the price to be paid in the disciplining of large global corporate entities for misbehavior that is not criminalized. Thus the calls for tort reform on the national level are supported by major corporations but opposed by trial lawyers who personally stand to benefit from the continuation of the contingency fee structure.[24]

This is an area, one could argue, that should be left entirely to the state judicial systems, not only to experiment with different types of changes in the tort laws and fee structures but to keep the decision from being made where national and international corporate interests can outbid consumers and victims for the attention of policy-makers. It also encourages experimentation with a variety of alternative dispute resolution mechanisms, experimentation that might be truncated by the adoption of national judicial standards.[25]

JUDICIAL FEDERALISM AND IDEOLOGY

Whenever arguments of this kind are made, inevitably questions of ideology are raised. In fact, in the area of federalism generally, it is often assumed, it seems, that all arguments are merely masks for some underlying ideological agenda. But we believe that arguments in support of judicial federalism can be, if not value free, then certainly ideologically neutral. We believe with Professor Gary Jacobsohn that to question the motives of a partisan in the federalism debate is wrong because it

22. Alexis De Tocqueville, Democracy in America 289–290 (Phillips Bradley ed., 1945).

23. See Phillip K. Howard, The Death of Common Sense: How Law Is Suffocating America (1994).

24. On the magnitude of the fees to be paid in the tobacco settlement, see Barry Meier, *The Spoils of Tobacco Wars; Big Settlement Puts Many Lawyers in the Path of a Windfall*, New York Times, Dec. 22, 1998, p. C1.

25. The argument against a national solution to tort reform is advanced in Robert L. Rabin, *Federalism and the Tort System*, 50 Rutgers L. Rev. 1 (1997). For other views, see Thomas A. Eaton & Susette M. Talarico, *Testing Two Assumptions About Federalism and Tort Reform*, 14 Yale L. & Pol'y Rev. 371 (1996) (discussing whether state control over products liability creates a race to the bottom); Victor E. Schwartz & Mark A. Behrens, *Federal Product Liability Reform in 1997: History and Public Policy Support Its Enactment Now*, 64 Tenn. L. Rev. 595 (1997) (arguing in favor of a national solution based on need for uniformity and consequences of interstate movement in goods).

assumes the very ground in dispute.[26] In fact we think that the interests of persons with a broad variety of ideological positions are served by a robust judicial federalism.

However, it is difficult to address ideology directly in that labels that were once relatively easy to interpret have become almost meaningless. A large part of the problem is due to a decline in the quality of political rhetoric. Sound-bite-driven phrases such as "the L word," "tax-and-spend liberal," "Christian conservative," "ultra-conservative," abound. Rather than try to parse terms, we will state for the purposes of discussion that liberalism, libertarianism, conservatism, and communitarianism are four of the major ideological perspectives that may have an interest in the state of judicial federalism.

For liberals, inalienable natural rights are limited only by social contract, the goal of which is to achieve the just society. The plain statement of this, the founding ideology of the United States is the Declaration of Independence. Of course the declaration was aspirational; it silently countenanced slavery without explanation. According to one author, the contract was dramatically and finally amended by Lincoln at Gettysburg, when he brought the equality of all Americans, white and nonwhite, into the ideological mix.[27]

In our estimation, the performance of judicial federalism is in no way illiberal, that is, it does not run counter to either the fundamental principles of the declaration nor does it violate the norm of equality as articulated by the Gettysburg Address and legitimated in the Fourteenth Amendment. If anything, the Fourteenth Amendment is a liberal document that assumes not only the existence of state judicial systems but their ability, ultimately, to enforce the fundamental principles of liberalism. (To be sure, the amendment of course advances weighty nationalist principles as well.)

For libertarians, the highest goal of society is to maximize individual freedom. The natural rights of human beings are seen as a goal, not something to be limited by "collective wisdom."[28] Libertarians include a broad range of historical and contemporary figures including Thomas Paine and Friedrich Hayek as well as Milton Friedman and Richard Epstein. Many libertarians believe that the term liberalism has been hijacked from them by statist and socialists, and that they are the true classic liberals. The maximization of individual freedom implies a variety of approaches to law and public policy. Certainly the hallmark of libertarianism, as Milton Friedman so eloquently puts it is "the freedom to choose."[29] Choice implies alternatives and judicial federalism, as we interpret it means the preservation of choices as long as possible. There are no guarantees under judicial federalism that libertarians will win all, or even most, of the public policy battles.

---

26. See Gary Jeffrey Jacobsohn, *Contemporary Constitutional Theory, Federalism, and the Protection of Rights* in Federalism and Rights 29–73 (Ellis Katz & G. Alan Tarr eds., 1996) (hereinafter Federalism and Rights).

27. Gary Wills, Lincoln at Gettysburg: Words that Remade America ch. 4 (1992).

28. See The Libertarian Reader xiv (David Boaz ed., 1997).

29. Milton & Rose Friedman, Free to Choose (1980).

But they certainly are not disadvantaged by it.

Conservatives are more interested in preserving "traditional" values, which is why they are most often, perhaps inappropriately, identified with religion. Even though a plurality, or even majority, of public officials might prefer the label conservative to liberal, the conservative has the hardest time finding a place at the ideological table. It may be that the traditional values of the United States tend to be the values of liberalism, and it is therefore not clear to many what is to be conserved.[30]

The key value that judicial federalism preserves is probably the one that is easiest for conservatives to articulate: subsidiarity, or local control. To the extent that state judicial systems are free to adopt innovative approaches or to fashion remedies that reflect local or regional differences, both the size and scope of judicial government is restrained, without contradicting the great national, liberal, principles of individual rights.

Finally, in recent years there has come into prominence an outpouring of writing from a large group of thinkers who are plainly reacting to the extreme individualism of the classical liberals and libertarians. This group of people has come to be known as the communitarians, and are exemplified by writers such as Amitai Etzioni, Robert Bellah, and Phillip Selznick. Just as every other ideology does, the communitarians claim that their roots go back as far as ancient history, but as an organized movement in the United States, communitarianism does not date from much before 1980. The "new communitarianism" is concerned with the balance between "social forces and the person, between community and autonomy, between the common good and liberty, between individual rights and responsibilities"[31]

And, if there were one key word that describes the operation of judicial federalism, it is indeed balance. Judicial federalism offers the opportunity to weigh alternatives over time, to keep an open mind, to reflect, and to develop visions of the good, without rushing headlong into the straitjacket of national policy. Thus, we suppose that the communitarians would have little to fear from a system of judicial federalism. Although the government is by no means the community, independent local governments, especially judges and courts, can foster community.

---

30. Typical of the difficulty of differentiating American conservatism from other ideologies, or for that matter from "world conservatism," is the rhetoric and behavior of two of the century's most celebrated putative conservative figures, Barry Goldwater and Ronald Reagan. In his call for radical deregulation of the economy and support of individual rights, Goldwater appeared to be very libertarian. Ronald Reagan was called a fiscal and social conservative, but did precious little to promote the agenda of so-called religious conservatives. For an excellent summary of the difficulties of separating the threads of liberalism and conservatism in American, especially as it relates to the characterizing of judges and justices, see J.M. Balkin, *Federalism and the Conservative Ideology*, 19 Urban Lawyer 459, 460–463 (1987).

31. The Essential Communitarian Reader (Amatai Etzioni ed., 1998).

THE FUNCTIONAL INEVITABILITY OF JUDICIAL FEDERALISM

Our point is not that judicial federalism is all things to all people. Rather that it is not a Trojan horse for states rights conservatism, or for libertarianism, or any "ism" for that matter. It is simply sound way of structurally dividing judicial power. Many commentators on federalism generally ask the very direct question: Why states? Are not states accidents? Have they not become so similar and alike that there is no functional reason for maintaining them? Are they not in Edward Rubin's and Malcolm Feeley's dismissive description "mere swatches of prairie"?[32] But the relative similarity of the states compared with 200 or 100 years ago is an argument for diversity of laws, not an argument against it. For it may show a tendency toward homogenization that could ultimately be dangerous. The states certainly do not mask ethnic or religious differences to any great degree and with few exceptions. But once again, this is cause for celebration, not dismay. The states are a convenience and an opportunity now, in addition to a given.

We turn the question of national culture on its head. We ask, if there is a national political/legal culture. Surely then one state must resemble that culture most closely. Which state would that be? Iowa? New York? Maine? California? Certainly not Alaska or Hawaii, you would answer. What about South Dakota? A fruitless, search no doubt. If we picked Nevada as our winner, a citizen of Utah would be shocked to learn about his neighbors' good fortune. But if there is no state that closely resembles this national culture, how can it be said to even exist?

But aren't there tremendous differences within states? And aren't most judicial behaviors registered at the local level? Why not just decentralize decision-making under one legal regimen? The answer is we believe that the independence of the states within the union to make legal decisions in its assigned, that is reserved, jurisdiction is the only thing that preserves the ability of local governments to act independently. Putting it another way, if we didn't have states, we would have to invent them. Luckily that is not the case. States are organic creatures, boundaries asleep in the bosom of history, not drawn with a straightedge on a map in a colonial sitting room. There was no intention on the part of the framers to create an undifferentiated mass to use the words of Chief Justice John Marshall in *McCulloch v. Maryland*.[33]

But the division of judicial power between states and federal government does not assume a passive judiciary. State courts make law and they make policy. They sometimes serve as legal entrepreneurs and as teachers to the community. Just as governors of states aspire for independent action and power, so too state courts

32. Edward L. Rubin & Malcolm Feeley, *Federalism: Some Notes on a National Neurosis*, 41 UCLA L. Rev. 903, 944 (1994).

33. "To suppose that the mere proposition of this fundamental law threw the American people into one aggregate mass, would be to assume what the instrument itself does not profess to establish. It is, therefore, a compact between the States, and all the powers which are not expressly relinquished by it, are reserved to the States." McCulloch v. Maryland, 17 U.S. 316, 381 (1819).

must see themselves as independent actors where, as Whitman says, speaking of the great city "[o]utside authority always enters after the precedence of inside authority."[34]

Some who read this will see in it the echoes of the discredited doctrine of states rights. The term itself has become identified with the racist resistance to equality for all citizens. The American States Rights party is an avowedly racist organization. But states have never had rights, the term referred to the right of an identifiable majority within the geographical boundaries of a state to behave differently from the norms of the national majority.

Courts and judges are the agents of the states, and therefore the agents of particular states with discrete identities. Although the United States has in general a much more mobile population than most of the world, state identities have not been wiped out. It is arrogant in the extreme to believe that the only way that majorities within these states could wish to have a destiny, culture, or way of life different from that dictated by some presumed national majority would be through trampling on the rights of the minority. There is more than ample evidence that exactly the opposite has often taken place.

It may be asked whether our argument is fundamentally empirical or normative. Of course all knowledge is empirical since we have only that knowledge we gain through observation using our senses. Our vision for America depends on, literally, our vision of America. But what is generally referred to as strict empiricism is hardly possible in this area of inquiry. The application of the social sciences to law and politics is helpful but limited.[35]

What norms, then, do we think that judicial federalism underpins? What is our vision? First, to the extent judicial federalism promotes heterogeneity and variety, it promotes the norm of personal liberty. We believe that it is clear that greater threats to liberty occur from homogeneity than from heterogeneity; from consolidation rather than from dispersal. Given the history of federal agencies such as the DEA, CIA, IRS, and FBI, the consolidation of power in the federal government is alarming to us. We also freely admit that our perspective on this question is from that of the white (for now) majority, and that had we lived the life of an African-American or Latino citizen, our opinion on this subject might be different.[36]

Secondly, we believe that the norm of diversity is important in itself. Although it is instrumental, in that it can lead to comparison, and thus foster experimentation in policy, at bottom it is reflective of the nature of the American nation, a nation of immigrants, pioneers, and inventors.

Finally, there is the norm of community. Governments certainly are not, nor can they create, communities. But they can encourage or discourage them. We believe

---

34. Walt Whitman, *Song of the Broadax* in Selected Poems 49 (Dover ed. 1991).

35. See generally John Monahan & Laurens Walker, Social Science in Law (4th ed. 1998).

36. See Derrick Bell, Faces at the Bottom of the Well: The Permanence of Racism (1992).

the sharing and dispersal of judicial power, including the opportunity for meaningful face-to-face encounters with local judicial officials that it affords, is more likely to foster community than a consolidation of judicial system with all officials facing east.

Any system that enhances some norms must, perforce, diminish others. It is clear that the norm of efficiency is not fostered by the dispersal of judicial power. It is certainly cheaper and easier to understand and deal with a court system with one set of rules, decisions, and rights than it is to deal with fifty-one. To the extent that judicial federalism allows or even encourages differential treatment of issues and people, the norm of uniformity is also clearly a victim. But we must be careful to point out that uniformity neither guarantees nor prevents equitable treatment. To confuse uniformity with justice in all cases would be a grave error.

FUTURE GOALS AND RESEARCH

Empirically then, what more would we like to know to test our vision against the facts on the ground? Certainly we should know much more about the operations of state courts, especially state trial courts. Although much has been written about these institutions over the last several years, they still tend to be the neglected stepchild of the field. And, what has been done tends usually to focus on their shortcomings.

We should want to know more about systems of monitoring state systems for the protection of rights and adherence to correct procedures, especially in areas where weaknesses have already been noted. Knowledge of processes for recruiting able and industrious judges, and knowledge of recruitment systems from around the world is of paramount concern if the promise of state judicial systems is to be realized.[37] The behavior of juries, including jury nullification, needs more study. Finally, still more light must be shed on injustices in the state system such as corrupt prosecutions and lack of adequate counsel.

It is hard to write a moderate book; it is very fatiguing to play defense for the whole game. We wish we didn't have to answer so many questions with "Yes, but." So much easier to write with great passion when great danger lurks. But, as

---

37. There has been relatively little comparative work done on federalism and rights in general, or judicial federalism in particular. On the former, see Koen Lenderts, *Federalism and Rights in the European Community*, and Irwin Cotler, *Can the Center Hold? Federalism and Rights in Canada*, in Federalism and Rights, *supra* note 26, at 139, 173; Vicki C. Jackson, *Ambivalent Resistance and Comparative Constitutionalism: Opening Up the Conversation on "Proportionality," Rights and Federalism*, 1 U. Pa. J. Const. L. 583 (1999). On the latter, it appears that the lack of literature may be due to the fact that many countries with some sort of federal structure, e.g., Germany, South Africa, do not have a comparable equivalent to American state courts. For one exploration of the topic, see Leslie F. Goldstein, *State Resistance to Authority in Federal Unions: The Early United States (1790–1860) and the European Community (1958–1994)*, 11 Studies Am. Pol. Dev. 149 (1997).

of this date, we can find no one who advocates doing away with judicial federalism and imposing one, unified system of justice on the entire nation. Thus, the logical question is what would we wish for the future and how might we get it?

Three very important things come to mind. The first is a greater appreciation of the value of local courts in the creation of the just society. The second is moving the argument on judicial federalism away from name-calling, blaming and "antinostalgia" to a debate over the best practical applications of the principles of justice. And the third goal might be a general increase in the reliance on local institutions of government for progressive measures: "going local,"[38] as one author has termed it.

And what policy measures might be recommended to get us from here to there, to arrive at a stronger judicial federalism? There are seven specific proposals that we would leave with the reader.

1. Increase the resources and freedom of action available to the state and local judicial systems. This includes a general (albeit rebuttable) presumption against national solutions to many things, be it tort reform or criminal or civil procedure.
2. Increase efforts to recruit a bench that is more reflective of the society at large, and of the evolving legal profession in particular, who would be selected and retained by merit criteria combined with some version of retention elections.
3. Reduce dramatically the federalization of the substantive criminal law.
4. Encourage state initiatives in creating and protecting state guaranteed rights and continuing to protect federally guaranteed rights.
5. Support improved training of state court personnel, prosecutors, and police.
6. Encourage more first-hand observation of court operations rather than relying solely on the valuable but limited perspective of things like Court TV.
7. Increase the professionalization of the ever-more competitive bar.

A unitary system of justice makes sense if there is truly one, national community of Americans, living in the same juridical culture. Many who criticize judicial federalism say that its adherents are nostalgic for days gone by. But there is even less evidence that we were ever one nation in the sense that the critics imply. There are times when Americans seem as one, in times of tragedy such as the assassination of John Kennedy, or in times of exultation like Neil Armstrong's stepping onto the moon. But more often staying together is a struggle, a struggle managed very well in the United States compared to other large and diverse nations around the world.

---

38. Michael H. Schuman, Going Local: Self-Reliant Communities in a Global Age (1998). Schuman makes the case that devolution is not just a conservative tool but can further the progressive agenda as well.

Bibliography

BOOKS, ARTICLES AND OTHER SOURCES

Abrahamson, Shirley S. *Criminal Law and State Constitutions: The Emergence of State Constitutional Law*, 63 Texas Law Review 1141 (1985).

Adler, Matthew D. & Seth F. Kreimer. *The New Etiquette of Federalism: New York, Printz, and Yeskey*, 1998 Supreme Court Review 71.

Allbritain, Nicole C. Comment, *One Step Closer to Merit-Based Judicial Selection: Ohio's New Limitations on Judicial Campaign Contributions and Expenditures*, 64 University of Cincinnati Law Review 1323 (1996).

Allen, Barbara. *Alexis de Tocqueville on the Covenantal Tradition of American Federal Democracy*, 28 Publius: The Journal of Federalism 1 (Spring 1998).

Alschuler, Albert W. *Racial Quotas and the Jury*, 44 Duke Law Journal 704 (1995).

Althouse, Ann. *Theoretical and Constitutional Issues: Enforcing Federalism After United States v. Lopez*, 38 Arizona Law Review 793 (1996).

Althouse, Ann. *Federal Jurisdiction and the Enforcement of Federal Rights: Can Congress Bring Back the Warren Era?*, 20 Law and Social Inquiry 1067 (1995).

Althouse, Ann. *How to Build a Separate Sphere: Federal Courts and State Power*, 100 Harvard Law Review 1485 (1987).

Amar, Akhil Reed. *The Bill of Rights as a Constitution*, 100 Yale Law Journal 1131 (1991).

Amar, Akhil Reed. *The Bill of Rights and the Fourteenth Amendment*, 101 Yale Law Journal 1193 (1992).

Amar, Akhil Reed. *Five Views of Federalism: "Converse-1983" in Context*, 47 Vanderbilt Law Review 1229 (1994).

Apple, James G. *Judicial Education Changes Direction*, State-Federal Judicial Observer 4 (March 1994).

Arendt, Hanna, The Origins of Totalitarianism (2d ed. 1958).

Ashenfelter, Orley, Theodore Eisenberg & Stewart J. Schwab. *Politics and the Judiciary: The Influence of Judicial Background on Case Outcomes*, 24 Journal of Legal Studies 257 (1995).

Baker, Lynn A. *The Revival of States' Rights: A Progress Report and a Proposal*, 22 Harvard Journal of Law & Public Policy 95 (1998).

Baker, Thomas E. *A Catalogue of Judicial Federalism in the United States*, 46 South Carolina Law Review 835 (1995).

Baker, Thomas E. *The Ambiguous Independent and Adequate State Ground in Criminal Cases: Federalism Along a Mobius Strip*, 19 Georgia Law Review 799 (1985).

Baldus, David, George Woodworth, David Zuckerman, Neil Alan Weiner & Barbara Broffitt. *Racial Discrimination and the Death Penalty in the Post-Furman Era: An Empirical and Legal Overview, With Recent Findings From Philadelphia*, 83 Cornell Law Review 1638 (1998).

Balkin, J.M. *Learning Nothing and Forgetting Nothing: Richard Epstein and the Takings Clause*, 18 Urban Lawyer 707 (1986).

Balkin, J.M. *Federalism and the Conservative Ideology*, 19 Urban Lawyer 459 (1987).

Barabak, Mark Z. *California and the West; Lungren Is Left Pondering What Might Have Been*, Los Angeles Times, December 28, 1998.

Barclay, Scott. *Posner's Economic Model and the Decision to Appeal*, 19 Justice System Journal 77 (1997).

Barone, Michael. Our Country: The Shaping of America From Roosevelt to Reagan (1990).

Bator, Paul M. *The State Courts and Federal Constitutional Litigation*, 22 William and Mary Law Review 605 (1981).

Bator, Paul M. *Finality in Criminal Law and Federal Habeas Corpus for State Prisoners*, 76 Harvard Law Review 441 (1963).

Baum, Lawrence. *Electing Judges* in Contemplating Courts (Lee Epstein ed., 1995).

Beatty, Jerry K. *State Court Evasion of United States Supreme Court Mandates During the Last Decade of the Warren Court*, 6 Valparaiso University Law Review 260 (1972).

Beavers, Staci L. & Jeffrey S. Walz. *Modeling Judicial Federalism: Predictors of State Court Protections of Defendants' Rights Under State Constitutions, 1969–1989*, 28 Publius: The Journal of Federalism 43 (Spring 1998).

Belknap, Michal R. Federal Law and Southern Order: Racial Violence and Constitutional Conflict in the Post-Brown South (1987).

Bell, Derrick. Faces at the Bottom of the Well: The Permanence of Racism (1992).

Bilionis, Louis D. *Legitimating Death*, 91 Michigan Law Review 1643 (1993).

Blalock, Jr., Herbert M. Social Statistics (rev. 2d ed. 1979).

Blume, John & Theodore Eisenberg. *Judicial Politics, Death Penalty Appeals, and Case Selection: An Empirical Study*, 72 Southern California Law Review 465 (1999).

Blumstein, James F. *Federalism and Civil Rights*, 47 Vanderbilt Law Review 1251 (1994).

Bolick, Clint. Grassroots Tyranny (1993).

Boot, Max. Out of Order: Arrogance, Corruption and Incompetence on the Bench (1998).

Boswell, J. The Life of Samuel Johnson, L.L.D. (Macmillan, 1908).

Bork, Robert H. The Tempting of America: The Political Seduction of the Law (1990).

Brace, Paul R. & Melinda Gann Hall. *The Interplay of Preferences, Case Facts, Context, and Rules in the Politics of Judicial Choice*, 59 Journal of Politics 1206 (1997).

Brace, Paul & Melinda Gann Hall. *Studying Courts Comparatively: The View From the American States*, 48 Political Research Quarterly 5 (1995).

Bradley, Craig M. *Are State Courts Enforcing the Fourth Amendment? A Preliminary Study*, 77 Georgetown Law Journal 251 (1988).

Bratton, William W. & Joseph A. McCahery. *The New Economics of Jurisdictional Competition: Devolutionary Federalism in a Second-Best World*, 86 Georgetown Law Journal 201 (1997).

Braveman, Daan. Protecting Constitutional Freedoms: A Role for Federal Courts (1989).

Brennan, Jr., William J. *The Bill of Rights and the States: The Revival of State Constitutions as Guardians of Individual Rights*, 61 New York University Law Review 535 (1986).

Brennan, Jr., William J. *State Constitutions and the Protection of Individual Rights*, 90 Harvard Law Review 489 (1977).

Briffault, Richard. *"What About the 'Ism'?": Normative and Formal Concerns in Contemporary Federalism*, 47 Vanderbilt Law Review 1303 (1994).

Bright, Stephen B. *Can Judicial Independence Be Attained in the South? Overcoming History, Elections, and Misperceptions About the Role of the Judiciary*, 14 Georgia State University Law Review 817 (1998).

Bright, Stephen B. *Is Fairness Irrelevant? The Evisceration of Federal Habeas Corpus Review and Limits on the Ability of State Courts to Protect Fundamental Rights*, 54 Washington and Lee Law Review 1 (1997).

Bright, Stephen B. *Counsel for the Poor: The Death Sentence Not for the Worst Crime but for the Worst Lawyer*, 103 Yale Law Journal 1835 (1994).

Bright, Stephen B. & Patrick J. Kennan. *Judges and the Politics of Death: Deciding Between the Bill of Rights and the Next Election in Capital Cases*, 75 Boston University Law Review 759 (1995).

Brinkley, Alan, Nelson W. Polsby & Kathleen M. Sullivan. New Federalist Papers: Essays in Defense of the Constitution (1997).

Brisbin Jr., Richard A. & John C. Kilwein. *U.S. Supreme Court Review of State High Court Decisions*, 78 Judicature 33 (1994).

Brod, Craig B. Note, *The Securities Exchange Act and the Rule of Exclusive Federal Jurisdiction*, 89 Yale Law Journal 95 (1979).

Broek, Jacobus ten. Equal Justice Under Law (1965).

Brown, Dorothy A. *The Invisibility Factor: The Limits of Public Choice Theory and Public Institutions*, 74 Washington University Law Quarterly 179 (1996).

Brown, George D. *Binding Advisory Opinions: A Federal Courts Perspective on the State School Finance Decisions*, 35 Boston College Law Review 543 (1994).

Brown, George D. *The Ideologies of Forum Shopping—Why Doesn't a Conservative Court Protect Defendants?*, 71 North Carolina Law Review 649 (1993).

Buchanan, James M. *Federalism and Individual Sovereignty*, 15 Cato Journal 259 (1995).

Butler, Paul. *Affirmative Action and the Criminal Law*, 68 University of Colorado Law Review 841 (1997).

Butler, Paul. *Racially Based Jury Nullification: Black Power in the Criminal Justice System*, 105 Yale Law Journal 677 (1995).

Calabresi, Steven G. *A Government of Limited and Enumerated Powers: In Defense of United States v. Lopez*, 94 Michigan Law Review 752 (1995).

Caldeira, Gregory A. *On the Reputation of State Supreme Courts*, 5 Political Behavior 83 (1983).

Caminker, Evan H. *Printz, State Sovereignty, and the Limits of Formalism*, 1997 Supreme Court Review 199.

Caminker, Evan H. *Precedent and Prediction: The Forward-Looking Aspects of Inferior Court Decisionmaking*, 73 Texas Law Review 1 (1994).

Canon, Bradley C. *Courts and Policy: Compliance, Implementation and Innovation* in The American Courts: Critical Assessment (John B. Gates & Charles A. Johnson eds., 1991).

Carp, Robert A. & Ronald Stidham. Judicial Process in America (4th ed. 1998).

Carrington, Paul D. *Judicial Independence and Democratic Accountability in Highest State Courts*, 61 Law and Contemporary Problems 79 (Summer 1998).

Cassel, Paul G. *The Guilty and the "Innocent": An Examination of Alleged Cases of Wrongful Conviction from False Confessions*, 22 Harvard Journal of Law and Public Policy 523 (1999).

Chapman, Ronald V. Comment, *Judicial Roulette: Alternatives to Single-Member Districts as a Legal and Political Solution to Voting-Rights Challenges to At-Large Judicial Elections*, 48 Southern Methodist University Law Review 457 (1995).

Chemerinsky, Erwin. *Formalism and Functionalism in Federalism Analysis*, 13 Georgia State University Law Review 959 (1997).

Chemerinsky, Erwin. *The Values of Federalism*, 47 Florida Law Review 499 (1995).

Chemerinsky, Erwin. *Parity Reconsidered: Defining a Role for the Federal Judiciary*, 36 UCLA Law Review 233 (1988).

Chemerinsky, Erwin & Larry Kramer. *Defining the Role of the Federal Courts*, 1990 Brigham Young University Law Review 67.

Choper, Jesse H. Judicial Review and the National Political Process (1980).

Clermont, Kevin M. & Theodore Eisenberg. *Do Case Outcomes Really Reveal Anything About the Legal System? Win Rates and Removal Jurisdiction*, 83 Cornell Law Review 581 (1998).

Clermont, Kevin M. & Theodore Eisenberg. *Exorcising the Evil of Forum-Shopping*, 80 Cornell Law Review 1507 (1995).

Clinton, Robert N., Richard A. Matasar & Michael G. Collins. Federal Courts: Theory and Practice (1996).

Clymer, Adam. *Federalism Awaites '00*, N.Y. Times, June 25, 1999, at A20.

Clymer, Steven D. *Unequal Justice: The Federalization of Criminal Law*, 70 Southern California Law Review 643 (1997).

Cogan, Neil H. *Moses and Modernism*, 92 Michigan Law Review 1347 (1993).

Collins, Michael G. *Article III Cases, State Court Duties, and the Madisonian Compromise*, 1995 Wisconsin Law Review 39.

Collins, Ronald K.L. *Reliance on State Constitutions—The Montana Disaster*, 63 Texas Law Review 1095 (1985).

Commager, Henry Steele. *Judicial Review and Democracy*, 19 Virginia Quarterly Review 417 (1943).

Cook, Jr., Julian Abele. *Dream Makers: Black Judges on Justice*, 94 Michigan Law Review 1479 (1996).

Cover, Robert M. *The Uses of Jurisdictional Redundancy: Interest, Ideology, and Innovation*, 22 William and Mary Law Review 639 (1981).

Cover, Robert M. & T. Alexander Aleinikoff. *Dialectical Federalism: Habeas Corpus and the Court*, 86 Yale Law Journal 1035 (1997).

Cray, Ed. Chief Justice: A Biography of Earl Warren (1997).

Croley, Steven P. *The Majoritarian Difficulty: Elective Judiciaries and the Rule of Law*, 62 University of Chicago Law Review 689 (1995).

Cross, Frank B. *Political Science and the New Legal Realism: A Case of Unfortunate Interdisciplinary Ignorance*, 92 Northwestern University Law Review 251 (1997).

Crowe, Nancy. The Impact of Gender and Race on the U.S. Courts of Appeals: 1981–1996 (Ph.D. dissertation, University of Chicago, 1999).

Culver, John H. & John T. Wold. *Rose Bird and the Politics of Judicial Accountability in California*, 70 Judicature 81 (1986).

Curriden, Mark. *The Changing Faces of Southern Courts*, 79 American Bar Association Journal 68 (June 1993).

Dalton, Harlon L. *Judicial Federalism and Individual Rights*, 31 Trial 56 (October 1995).

Developments in the Law—Section 1983 and Federalism, 90 Harvard Law Review 1133 (1977).

Diehm, James W. *New Federalism and Constitutional Criminal Procedure: Are We Repeating the Mistakes of the Past?*, 55 Maryland Law Review 223 (1996).

DiIulio, Jr., John J. *White Lies About Black Crime*, 118 Public Interest 30 (Winter 1995).

DiIulio, Jr., John J. *The Question of Black Crime*, 117 Public Interest 3 (Fall 1994).

Dolbeare, Kenneth M. Trial Courts in Urban Politics: State Court Policy Impact and Functions in a Local Political System (1967).

Dorf, Michel C. *Instrumental and Non-Instrumental Federalism*, 28 Rutgers Law Journal 825 (1998).

Dorf, Michael C. *The Supreme Court, 1997 Term—Foreward: The Limits of Socratic Deliberation*, 112 Harvard Law Review 4 (1998).

Dreyfuss, Rochelle Copper. *Specialized Adjudication*, 1990 Brigham Young University Law Review 377.

Dubois, Paul. From Ballot to Bench: Judicial Elections and the Quest for Accountability (1980).

Ducat, Craig, Mikel Wyckoff & Victor Flango. *State Judges and Federal Constitutional Rights*, 4 Research Law and Policy Studies 155 (1995).

Dworkin, Ronald. Taking Rights Seriously (1977).

Eaton, Thomas A. & Susette M. Talarico. *Testing Two Assumptions About Federalism and Tort Reform*, 14 Yale Law and Policy Review 371 (1996).

Edwards, Lee. *In Our Hearts We Know Goldwater Was Right*, Kansas City Star, June 4, 1998.

Egan, Timothy. *The War on Crack Retreats, Still Taking Prisoners*, New York Times, February 28, 1999, at A1.

Eisenberg, Theodore. *Litigation Models and Trial Outcomes in Civil Rights and Prisoner Cases*, 77 Georgetown Law Journal 1567 (1989).

Eisenberg, Theodore & Stewart Schwab. *What Shapes Perceptions of the Federal Court System?*, 56 University of Chicago Law Review 501 (1989).

Eisenberg, Theodore & Stewart Schwab. *The Reality of Constitutional Tort Litigation*, 72 Cornell Law Review 641 (1987).

Elazar, Daniel J. American Federalism: A View From the States (3d ed. 1984).

Eldredge, Dirk Chase. Ending the War on Drugs: A Solution for America, a Conservative Republican Calls for an End to Prohibition (1998).

Elson, Alex. *The Case for an In-Depth Study of the American Law Institute*, 23 Law and Social Inquiry 625 (1998).

Ely, John Hart. Democracy and Distrust: A Theory of Judicial Review (1980).

Emmert, Craig F. & Carol Ann Traut. *State Supreme Court Courts, State Constitutions, and Judicial Policymaking*, 16 Justice System Journal 16 (1992).

Epstein, Richard. Private Property and the Power of Eminent Domain (1985).

Eskridge, Jr., William E. & Philip P. Frickey. *Quasi-Constitutional Law: Clear Statement Rules as Constitutional Lawmaking*, 45 Vanderbilt Law Review 593 (1992).

Esler, Michael. *State Supreme Court Commitment to State Law*, 78 Judicature 25 (1994).

The Essential Communitarian Reader (Amatai Etzioni ed., 1998).

Estreicher, Samuel & John E. Sexton. Redefining the Supreme Court's Role: A Theory of Managing the Federal Judicial Process (1986).

Fallon, Jr., Richard H. *Reflections on the Hart and Wechsler Paradigm*, 47 Vanderbilt Law Review 953 (1994).

Fallon, Jr., Richard H. *Individual Rights and the Powers of Government*, 27 Georgia Law Review 343 (1993).

Fallon, Richard H., Daniel J. Meltzer & David L. Shapiro. Hart & Wechsler's The Federal Courts and the Federal System (4th ed. 1996).

Fallon, Jr., Richard H. *The Ideologies of Federal Courts Law*, 74 Virginia Law Review 1141 (1988).

Farole, Jr., Donald J. Interest Groups and Judicial Federalism: Organizational Litigation in State Judiciaries (1998).

Faust, Richard, Tina J. Rubenstein & Larry W. Yackle. *The Great Writ in Action: Empirical Light on the Federal Habeas Corpus Debate*, 18 New York University Review of Law and Social Change 649 (1991).

Federalism and Rights (Ellis Katz & G. Alan Tarr eds., 1996).

Fink, Howard & Mark V. Tushnet. Federal Jurisdiction: Policy and Practice (1984).

Fink, Howard P., et al. Federal Courts in the 21st Century: Cases and Materials (1996).

Fischel, William A. *How Serrano Caused Proposition 13*, 12 Journal of Law and Politics 607 (1996).

Flango, Victor E. *Litigant Choice Between State and Federal Courts*, 46 South Carolina Law Review 961 (1995).

Flango, Victor E. Habeas Corpus in State and Federal Courts (National Center for State Courts 1994).

Flango, Victor E. *How Would the Abolition of Federal Diversity Jurisdiction Affect State Courts?*, 74 Judicature 35 (1990).

Flemming, Gregory N. et al. *An Integrated Model of Privacy Decision Making in State Supreme Courts*, 26 American Politics Quarterly 35 (1998).

Franklin, Marc. *Suing Media for Libel: A Litigation Study*, 1981 American Bar Foundation Research Journal 795.

Franklin, Marc. *Winners and Losers and Why: A Study of Defamation Litigation*, 1980 American Bar Foundation Research Journal 455.

Friedman, Barry. *Valuing Federalism*, 82 Minnesota Law Review 317 (1997).

Friedman, Barry. Book Review, 12 Constitutional Commentary 441 (1995).

Friedman, Barry. *Pas De Deux: The Supreme Court and the Habeas Courts*, 66 Southern California Law Review 2467 (1993).

Friedman, Barry. *Trumping Rights*, 27 Georgia Law Review 435 (1993).

Friedman, Barry. *Habeas and Hubris*, 45 Vanderbilt Law Review 797 (1992).

Friedman, Lawrence W., et al. *State Supreme Courts: A Century of Style and Citation*, 33 Stanford Law Review 773 (1981).

Friendly, Henry J. *Is Innocence Irrelevant? Collateral Attacks on Criminal Judgments*, 38 University of Chicago Law Review 142 (1970).

Friesen, Jennifer. *State Courts as Sources of Constitutional Law: How to Become Independently Wealthy*, 72 Notre Dame Law Review 1065 (1997).

Friesen, Jennifer. State Constitutional Law: Litigating Individual Rights, Claims and Defenses (2d ed. 1996).

Fyfe, James J. *Enforcement Workshop*, 19 Criminal Law Bulletin 253 (1983).

Galanter, Marc. *The Faces of Mistrust: The Image of Lawyers in Public Opinion, Jokes, and Political Discourse*, 66 University of Cincinnati Law Review 805 (1998).

Galanter, Marc. *Why the "Hayes" Come Out Ahead: Speculations on the Limits of Legal Change*, 9 Law and Society Review 95 (1974).

Galie, Peter J. *State Courts and Economic Rights*, 496 Annals of the American Academy of Political and Social Science 76 (March 1988).

Gardner, James A. *Southern Character, Confederate Nationalism, and the Interpretation of State Constitutions: A Case Study in Constitutional Argument*, 76 Texas Law Review 1219 (1998).

Gardner, James A. *The "State-as-Laboratories" Metaphor in State Constitutional Law*, 30 Valparaiso University Law Review 475 (1996).

Gardner, James A. *What Is a State Constitution?*, 24 Rutgers Law Journal 1025 (1993).

Gardner, James A. *The Failed Discourse of State Constitutionalism*, 90 Michigan Law Review 761 (1992).

Garrett, Elizabeth. *Enhancing the Political Safeguards of Federalism? The Unfunded Mandates Reform Act of 1995*, 45 University of Kansas Law Review 1113 (1997).

George, Tracey E. & Lee Epstein. *On the Nature of Supreme Court Decision Making*, 86 American Political Science Review 323 (1992).

Gibson, James L. *Pluralism, Federalism and the Protection of Civil Liberties*, 43 Western Political Quarterly 511 (1991).

Ginsburg, Ruth Bader. *Speaking in a Judicial Voice*, 67 New York University Law Review 1185 (1992).

Glendon, Mary Ann. Rights Talk: The Impoverishment of Political Discourse (1991).

Glennon, Robert J. *The Jurisdictional Legacy of the Civil Rights Movement*, 61 Tennessee Law Review 869 (1994).

Goldstein, Leslie F. *State Resistance to Authority in Federal Unions: The Early United States (1790–1860) and the European Community (1958–1994)*, 11 Studies in American Political Development 149 (1997).

Greenberg, Reuben M. *Race, the Criminal Justice System, and Community-Oriented Policing*, 20 Harvard Journal of Law and Public Policy 397 (1997).

Greenhouse, Linda. *47% in Poll View Legal System as Unfair to Poor and Minorities*, New York Times, February 24, 1999, p. A12.

Greenhouse, Linda. *States Are Given New Legal Shield by Supreme Court*, N.Y. Times, June 24, 1999, at A1.

Gross, Samuel R. *Crime, Politics, and Race*, 20 Harvard Journal of Law and Public Policy 405 (1997).

Grossman, Joel, et al. *Measuring the Pace of Civil Litigation in Federal and State Trial Courts*, 65 Judicature 86 (1981).

Gruhl, John. *State Supreme Courts and the U.S. Supreme Court's Post—Miranda Rulings*, 72 Journal of Criminal Law and Criminology 886 (1981).

Guinier, Lani. The Tyranny of the Majority: Fundamental Fairness in Representative Democracy (1994).

Haas, Kenneth C. *The "New Federalism" and Prisoner's Rights: State Supreme Courts in Comparative Perspective*, 34 Western Political Quarterly 552 (1981).

Hajnacki, Marie & Lawrence Baum. *Choosing Judicial Candidates: How Voters Explain Their Decisions*, 75 Judicature 300 (1992).

Hall, Kermit L., William M. Wiecek, & Paul Finkleman. American Legal History (2d ed. 1996).

Hall, Kermit. The Magic Mirror: Law in American History (1989).

Hall, Melinda Gann. Competition in Judicial Elections, 1980–1995 (1998).

Hansen, Mark. *A Run for the Bench*, 84 American Bar Association Journal 68 (October 1998).

Hanson, Roger A. & Henry W.K. Daley. Federal Habeas Corpus Review: Challenging State Court Criminal Convictions (U.S. Department of Justice, Bureau of Justice Statistics 1995).

Harr, Jonathan. A Civil Action (1995).

Harriger, Katy J. *The Federalism Debate in the Transformation of Federal Habeas Corpus Law*, 27 Publius: The Journal of Federalism 1 (Summer 1997).

Hart, Jr., Henry M., & Herbert Wechsler. The Federal Courts and the Federal System (1953).

Hartnett, Edward. *Why is the Supreme Court of the United States Protecting State Judges From Popular Democracy?*, 75 Texas Law Review 907 (1997).

Hasen, Richard L. *"High Court Wrongly Elected": A Public Choice Model of Judging and Its Implications for the Voting Rights Act*, 75 North Carolina Law Review 1305 (1997).

Heinz, John P., Edward O. Lawmann, Robert L. Nelson & Ethan Michelson. *The Changing Character of Lawyers' Work: Chicago in 1975 and 1995*, 32 Law and Society Review 751 (1998).

Heise, Michael. *Equal Educational Opportunity, Hollow Victories, and the Demise of School Finance Equity Theory: An Empirical Perspective and Alternative Explanation*, 32 Georgia Law Review 543 (1998).

Heise, Michael. *State Constitutional Litigation, Educational Finance, and Legal Impact: An Empirical Analysis*, 63 University of Cincinnati Law Review 1735 (1995).

Hellman, Arthur D. *Light on a Darkling Plain: Intercircuit Conflicts in the Perspective of Time and Experience*, 1998 Supreme Court Review 247.

Hellman, Arthur D. *The Shrunken Docket of the Rehnquist Court*, 1996 Supreme Court Review 403.

Hellman, Arthur D. *By Precedent Unbound: The Nature and Extent of Unresolved Intercircuit Conflict*, 56 University of Pittsburgh Law Review 693 (1995).

Hellman, Arthur D. *Case Selection in the Burger Court: A Preliminary Inquiry*, 60 Notre Dame Law Review 947 (1985).

Herman, Susan N. *Why Parity Matters*, 71 Boston University Law Review 651 (1991).

Herman, Susan N. *Beyond Parity: Section 1983 and the State Courts*, 54 Brooklyn Law Review 1057 (1989).

Hershkoff, Helen. *Positive Rights and State Constitutions: The Limits of Federal Rationality Review*, 112 Harvard Law Review 1131 (1999).

Higginbotham, A. Leon. *Seeking Pluralism in Judicial Systems: The American Experience and the South African Challenge*, 42 Duke Law Journal 1028 (1993).

Hills, Jr., Roderick M. *The Political Economy of Cooperative Federalism: Why State Autonomy Makes Sense and "Dual Sovereignty" Doesn't*, 96 Michigan Law Review 813 (1998).

Hoffman, Joseph L. & Lauren K. Robel. *Federal Court Supervision of State Criminal Justice Administration*, 543 Annals of the American Academy of Political and Social Science 154 (January 1996).

Holleran, Scott. *Who Stands Up for Individual Rights Today? Not Republicans*, Arizona Republic, Nov. 30, 1998.

Hollon, Greg. Note, *After the Federalization Binge: A Civil Liberties Hangover*, 31 Harvard Civil Rights-Civil Liberties Law Review 499 (1996).

Holmes, Malcolm D., et al. *Judges' Ethnicity and Minority Sentencing: Evidence Concerning Hispanics*, 74 Social Science Quarterly 496 (1993).

Holmes, Steven A. *Right to Abortion Quietly Advances in State Courts*, New York Times, December 6, 1998.

Hovenkamp, Herbert. *The Indirect-Purchaser Rule and Cost-Plus Sales*, 103 Harvard Law Review 1717 (1990).

Hovenkamp, Herbert. *State Antitrust in the Federal Scheme*, 58 Indiana Law Journal 375 (1983).

Howard, Phillip K. The Death of Common Sense: How Law Is Suffocating America (1994).

Hyman, Harold M. *Federalism: Legal Fiction and Historical Artifact?*, 1987 Brigham Young University Law Review 905.

Ifill, Sherrilyn A. *Judging the Judges: Racial Diversity, Impartiality and Representation on State Trial Courts*, 39 Boston College Law Review 95 (1997).

Ignatieff, Michael. The Needs of Strangers (1984).

Inman, Robert P. & Daniel L. Rubinfeld. *Rethinking Federalism*, 11 Journal of Economic Perspectives 43 (1997).

Israel, Jerold. *Federal Criminal Procedure as a Model for the States*, 543 Annals of the American Academy of Political and Social Science 130 (January 1996).

Jackson, Vicki C. *Coeur D'Alene, Federal Courts and the Supremacy of Federal Law: The Competing Paradigms of Chief Justices Marshall and Rehnquist*, 15 Constitutional Commentary 301 (1998).

Jackson, Vicki C. *Federalism and the Uses and Limits of Law: Printz and Principle?*, 111 Harvard Law Review 2180 (1998).

Jackson, Vicki C. *Ambivalent Resistance and Comparative Constitutionalism: Opening Up the Conversation on "Proportionality," Rights and Federalism*, 1 University of Pennsylvania Journal of Constitutional Law 583 (1999).

Jackson, Vicki C. *Printz and Testa: The Infrastructure of Federal Supremacy*, 32 Indiana Law Review 111 (1998).

Jacobsohn, Gary Jeffrey. *Contemporary Constitutional Theory, Federalism, and the Protection of Rights* in Federalism and Rights (Ellis Katz & G. Alan Tarr eds., 1996).

Jaffe, Louis. English and American Judges as Lawmakers (1969).

Jeffries, Jr., John C. *In Praise of the Eleventh Amendment and Section 1983*, 84 Va. L. Rev. 47 (1998).

Joseph, Gregory P., & Stephen A. Saltzburg. Evidence in America: The Federal Rules in the States (Supp. 1992).

Judicial Conference of the United States, Committee on Long Range Planning, Long Range Plan for the Federal Courts (1995).

Kahn, Paul W. *State Constitutionalism and the Problems of Fairness*, 30 Valparaiso University Law Review 459 (1996).

Kahn, Paul W. *Interpretation and Authority in State Constitutionalism*, 106 Harvard Law Review 1147 (1993).

Kaplan, John, Jerome H. Skolnick & Malcolm Feeley. Criminal Justice (5th ed. 1991).

Karlan, Pamela S. *Race, Rights, and Remedies in Criminal Adjudication*, 96 Michigan Law Review 2001 (1998).

Kennedy, Randall. Race, Crime, and the Law (1997).

Kenny, Michael P. *RICO and Federalism: A Case for Concurrent Jurisdiction*, 31 Boston College Law Review 239 (1990).

Kilwein, John C., & Richard A. Brisbin, Jr. *Policy Convergence in a Federal Judicial System: The Application of Intensified Scrutiny Doctrines by State Supreme Courts*, 41 American Journal of Political Science 122 (1997).

Kincaid, John. *Federal Democracy and Liberty*, 32 PS: Political Science & Politics 211 (1999).

Kopel, David B., & Glenn H. Reynolds. *Taking Federalism Seriously: Lopez and the Partial Birth Abortion Ban Act*, 30 Connecticut Law Review 59 (1998).

Kramer, Larry. *Understanding Federalism*, 47 Vanderbilt Law Review 1485 (1994).

Kramer, Larry. *Diversity Jurisdiction*, 1990 Brigham Young University Law Review 97.

Kramer, Paul. Waiting for Godot?—The New Judicial Federalism 1987–1992: Reality or Hoax? (September 1996).

Kritzer, Herbert. *Adjudication to Settlement: Shading in the Gray*, 70 Judicature 161 (1986).

Kritzer, Herbert, et al. *Courts and Litigation Investment: Why Do Lawyers Spend More Time on Federal Cases?*, 9 Justice System Journal 7 (1984).

Lamb, Charles. *Judicial Policy-Making and Information Flow to the Supreme Court,* 29 Vanderbilt Law Review 45 (1976).

Lassiter, Christo. *The O.J. Simpson Verdict: A Lesson in Black and White*, 1 Michigan Journal of Race and Law 69 (1996).

Latzer, Barry. *Toward the Decentralization of Criminal Procedure: State Constitutional Law and Selective Disincorporation*, 87 Journal of Criminal Law and Criminology 63 (1996).

Latzer, Barry. *The Hidden Conservatism of the State Court "Revolution,"* 74 Judicature 190 (1991).

Lauman, Edward O., & John P. Heinz. Chicago Lawyers: The Professions of the Bar (1982).

Ledewitz, Bruce. *The Role of Lower State Courts in Adopting State Law to Changed Federal Interpretations*, 67 Temple Law Review 1003 (1994).

Lee, Evan Tsen. *On the Received Wisdom in Federal Court*, 147 University of Pennsylvania Law Review 1111 (1999).

Lee, Evan Tsen. *Section 2254(d) of the New Habeas Statute: An (Opinionated) User's Manual*, 51 Vanderbilt Law Review 103 (1998).

Lee, Evan Tsen & Ashutoh Bhagwat. *The McCleskey Puzzle: Remedying Prosecutorial Discrimination Against Black Victims in Capital Sentencing*, 1998 Supreme Court Review 145.

Lee, Evan Tsen. *The Theories of Federal Habeas Corpus*, 72 Washington University Law Quarterly 151 (1994).

Legal Rights: Historical and Philosophical Perspectives (Austin Sarat & Thomas R. Kearns eds., 1996).

Lemann, Nicholas. *Justice for Blacks?*, New York Review of Books 25 (March 5, 1998).

Lenz, Timothy O. *"Rights Talk" About Privacy in State Courts*, 60 Albany Law Review 1613 (1997).

Lessig, Lawrence. *Translating Federalism: United States v. Lopez,* 1995 Supreme Court Review 125.

Leyden, Liz. *Study Contrasts N.Y. Prison, Education Priorities*, Washington Post, November 30, 1998.

The Libertarian Reader (David Boaz ed., 1997).

Liebman, James S., & William F. Ryan. *"Some Effectual Power": The Quantity and Quality of Decisionmaking That Article III and the Supremacy Clause Demand of the Federal Courts*, 98 Columbia Law Review 696 (1998).

Liebman, James S. & Randy Hertz. Federal Habeas Corpus Practice and Procedure (2 vols., 2d ed. 1994).

Liebman, James S. *More than "Slightly Retro": The Rehnquist Court's Rout of Habeas Corpus Jurisdiction in Teague v. Lane*, 18 New York University Review of Law and Social Change 537 (1991).

Lippman, Jr., Theo. *"Mr. Conservative" Was a Loser of World-Class Proportions*, The Baltimore Sun, June 2, 1998.

Loss, Louis. *The SEC Proxy Rules and State Law*, 73 Harvard Law Review 1249 (1960).

Lund, Nelson. *Federalism and Civil Liberties*, 45 Kansas Law Review 1045 (1997).

Lyles, Kevin L. The Gatekeepers: Federal District Courts in the Political Process (1997).

Maclin, Tracey. *Race and the Fourth Amendment*, 51 Vanderbilt Law Review 333 (1998).

Maggs, Gregory E. *Reducing the Costs of Statutory Ambiguity: Alternative Approaches and the Federal Courts Study Committee*, 29 Harvard Journal on Legislation 123 (1992).

Maier, Thomas. *Suicide Law: Year 1 / Few in Oregon Have Asked for Help in Dying*, Newsday, November 3, 1998.

Malloy, S. Elizabeth Wilborn. *Whose Federalism?*, 32 Indiana Law Review 45 (1998).

Maltz, Earl M. *False Prophet—Justice Brennan and the Theory of State Constitutional Law*, 15 Hastings Constitutional Law Quarterly 429 (1988).

Maltz, Earl M. *The Dark Side of State Court Activism*, 63 Texas Law Review 995 (1985).

Martin, James A., & Elizabeth A. Prescott. *The Magnitude and Sources of Delay in Ten State Appellate Courts*, 6 Justice System Journal 305 (1981).

Marvell, Thomas B. *The Rationales for Federal Question Jurisdiction: An Empirical Examination of Student Rights Litigation*, 1984 Wisconsin Law Review 1315.

Marvell, Thomas. Appellate Courts and Lawyers: Information Gathering in the Adversary System (1978).

Mash, Kenneth Mitchell. Uniformity in the Balance: An Examination of Section 1983 and Federal Jurisdiction (Ph.D. dissertation, Penn State University 1997).

Mason, Margaret P.P. Note, *Courting Reversal: The Supervisory Role of State Supreme Courts*, 87 Yale Law Journal 1191 (1978).

Matasar, Richard A. & Gregory S. Bruch. *Procedural Common Law, Federal Jurisdiction Policy, and the Abandonment of the Adequate and Independent State Grounds Doctrine*, 86 Columbia Law Review 1291 (1986).

Mather, Lynn. *Policy Making in State Trial Courts* in The American Courts: A Critical Assessment (John B. Gates & Charles A. Johnson eds., 1991).

McAdams, John C. *Racial Disparity and Death Penalty*, 61 Law and Contemporary Problems 153 (Autumn 1998).

McConkie, Pace Jefferson. *Civil Rights and Federalism Fights: Is There a "More Perfect Union" for the Heirs to the Promise of Brown*?, 1996 Brigham Young University Law Review 389.

McConnell, Grant. Private Power and American Democracy (1966).

McConnell, Michael W. *Federalism: Evaluating the Founders' Design*, 54 University of Chicago Law Review 1484 (1987).

McFadden, Patrick M. Electing Justice: The Law and Ethics of Judicial Election Campaigns (1990).

McKenzie, Richard B. *Clinton Confidential: The Best-Kept Secret of the Clinton Years Is Economic*, Reason, November 1996.

Meador, Daniel J. *Federal Law in State Supreme Courts*, 3 Constitutional Commentary 347 (1986).

Meador, Daniel J. *Straightening Out Federal Review of State Criminal Cases*, 44 Ohio State Law Journal 273 (1983).

Meier, Barry. *The Spoils of Tobacco Wars; Big Settlement Puts Many Lawyers in the Path of a Windfall*, New York Times, December 22, 1998.

Meltsner, Michael. *Southern Appellate Courts: A Dead End*, in Southern Justice (Lawrence Friedman ed., 1965).

Meltzer, Daniel J. *State Court Forfeitures of Federal Rights*, 99 Harvard Law Review 1128 (1986).

Mendoza, Martha. *Civil Rights Cases Lowest on Federal Priority List*, Cincinnati Enquirer, March 21, 1994, p. A9.

Miller, Neal. *An Empirical Study of Forum Choices in Removal Cases Under Diversity and Federal Question Jurisdiction*, 41 American University Law Review 369 (1992).

Milton & Rose Friedman. Free to Choose (1980).

Monahan, John & Laurens Walker. Social Science and the Law (4th ed. 1998).

Morrison, Nina. Note, *Curing "Constitutional Amnesia": Criminal Procedure Under State Constitutions*, 73 New York University Law Review 880 (1998)

Mosk, Stanley. *States' Rights—and Wrongs*, 72 New York University Law Review 552 (1997).

Nagel, Robert F. *The Term Limits Dissent: What Nerve*, 38 Arizona Law Review 843 (1996).

Nardulli, Peter F. *The Caseload Controversy and the Study of Criminal Courts,* 70 Journal of Criminal Law and Criminology 89 (1979).

Neuborne, Burt. *The Myth of Parity*, 90 Harvard Law Review 1105 (1977).

Neuborne, Burt. *Parity Revisited: The Uses of a Judicial Forum of Excellence*, 44 DePaul Law Review 797 (1995).

Neuborne, Burt. *Toward Procedural Parity in Constitutional Litigation*, 22 William and Mary Law Review 725 (1981).

Newman, Jon O. *Restructuring Federal Jurisdiction: Proposals to Preserve the Federal Judicial System*, 56 University of Chicago Law Review 761 (1989).

Nichol, Gene R. *Federalism, State Courts, and Section 1983*, 73 Virginia Law Review 959 (1987).

Nolan, Thomas J. *Racism in the Criminal Justice System: Problems and Suggestions*, 20 Harvard Journal of Law & Public Policy 417 (1997).

Note, *Blown Away? The Bill of Rights After Oklahoma City*, 109 Harvard Law Review 2074 (1996).

Note, *Exclusive Jurisdiction of the Federal Courts in Private Civil Actions*, 70 Harvard Law Review 509 (1957).

Note, *Forum Shopping Reconsidered*, 103 Harvard Law Review 1677 (1990).

Oakley, John B. & Arthur F. Coon. *The Federal Rules in State Courts: A Survey of State Court Systems of Civil Procedure*, 61 Washington Law Review 1367 (1986).

Oakley, John B. & Robert Thompson. *Law Clerks in Judges' Eyes: Tradition and Innovation in the Use of Legal Staff by American Judges,* 67 California Law Review 1286 (1979).

Ostrom, Brian J. & Neal B. Kauder. Examining the Work of the State Courts (1993).

Parker, Richard D. Here the People Rule (1994).

Percy, Stephen L. *ADA, Disability Rights, and Evolving Regulatory Federalism*, 23 Publius: The Journal of Federalism 87 (Fall 1993).

Perry, Michael J. *Is the Idea of Human Rights Ineliminably Religious?* in Legal Rights: Historical and Philosophical Perspective (Austin Sarat & Thomas R. Kearns eds., 1996).

Peters, Ellen A. *Capacity and Respect: A Perspective on the Historic Role of the State Courts in the Federal System*, 73 New York University Law Review 1065 (1998).

Peterson, Todd David. *Studying the Impact of Race and Ethnicity in the Federal Courts*, 64 George Washington Law Review 173 (1996).

Pinello, Daniel R. *Linking Party to Judicial Ideology in American Courts: A Meta-Analysis*, 20 Justice System Journal 219 (1999).

Polsby, Daniel D. *Recontextualizing the Context of the Death Penalty*, 44 Buffalo Law Review 527 (1996).

Posner, Richard A. Economic Analysis of Law (5th ed. 1998).

Posner, Richard A. The Federal Courts: Challenge and Reform (1996).

Priest, George & Benjamin Klein. *The Selection of Disputes for Litigation*, 13 Journal of Legal Studies 1 (1984).

Rabin, Robert L. *Federalism and the Tort System*, 50 Rutgers Law Review 1 (1997).

Rathjen, Gregory J. *Lawyers and the Appellate Choice: An Analysis of Factors Affecting the Decision to Appeal*, 6 American Politics Quarterly 387 (1978).

Reagan, President Ronald. Address to the National Conference of State Legislatures (17 Weekly Comp. Pres. Doc. 836, July 30, 1981).

Redish, Martin H. Federal Jurisdiction: Tensions in the Allocation of Judicial Power (2d ed. 1990).

Redish, Martin H. *Judicial Parity, Litigant Choice and Democratic Theory: A Comment on Federal Jurisdiction and Constitutional Rights*, 36 UCLA Law Review 329 (1988).

Redish, Martin H. & John E. Muench. *Adjudication of Federal Causes of Action in State Court*, 75 Michigan Law Review 311 (1976).

Redish, Martin H. & Steven G. Sklaver. *Federal Power to Commandeer State Courts: Implications for the Theory of Judicial Federalism*, 32 Indiana Law Review 71 (1998).

Reed, Douglas S. *Twenty-Five Years After Rodriguez: School Finance Litigation and the Impact of the New Judicial Federalism*, 32 Law and Society Review 175 (1998).

Remington, Frank J. *Post-Conviction Review—What State Trial Courts Can Do to Reduce Problems*, 72 Judicature 53 (1988).

Remington, Frank J. *State Prisoner Access to Post-Conviction Relief—A Lessening Role for Federal Courts: An Increasingly Important Role for State Courts*, 44 Ohio State Law Journal 287 (1983).

Resnik, Judith. *Rereading "The Federal Courts": Revising the Domain of Federal Courts Jurisprudence at the End of the Twentieth Century*, 47 Vanderbilt Law Review 1021 (1994).

Revesz, Richard L. *Specialized Courts and the Administrative Lawmaking System*, 138 University of Pennsylvania Law Review 1111 (1990).

Ribstein, Larry E. & Bruce H. Kobayashi. *An Economic Analysis of Uniform State Laws*, 25 Journal of Legal Studies 131 (1996).

Riker, William H. Federalism: Origin, Operation, Significance (1964).

Robinson, Paul H. An Empirical Study of Federal Habeas Corpus Review of State Court Judgments (Federal Justice Research Program, Office for Improvements in the Administration of Justice) (1979).

Rodriguez, Alex. *Freed from Death Row; Wrongfully Convicted Speak Against Capital Punishment*, Chicago Sun-Times, November 15, 1998.

Rodriguez, Daniel B. *State Constitutional Theory and Its Prospects*, 28 Northern Mexico Law Review 271 (1998).

Romans, Neil. *The Role of State Supreme Courts in Judicial Policy Making:* Escobedo, Miranda *and the Use of Judicial Impact Analysis*, 27 Western Political Quarterly 38 (1969).

Rosen, Mark. *Our Nonuniform Constitution: Geographical Variations of Constitutional Requirements in the Aid of Community*, 77 Texas Law Review 1129 (1999).

Rosenfeld, Felicia A. Note, *Fulfilling the Goals of Michigan v. Long: The State Court Reaction*, 56 Fordham Law Review 1041 (1988).

Rothman, Stanley & Stephen Powers. *Execution by Quota?*, 116 Public Interest 3 (Summer 1994).

Rothschild, Gita F. *Forum Shopping*, 24 Litigation 40 (Spring 1998).

Rovella, David E. *"Race Pervades Death Penalty,"* National Law Journal, June 8, 1998.

Rovella, David E. *State AGs Look for New Targets*, National Law Journal, January 26, 1998.

Rubin, Edward L. *The New Legal Process, the Synthesis of Discourse, and the Microanalysis of Institutions*, 109 Harvard Law Review 1393 (1996).

Rubin, Edward L. & Malcolm Feeley. *Federalism: Some Notes on a National Neurosis*, 41 UCLA Law Review 903 (1994).

Ryan, John Paul, Alan Ashman, Bruce D. Sales & Sandra Shane-DuBow. American Trial Judges: Their Work Styles and Performance (1980).

Samborn, Randall. *Habeas Corpus Statistics Reveal Caseload Is Light*, National Law Journal, October 17, 1994.

Sandel, Michael J. Democracy's Discontent (1996).

Schapiro, Robert A. *Identity and Interpretation in State Constitutional Law*, 84 Virginia Law Review 389 (1998).

Scheiber, Harry N. *Federalism and the Legal Process: Historical and Contemporary Analysis of the American System*, 14 Law and Society Review 663 (1980).

Scheuerman, Kurt E. Comment, *Rethinking Judicial Elections*, 72 Oregon Law Review 459 (1993).

Schiedegger, Kent S. *Habeas Corpus, Relitigation, and the Legislative Power*, 98 Columbia Law Review 888 (1998).

Schlag, Peter. *Rights in the Post-Modern Condition* in Legal Rights: Historical and Philosophical Perspectives (Austin Sarat & Thomas R. Kearns eds., 1996).

Schoshinski, Maura Anne. Comment, *Towards an Independent, Fair, and Competent Judiciary: An Argument for Improving Judicial Elections*, 7 Georgetown Journal of Legal Ethics 839 (1994).

Schuman, Michael H. Going Local: Self-Reliant Communities in a Global Age (1998).

Schwartz, Victor E., & Mark A. Behrens. *Federal Product Liability Reform in 1997: History and Public Policy Support Its Enactment Now*, 64 Tennessee Law Review 595 (1997).

Schwarzer, William W., & Russell R. Wheeler. On the Federalization of the Administration of Civil and Criminal Justice (Federal Judicial Center 1994).

Scuggs, Anna M., Jean-Claude Mazzola, & Mary E. Zaug. *Recent Voting Rights Act Challenges to Judicial Elections*, 79 Judicature 34 (1995).

Shapiro, David L. Federalism: A Dialogue (1995).

Shapiro, David L. *Federal Habeas Corpus: A Study in Massachusetts*, 87 Harvard Law Review 321 (1973).

Shapiro, Fred R. *The Most-Cited Law Review Articles Revisited*, 71 Chicago-Kent Law Review 751 (1996).

Sheldon, Charles H. & Linda J. Maule. Choosing Justice: The Recruitment of State and Federal Judges (1997).

Shepard, Randall T. *The Maturing Nature of State Constitution Jurisprudence*, 30 Valparaiso University Law Review 421 (1996).

Sheran, Robert J., & Barbara Isaacman. *State Cases Belong in State Courts*, 12 Creighton Law Review 1 (1978).

Siegelman, Peter & John J. Donohue III. *Studying the Iceberg From Its Tip: A Comparison of Published and Unpublished Employment Discrimination Cases*, 24 Law and Society Review 1133 (1990).

Simon, Jonathan & Jerome H. Skolnick. *Federalism: The Exclusionary Rule and the Police* in Power Divided: Essays on the Theory and Practice of Federalism (Harry N. Scheiber & Malcolm M. Feeley eds., 1989).

Sisk, Gregory C., Michael Heise & Andrew P. Morriss. *Charting the Influences on the Judicial Mind: An Empirical Study of Judicial Reasoning*, 73 New York University Law Review 1377 (1998).

Sklansky, David A. *Traffic Stops, Minority Motorists, and the Future of the Fourth Amendment*, 1997 Supreme Court Review 271.

Skolnick, Jerome H. Justice Without Trial (1964).

Smith, Christopher E. & Darwin L. Burke. *Judges' Views on Habeas Corpus: A Comparison of State and Federal Judges*, 22 Oklahoma City University Law Review 1125 (1997).

Solimine, Michael E. *Competitive Federalism and Interstate Recognition of Marriage*, 32 Creighton Law Review 83 (1998).

Solimine, Michael E. *Against Judicial Devolution*, 78 Judicature 313 (1995).

Solimine, Michael E. *Constitutional Restrictions on the Partisan Appointment of Federal and State Judges*, 61 University of Cincinnati Law Review 955 (1993).

Solimine, Michael E. *Rethinking Exclusive Federal Jurisdiction*, 52 University of Pittsburgh Law Review 383 (1991).

Solimine, Michael E., & James L. Walker. *Constitutional Litigation in Federal and State Courts: An Empirical Analysis of Judicial Parity*, 10 Hastings Constitutional Law Quarterly 213 (1983).

Solimine, Michael E., & James L. Walker. *The Supreme Court, Judicial Review, and the Public: Leadership Versus Dialogue*, 11 Constitutional Commentary 1 (1994).

Solimine, Michael E., & James L. Walker. *Federalism, Liberty and State Constitutional Law*, 23 Ohio Northern University Law Review 1457 (1997).

Solimine, Michael E., & James L. Walker. *The Next Word: Congressional Response to Supreme Court Statutory Decisions*, 65 Temple Law Review 425 (1992).

Solimine, Michael E., & James L. Walker. *State Court Protection of Federal Constitutional Rights*, 12 Harvard Journal of Law and Public Policy 127 (1989).

Solimine, Michael E., & Susan E. Wheatley. *Rethinking Feminist Judging*, 70 Indiana Law Journal 891 (1995).

Songer, Donald R., et al. *An Empirical Study of the Rational Actor Theory of Litigation*, 57 Journal of Politics 1119 (1995).

Special Project, *The Continuing Evolution of Criminal Constitutional Law in State Courts*, 47 Vanderbilt Law Review 795 (1994).

Spohn, Cassia. *The Sentencing Decisions of Black and White Judges: Expected and Unexpected Similarities*, 24 Law and Society Review 1197 (1990).

Stacy, Tom. *Does Federalism Promote Liberty?*, 5 Kansas Journal of Law and Public Policy 15 (1996).

Stacy, Tom & Kim Dayton. *The Underfederalization of Crime*, 6 Cornell Journal of Law and Public Policy 247 (1997).

Steiker, Jordon. *Restructuring Post-Conviction Review of Federal Constitutional Claims Raised by State Prisoners: Confronting the New Face of Excessive Proceduralism*, 1998 University of Chicago Legal Forum 315.

Steinglass, Steven H. Section 1983 Litigation in State Courts (2 vols., 1998 ed.).

Steinglass, Steven H. *The Emerging State Court § 1983 Action: A Procedural Review*, 38 University of Miami Law Review 381 (1984).

Stewart, Richard B. *Federalism and Rights*, 19 Georgia Law Review 917 (1985).

Stone, Christopher. *Should Trees Have Standing? Toward Legal Rights for Natural Objects*, 45 Southern California Law Review 450 (1972).

Stumpf, Harry P. American Judicial Politics (2d ed. 1998).

Stuntz, William J. *The Uneasy Relationship Between Criminal Procedure and Criminal Justice*, 107 Yale Law Journal 1 (1997).

Sunstein, Cass. Book Review, New Republic 33 (September 2, 1991).

Sunstein, Cass. *Interpreting Statutes in the Regulatory State*, 103 Harvard Law Review 405 (1989).

Symposium, *The ABA's Proposal Moratorium on the Death Penalty*, 61 Law & Contemp. Prob. 1 (Autumn 1998).

Symposium, *The New Judicial Federalism: A New Generation*, 30 Valparaiso University Law Review 421 (1996).

Symposium, *State Constitutional Commentary*, 59 Albany Law Review 1539 (1996).

Symposium, *The Emergence of State Constitutional Law*, 63 Texas Law Review 959 (1985).

Synder, Brad. Note, *Disparate Impact on Death Row: M.L.B. and the Indigent's Right to Counsel at Capital State Postconviction Hearings*, 107 Yale Law Journal 2211 (1998).

Tarr, G. Alan. Understanding State Constitutions (1998).

Tarr, G. Alan. *State Constitutional Politics: An Historical Perspective* in Constitutional Politics in the States: Contemporary Controversies and Historical Patterns (G. Alan Tarr ed., 1996).

Tarr, G. Alan & Mary Cornelia Aldis Porter. State Supreme Courts in State and Nation (1988).

Taslitz, Andrew E. *An African-American Sense of Fact: The O.J. Trial and Black Judges on Justice*, 7 Boston University Public Interest Law Journal 219 (1998).

Thompson, Charles & John B. Oakley. *From Information to Opinion in Appellate Courts*, 1986 Arizona State Law Journal 1 (1986).

Tobias, Carl W. *Rule 11 and Civil Rights Litigation*, 37 Buffalo Law Review 485 (1988–89).

Tocqueville, Alexis De. Democracy in America (Phillips Bradley ed., 1945).

Tokaji, Daniel P., & Mark D. Rosenbaum. *Promoting Equality by Protecting Local Power: A Neo-Federalist Challenge to State Affirmative Action Bars*, 10 Stanford Law and Policy Review 129 (1999).

Tonry, Michael. Malign Neglect: Race, Crime and Punishment in America (1995).

Tribe, Laurence. American Constitutional Law (2d ed. 1988).

Trotter, Jr., Joseph A. & Caroline S. Cooper. *State Trial Court Delay: Efforts at Reform,* 31 American University Law Review 213 (1982).

Tushnet, Mark. *What Then Is the American?*, 38 Arizona Law Review 873 (1996).

Tushnet, Mark. *The Politics of Constitutional Law* in The Politics of Law (David Kairys ed., rev. ed. 1990).

Tushnet, Mark. *An Essay on Rights*, 62 Texas Law Review 1394 (1984).

Tushnet, Mark, & Larry W. Yackle. *Symbolic Statutes and Real Laws: The Pathologies of the Antiterrorism and Effective Death Penalty Act and the Prison Litigation Reform Act*, 47 Duke Law Journal 1 (1997).

Uelman, Gerald F. *Crocodiles in the Bathtub: Maintaining the Independence of State Supreme Courts in an Era of Judicial Politicization*, 72 Notre Dame Law Review 1133 (1997).

Ulen, Thomas S. *Economic and Public-Choice Forces in Federalism*, 6 George Mason Law Review 921 (1998).

U.S. Department of Justice, Office of Legal Policy, Federal Habeas Corpus: Review of State Judgments (1988).

Vazquez, Carlos Manuel. *What Is Eleventh Amendment Immunity?*, 106 Yale L.J. 1683 (1997).

Vines, Kenneth. *Southern State Supreme Courts and Race Relations,* 18 Western Political Quarterly 5 (1965).

Waldron, Jeremy. *Rights and Needs: The Myth of Disjunction* in Legal Rights: Historical and Philosophical Perspectives (Austin Sarat & Thomas R. Kearns eds., 1996).

Walker, Jack L. *The Diffusion of Innovations Among the American States*, 63 American Political Science Review 880 (1969).

Waltenburg, Eric N. & Bill Swinford. Litigating Federalism: The States Before the U.S. Supreme Court (1999).

Wechsler, Herbert. *The Political Safeguards of Federalism: The Role of the States in the Composition and Selection of the National Government*, 54 Columbia Law Review 543 (1954).

Weinberg, Louise. *Fear and Federalism*, 23 Ohio Northern University Law Review 1295 (1997).

Weinberg, Louise. Federal Courts: Cases and Comments on Judicial Federalism and Judicial Power (1994).

Weinberg, Louise. *The New Judicial Federalism*, 29 Stanford Law Review 1191 (1977).

Weiner, Scott D. Note, *Popular Justice: State Judicial Elections and Procedural Due Process*, 31 Harvard Civil Rights-Civil Liberties Law Review 187 (1996).

Weisberg, Robert. *Deregulating Death*, 1983 Supreme Court Review 305.

Wells, Michael. *Naked Politics, Federal Courts Law, and the Canon of Acceptable Arguments*, 47 Emory Law Journal 89 (1998).

Wells, Michael. *Who's Afraid of Henry Hart?*, 14 Constitutional Commentary 175 (1997).

Wenzel, James P., Shaun Bowler & David J. Lanoue. *Legislating From the State Bench: A Comparative Analysis of Judicial Activism*, 25 American Politics Quarterly 363 (1997).

Wheeler, Stanton, et al. *Do the "Haves" Come Out Ahead? Winning and Losing in State Supreme Courts*, 1870–1970, 21 Law and Society Review 403 (1987).

Whitman, Walt. *Song of the Broadax* in Selected Poems (Dover ed. 1991).

Williams, Robert F. State Constitutional Law: Cases and Materials (2d ed. 1993).

Wills, Gary. Lincoln at Gettysburg: Words that Remade America (1992).

Woolhandler, Ann. *Demodeling Habeas*, 45 Stanford Law Review 575 (1993).

Wortley, Scott, John Hagan, & Ross Macmillan. *Just Des(s)erts? The Racial Polarization of Criminal Injustice*, 31 Law and Society Review 637 (1997).

Yackle, Larry W. Federal Courts (1999).

Yackle, Larry W. *A Primer on the New Habeas Corpus Statute*, 44 Buffalo Law Review 381 (1996).

Yackle, Larry W. Reclaiming the Federal Courts (1994).

Yackle, Larry W. *The Habeas Hagioscope*, 66 Southern California Law Review 2331 (1993).

Yoo, John C. *The Judicial Safeguards of Federalism*, 70 Southern California Law Review 1311 (1997).

Zeigler, Donald H. *Gazing Into the Crystal Ball: Reflections on the Standards State Judges Should Use to Ascertain Federal Law*, 40 William and Mary Law Review 1143 (1999).

Zimmerman, Joseph F. *Interstate Cooperation: The Roles of the State Attorneys General*, 28 Publius: The Journal of Federalism 71 (Winter 1998).

Zimring, Franklin E. *The Wages of Ambivalence: On the Context and Prospect of New York's Death Penalty*, 44 Buffalo Law Review 303 (1996).

Table of Cases

Adamson v. California, 332 U.S. 46 (1947).
Agency Holding Corp. v. Malley-Duff & Assoc., Inc., 483 U.S. 143 (1987).
Alabama v. Engler, 85 F.3d 1205 (6th Cir. 1995).
Alden v. Maine, 119 S.Ct. 2240 (1999).
Arizona v. Evans, 514 U.S. 1 (1995).
Atascadero State Hosp. v. Scanlon, 473 U.S. 234 (1985).
Atherton v. FDIC, 519 U.S. 213 (1997).
Ballew v. Georgia, 435 U.S. 223 (1978).
Barron v. Baltimore, 32 U.S. 243 (1833).
Belton v. Gebhart, 87 A.2d 862 (Del. Ct. Chancery 1952).
Bowers v. Hardwick, 478 U.S. 186 (1986).
Brown v. Allen, 344 U.S. 443 (1953).
Brown v. Texas, 522 U.S. 940 (1998).
Buckley v. Valeo, 424 U.S. 1 (1976)
Calderon v. Ashmus, 523 U.S. 740 (1998).
Calderon v. Thompson, 523 U.S. 538 (1998).
California Board of Regents v. Bakke, 438 U.S. 265 (1978).
Chisom v. Roemer, 501 U.S. 380 (1991).
City of Boerne v. Flores, 521 U.S. 507 (1997).
Coleman v. Thompson, 501 U.S. 722 (1991).
Compania General de Tabacos de Filipinas v. Collector, 275 U.S. 87 (1927).
Cousin v. Sundquist, 145 F.3d 818 (6th Cir. 1998).
Deakins v. Monaghan, 484 U.S. 193 (1988).
Dennis v. United States, 341 U.S. 494 (1951).
Developed in United States v. Leon, 468 U.S. 897 (1984).
Dombrowski v. Pfister, 380 U.S. 479 (1965).
Engle v. Isaac, 456 U.S. 107 (1982).
Fair Assessment in Real Estate Association v. McNary, 454 U.S. 100 (1981).
Fay v. Noia, 372 U.S. 391 (1963).
Felder v. Casey, 487 U.S. 131 (1988).
Florida Prepaid Postsecondary Ed. Exp. Bd. v. College Savings Bank, 119 S.Ct. 2198 (1999).

Freeman v. Bee Machine Co., 319 U.S. 448 (1943).
Furman v. Georgia, 408 U.S. 238 (1972).
Garcia v. San Antonio Metropolitan Transit Authority, 469 U.S. 528 (1985).
Gebhart v. Belton, 91 A.2d 137 (Del. 1952).
General Inv. Co. v. Lake Shore & M.S. Ry., 260 U.S. 261 (1922).
Gertz v. Robert Welch, Inc., 418 U.S. 323 (1974).
Gregg v. Georgia, 428 U.S. 153 (1976).
Gulf Offshore Co. v. Mobil Oil Corp., 453 U.S. 473 (1981).
Harris v. Alabama, 513 U.S. 504 (1995).
Harris v. Reed, 489 U.S. 255 (1989).
Hathorn v. Lovorn, 457 U.S. 255 (1982).
Hoffman v. Pursue, Ltd., 420 U.S. 592 (1975).
Howlett v. Rose, 496 U.S. 356 (1990).
Huffman v. Pursue, Ltd., 420 U.S. 592 (1975).
Idaho v. Coeur d'Alene Tribe of Idaho, 521 U.S. 261 (1997).
Int'l Science & Tech. Inst., Inc. v. Ivacon Commm., Inc., 106 F.3d 1146 (4th Cir. 1997).
Johnson v. Fankell, 520 U.S. 911 (1997).
Johnson v. Texas, 755 S.W.2d 92 (Tex. Ct. Crim. App. 1988).
Juidice v. Vail, 430 U.S. 327 (1977).
Korematsu v. United States, 323 U.S. 214 (1944).
Kruse v. City of Cincinnati, 142 F.3d 907 (6th Cir. 1998).
Lindl v. Murphy, 96 F.3d 856 (7th Cir. 1996).
Lochner v. New York, 69 N.E. 373 (N.Y. 1904).
Maine v. Thiboutot, 448 U.S. 1 (1980).
Mapp v. Ohio, 367 U.S. 643 (1961).
Marrese v. American Academy of Orthopaedic Surgeons, 470 U.S. 373 (1985).
Martinez v. California, 444 U.S. 277 (1980).
McCleskey v. Kemp, 481 U.S. 279 (1987).
McCleskey v. Zant, 499 U.S. 467 (1991).
McCulloch v. Maryland, 17 U.S. 316 (1819).
Merrell Dow Pharmaceuticals, Inc. v. Thompson, 478 U.S. 804 (1986).
Michigan v. Long, 463 U.S. 1032 (1983).
Miller v. California, 413 U.S. 15 (1973).
Milwaukee Branch of the NAACP v. Thompson, 116 F.3d 1194 (7th Cir. 1997).
Miranda v. Arizona, 384 U.S. 436 (1966).
Mitchum v. Foster, 407 U.S. 225 (1972).
Moore v. Sims, 442 U.S. 415 (1979).
New State Ice Co. v. Liebman, 285 U.S. 262 (1932).
New York v. United States, 505 U.S. 157 (1992).
New York Times v. Sullivan, 376 U.S. 254 (1964).
Ohio v. Robinette, 519 U.S. 33 (1996).
O'Sullivan v. Boerckel, 119 S.Ct. 1728 (1999).
Patsy v. Florida Bd. of Regents, 457 U.S. 496 (1982).
Pennsylvania v. LaBron, 518 U.S. 938 (1996).
Pennzoil v. Texaco, 481 U.S. 1 (1987).
Plessy v. Ferguson, 163 U.S. 537 (1896).
Powell v. State, 510 S.E. 2d 18 (Ga. 1998).
Printz v. United States, 521 U.S. 898 (1997).
Richmond v. J.A. Croson Co., 488 U.S. 469 (1989).

Rivet v. Regions Bank of Louisiana, 522 U.S. 470 (1998).
Roe v. Wade, 410 U.S. 713 (1973).
Romer v. Evans, 882 P.2d 1335 (Colo. 1994).
Romine v. CompuServe Corp., 160 F.3d 337 (6th Cir. 1998).
Roth v. United States, 354 U.S. 476 (1957).
Ruhrgas AG v. Marathon Oil Co., 119 S.Ct. 1563 (1999).
San Antonio Independent School District v. Rodriguez, 411 U.S. 1 (1973).
Schneckloth v. Bustamonte, 412 U.S. 218 (1973).
Seminole Tribe of Florida v. Florida, 517 U.S. 44 (1996).
Steffel v. Thompson, 415 U.S. 452 (1974).
Stone v. Powell, 428 U.S. 465 (1976).
Suster v. Marshall, 149 F.3d 523 (6th Cir. 1998).
Tafflin v. Levitt, 493 U.S. 455 (1990).
Teague v. Lane, 489 U.S. 288 (1989).
Teamsters v. Lucas Flour Co., 369 U.S. 95 (1962).
Testa v. Katt, 330 U.S. 386 (1947).
Texas v. Johnson, 491 U.S. 397 (1989).
U.S. Term Limits Inc. v. Thornton, 514 U.S. 779 (1995).
United States v. Leon, 468 U.S. 897 (1984).
United States v. Lopez, 514 U.S. 549 (1995).
Village of Bolingbrook v. Citizens Utilities Co., 864 F.2d 481 (7th Cir. 1988).
Wainright v. Sykes, 433 U.S. 72 (1977).
Washington v. Glucksberg, 521 U.S. 702 (1997).
Young, Ex Parte, 209 U.S. 123 (1908).
Younger v. Harris, 401 U.S. 37 (1971).

Index

Abortion, 2, 27
Abstention, 31
Affirmative Action, 130
African-American judges, 109–114
Age Discrimination in Employment Act, 74
Althouse, Ann, 58
American Bar Association, 114
American Civil Liberties Union, 14 n.3
American Law Institute, 7
American Political Science Association, 10 n.28
Americans with Disabilities Act, 20, 131
Anti-Injunction Act, 33
Antiterrorism and Effective Death Penalty Act, 121–122, 125–126
Antitrust: federal, 83–84; state, 75
Appeals, 44 n.47

Bankruptcy, 84
Bill of Rights, 23, 88, 94
Bird, Rose, 118, 132–133
Black, Hugo, 24, 31
Bork, Robert, 19
Brady Handgun Violence Prevention Act, 1 n.1
Brennan, William J., 5, 58, 89
Buchanan, James, 19

Campaign finance reform, 25, 42 n.40
Chemerinsky, Erwin, 53–54
Citations in Judicial Opinions, 77–79
Civil cases, 63–65
Civil Rights Act (42 U.S.C. § 1983), 33, 64 n.2, 75–79
Civil Rights Act of 1964 (Title VII), 67, 72, 74, 75
Civil Rights Movement, 35–36
Civil War, 2, 35–36
Clinton, Bill, 4, 122
Communitarianism, 138
Congress, 29–30, 50, 64, 67, 80–81, 85, 115, 121–122, 135
Constitution (U.S.), Article III, 29–30, 97 n.31
Copyright cases, 64, 84
Criminal cases, 63–64

De Tocqueville, 17 n.15, 135
Death penalty and state courts, 114–119
Declaration of Independence, 137
Defense of Marriage Act, 135
Delay in court, 44 n.46
Diversity Jurisdiction, 80
Dolbeare, Kenneth, 38
Drug policy, 26, 134

Eighth Amendment, 114
Eleventh Amendment, 30 n.4, 59–60, 131 n.7
Ely, John Hart, 19
Employee Retirement Income Security Act, 64 n.5, 65 n.7
Equal Protection Clause, 45, 51
Exclusionary rule, 7 n.19, 25

Fair Labor Standards Act, 60 n.84
Federal Courts Study Committee, 65 n.7
Federal Employees Liability Act, 65 n.7
Federal Judges, 37–39, 65

Federal Jurisdiction, exclusive, 66–68
Federal Rules of Civil Procedure, 38 n.29, 74
Federal Rules of Evidence, 38 n.29, 74
Federalism: comparative, 141; competition, 26; experimentation, 24–25, 98; political safeguards of, 80–81
Feeley, Malcolm, 139
First Amendment, 45, 50
Forum shopping, 65, 68–69
Fourteenth Amendment, 24, 131 n.7, 137
Fourth Amendment, 32, 45, 50–51, 54
Friedman, Barry, 9
Friedman, Milton, 137

Gardner, James, 89–90, 93–95
Gettysburg Address, 137
Glendon, Mary Ann, 15–16
Goldwater, Barry, 3
Gore, Al, 4
Gun-Free School Zones Act, 1 n.1, 133 n.14

Habeas Corpus, 32, 119–127
Harlan, John, 31
Hart, Henry, 33
Hellman, Arthur, 58
Holmes, Oliver Wendell, 19, 64

Information flow in courts, 55–57, 94, 103
Interest groups, 26 n.46, 57

Jacobsohn, Gary, 136
Judges, election of, 41–42, 103, 111–11-3, 118–119
Judges, qualifications of, 39
Judicial Federalism: and ideology, 136–138; and rights, 22–27, 129–136; approaches, 7–9; defined, 4–6; economic analysis, 9, 72–73; future goals and research, 141–142; inevitablity of, 139–141
Juries, 112–113
Jury trial, 24

Kramer, Larry, 9

Labor Management Relations Act, 66–67, 72
Law and Society Association, 10 n.28
Law Clerks, 38
Lawyers, 56
Legal Process Model, 33–34
Legal Realism Model, 34, 58
Libertarianism, 137
Liebman, James, 123–124

Madison Compromise, 29–30, 68
Madison, James, 30
Marshall, John, 23, 139

National Center for State Courts, 122–124
Neuborne, Burt, 35, 37, 39, 41, 43, 49
Nixon, Richard, 3

Outer Continental Shelf Lands Act, 67
O'Connor, Sandra Day, 97

Parity between federal and state courts: definition of, 58–59; empirical study of, 42–55; history and evidence, 34–42, 74
Patent cases, 64, 72, 84
Perry, Michael, 19
Posner, Richard A., 72
Powell, Lewis, 32
Publication of Opinions, 44

Race and gender task forces, 105 n.1
Race and schools, 131
Race and the criminal process, 106–109
Racial Justice Act, 115–116
Racketeer Influenced and Corrupt Organizations Act, 7 n.19, 67, 74–75
Reagan, Ronald, 2 n.2, 3, 138 n.30
Redish, Martin, 66
Removal of cases from state to federal court, 69, 82–83
Repeat players in litigation, 56
Right-to-die, 26, 135
Rights: discourse on, 18-22; measure, 13–16, 100; federalism and, 16–18, 22–27, 72–73, 96, 101, 130–131; majorities and, 27–28
Riker, William, 27
Rubin, Edward, 139

School funding cases, 92–93
Sodomy, 26
Specialization of lawyers, 70, 73
State Appellate Courts, 44, 57–58
State Attorneys General, 60 n.84, 75 n.45, 120
State constitutional law: and judicial elections, 103; empirical studies, 90, 94; general, 88–90; relation to liberty, 94–96; relation to parity, 91–93, 96; relation to Supreme Court review, 96–104
State constitutions, 94–96
State judges, 38–40
State political culture, 1 n.1, 94–96, 139–140
States rights, 140
Stevens, John Paul, 98, 117
Supremacy Clause, 2, 26
Supreme Court (U.S.), 57, 73, 133

Telephone Consumer Protection Act, 65 n.7
Tenth Amendment, 3
Tobacco suits, 136
Tort reform, 136
Truth in Lending Act, 65 n.7

Uniformity of federal law, 71–73, 96, 101

Violence Against Women Act, 82 n.69
Voting Rights Act, 110–112

Waldron, Jeremy, 21
Warren, Earl, 132
Wechsler, Herbert, 33
Whitman, Walt, 140
Wilson, James, 30
Workload, judicial, 80

Yackle, Larry, 34, 58, 91–93

Zimring, Franklin, 115

About the Author

MICHAEL E. SOLIMINE is Donald P. Klekamp Professor of Law, University of Cincinnati College of Law. Professor Solimine clerked for a U.S. District Judge and was a litigation associate in a law firm prior to joining the College of Law in 1987.

JAMES L. WALKER is Professor of Political Science, Wright State University. His teaching and publications are in the areas of constitutional law and civil liberties.

ISBN 0-313-30634-6

90000>

EAN

9 780313 306341

HARDCOVER BAR CODE